EVIL EMPIRE™

LAND OF THE FREE

BOOM!
STUDIOS

BOOM! STUDIOS

EVIL EMPIRE Volume Three, July 2016. Published by BOOM! Studios, a division of Boom Entertainment, Inc. Evil Empire is ™ & © 2016 Boom Entertainment, Inc. Originally published in single magazine form as EVIL EMPIRE No. 9-12. ™ & © 2014, 2015 Boom Entertainment, Inc. All rights reserved. BOOM! Studios™ and the BOOM! Studios logo are trademarks of Boom Entertainment, Inc. registered in various countries and categories. All characters, events, and institutions depicted herein are fictional. Any similarity between any of the names, characters, persons, events, and/or institutions in this publication to actual names, characters, and persons, whether living or dead, events, and/or institutions is unintended and purely coincidental. BOOM! Studios does not read or accept unsolicited submissions of ideas, stories, or artwork.

A catalog record of this book is available from OCLC and from the BOOM! Studios website, www.boom-studios.com, on the Librarians Page.

BOOM! Studios, 5670 Wilshire Boulevard, Suite 450, Los Angeles, CA 90036-5679. Printed in China. First Printing.

ISBN: 978-1-60886-813-1, eISBN: 978-1-61398-484-0

exc. 0.0 *So the question is, where does this leave us?*

CREATED AND WRITTEN BY
MAX BEMIS

ILLUSTRATED BY
VICTOR SANTOS

COLORED BY
CHRIS BLYTHE
(CHAPTER NINE)
JUAN MANUEL TUMBURÚS
(CHAPTERS TEN THROUGH TWELVE)

LETTERED BY
ED DUKESHIRE

COVER BY
JAY SHAW

DESIGNER
SCOTT NEWMAN

ASSOCIATE EDITOR
JASMINE AMIRI

EDITOR
DAFNA PLEBAN

CHAPTER
NINE

....
fig. 1

exc. 1.0 **A trend can be a *virus*. A virus eating away
at the vestiges of people's sanity.**

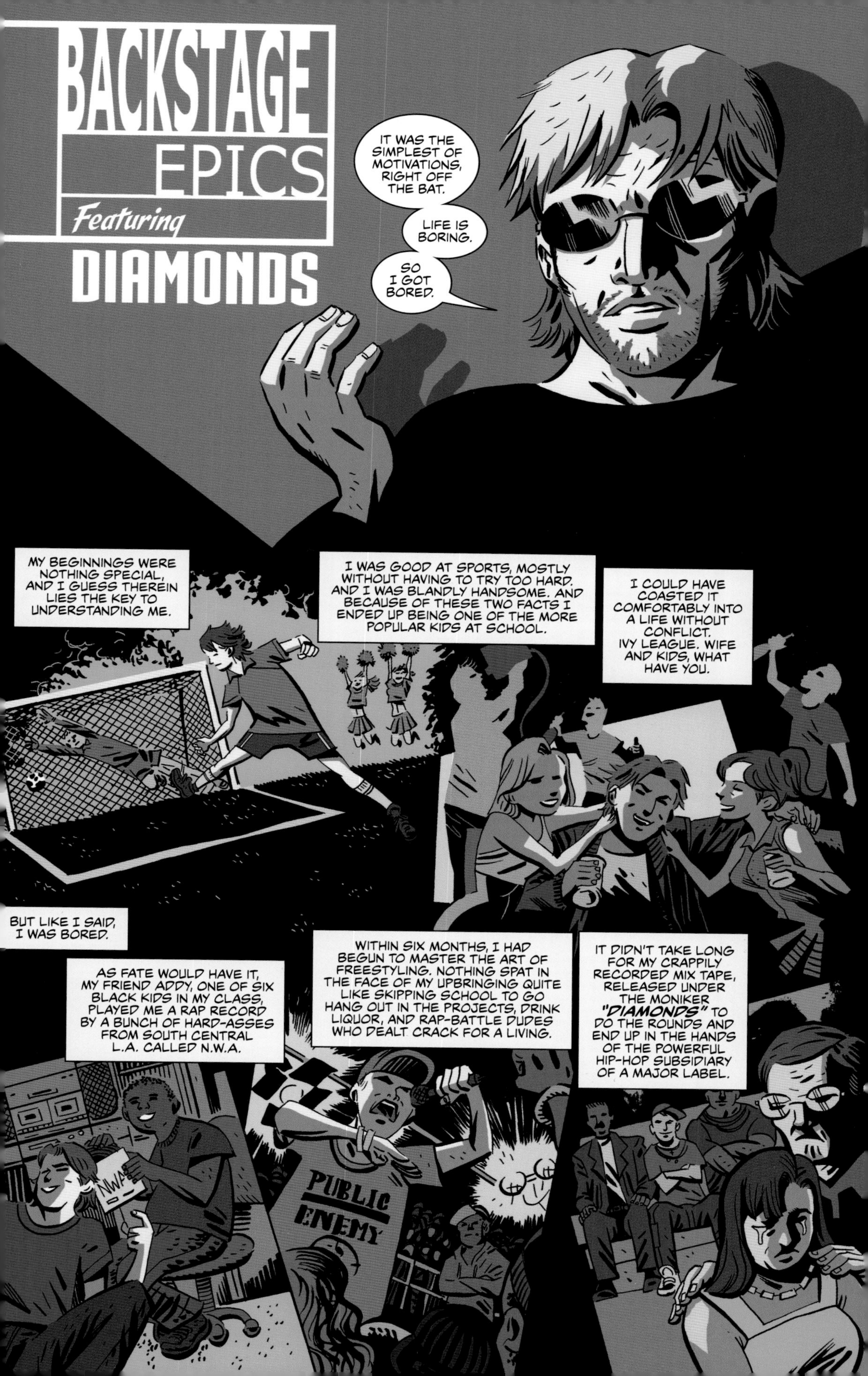
BACKSTAGE EPICS
Featuring
DIAMONDS
IT WAS THE SIMPLEST OF MOTIVATIONS, RIGHT OFF THE BAT.
LIFE IS BORING.
SO I GOT BORED.
MY BEGINNINGS WERE NOTHING SPECIAL, AND I GUESS THEREIN LIES THE KEY TO UNDERSTANDING ME.
I WAS GOOD AT SPORTS, MOSTLY WITHOUT HAVING TO TRY TOO HARD. AND I WAS BLANDLY HANDSOME. AND BECAUSE OF THESE TWO FACTS I ENDED UP BEING ONE OF THE MORE POPULAR KIDS AT SCHOOL.
I COULD HAVE COASTED IT COMFORTABLY INTO A LIFE WITHOUT CONFLICT. IVY LEAGUE. WIFE AND KIDS, WHAT HAVE YOU.
BUT LIKE I SAID, I WAS BORED.
AS FATE WOULD HAVE IT, MY FRIEND ADDY, ONE OF SIX BLACK KIDS IN MY CLASS, PLAYED ME A RAP RECORD BY A BUNCH OF HARD-ASSES FROM SOUTH CENTRAL L.A. CALLED N.W.A.
NWA
WITHIN SIX MONTHS, I HAD BEGUN TO MASTER THE ART OF FREESTYLING. NOTHING SPAT IN THE FACE OF MY UPBRINGING QUITE LIKE SKIPPING SCHOOL TO GO HANG OUT IN THE PROJECTS, DRINK LIQUOR, AND RAP-BATTLE DUDES WHO DEALT CRACK FOR A LIVING.
PUBLIC ENEMY
IT DIDN'T TAKE LONG FOR MY CRAPPILY RECORDED MIX TAPE, RELEASED UNDER THE MONIKER "DIAMONDS" TO DO THE ROUNDS AND END UP IN THE HANDS OF THE POWERFUL HIP-HOP SUBSIDIARY OF A MAJOR LABEL.

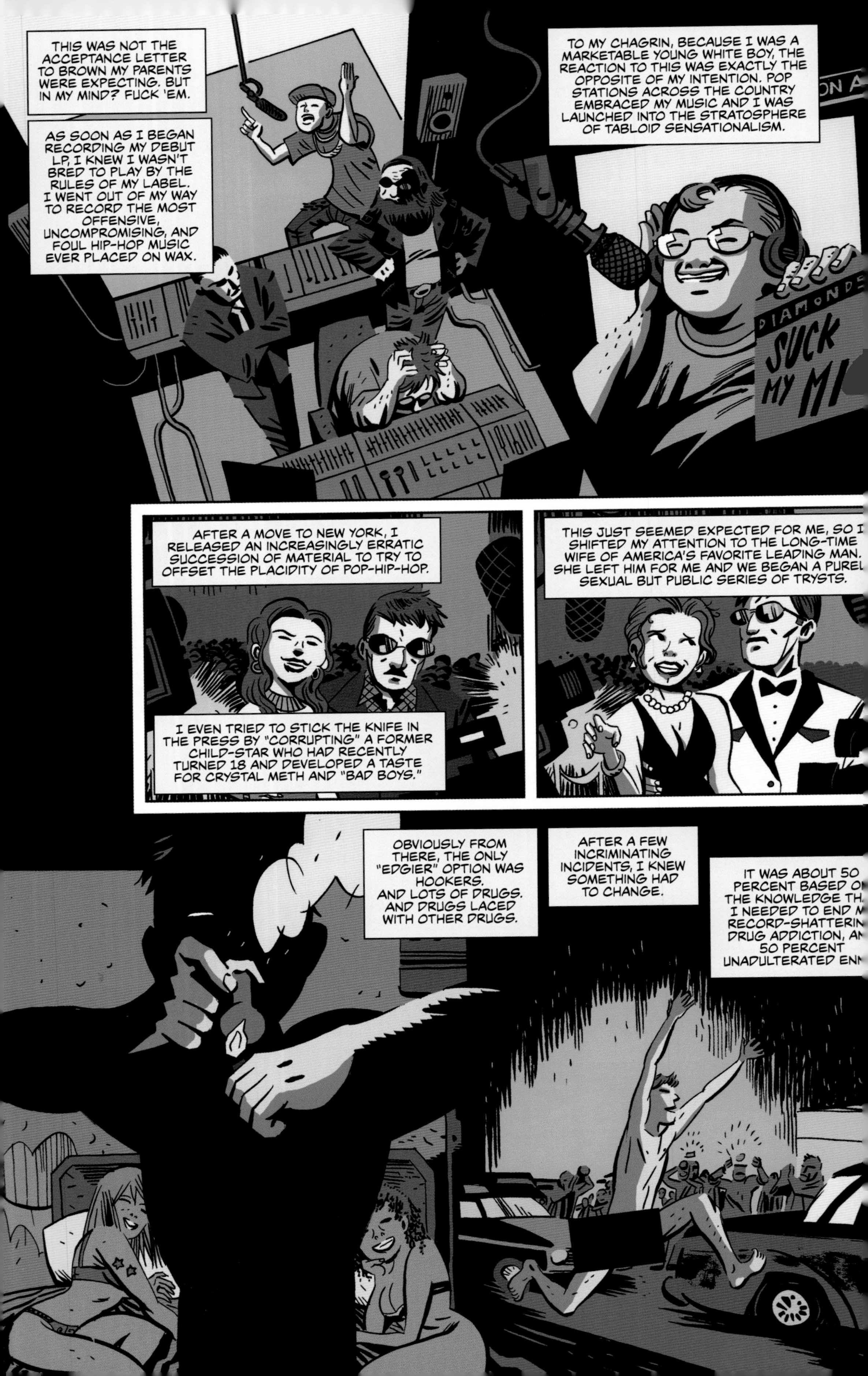
THIS WAS NOT THE ACCEPTANCE LETTER TO BROWN MY PARENTS WERE EXPECTING. BUT IN MY MIND? FUCK 'EM.
AS SOON AS I BEGAN RECORDING MY DEBUT LP, I KNEW I WASN'T BRED TO PLAY BY THE RULES OF MY LABEL. I WENT OUT OF MY WAY TO RECORD THE MOST OFFENSIVE, UNCOMPROMISING, AND FOUL HIP-HOP MUSIC EVER PLACED ON WAX.
TO MY CHAGRIN, BECAUSE I WAS A MARKETABLE YOUNG WHITE BOY, THE REACTION TO THIS WAS EXACTLY THE OPPOSITE OF MY INTENTION. POP STATIONS ACROSS THE COUNTRY EMBRACED MY MUSIC AND I WAS LAUNCHED INTO THE STRATOSPHERE OF TABLOID SENSATIONALISM.
SUCK MY MI
AFTER A MOVE TO NEW YORK, I RELEASED AN INCREASINGLY ERRATIC SUCCESSION OF MATERIAL TO TRY TO OFFSET THE PLACIDITY OF POP-HIP-HOP.
I EVEN TRIED TO STICK THE KNIFE IN THE PRESS BY "CORRUPTING" A FORMER CHILD-STAR WHO HAD RECENTLY TURNED 18 AND DEVELOPED A TASTE FOR CRYSTAL METH AND "BAD BOYS."
THIS JUST SEEMED EXPECTED FOR ME, SO I SHIFTED MY ATTENTION TO THE LONG-TIME WIFE OF AMERICA'S FAVORITE LEADING MAN. SHE LEFT HIM FOR ME AND WE BEGAN A PUREL SEXUAL BUT PUBLIC SERIES OF TRYSTS.
OBVIOUSLY FROM THERE, THE ONLY "EDGIER" OPTION WAS HOOKERS. AND LOTS OF DRUGS. AND DRUGS LACED WITH OTHER DRUGS.
AFTER A FEW INCRIMINATING INCIDENTS, I KNEW SOMETHING HAD TO CHANGE.
IT WAS ABOUT 50 PERCENT BASED O THE KNOWLEDGE TH I NEEDED TO END M RECORD-SHATTERI DRUG ADDICTION, A 50 PERCENT UNADULTERATED EN

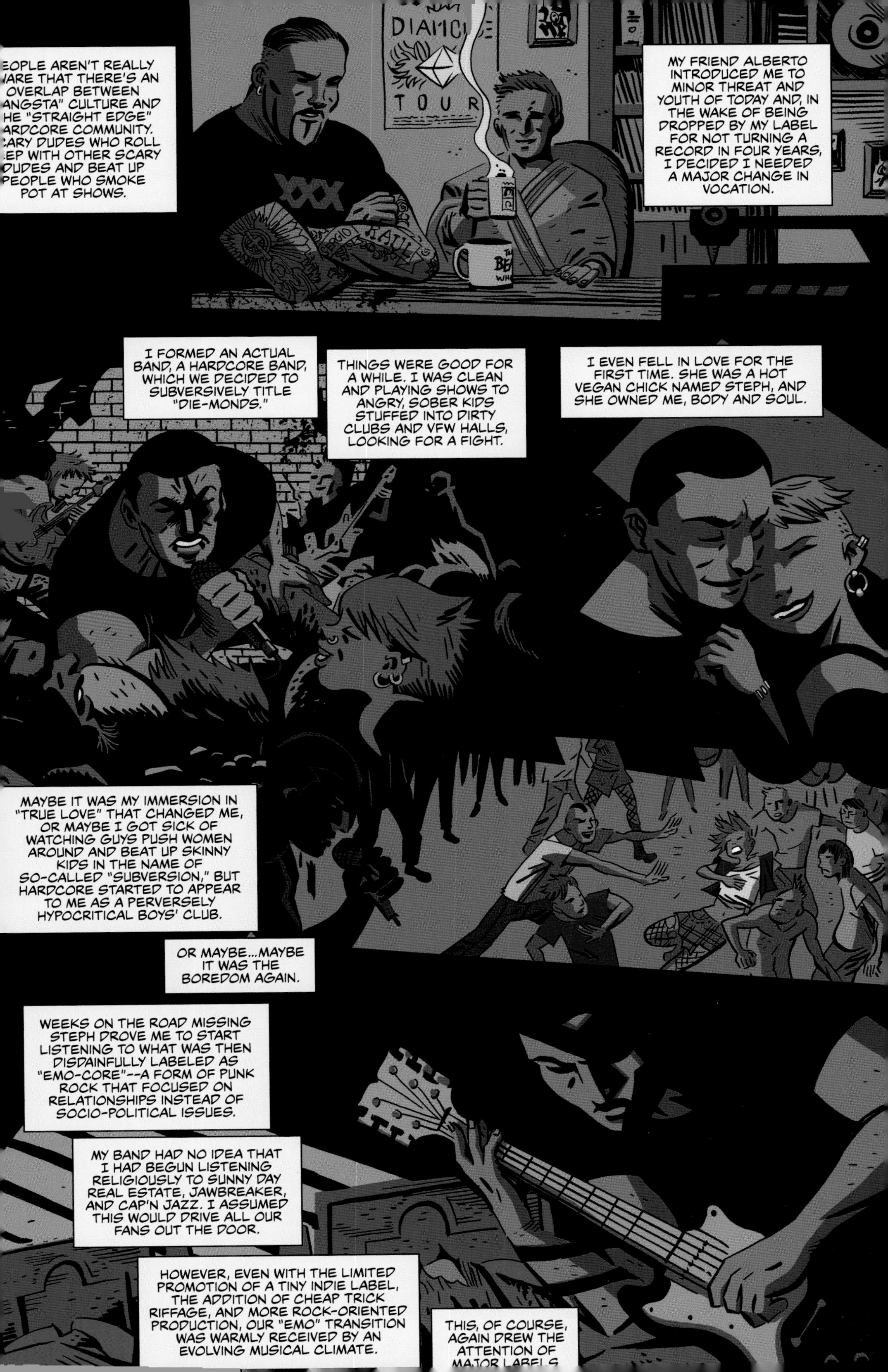

EOPLE AREN'T REALLY WARE THAT THERE'S AN OVERLAP BETWEEN ANGSTA" CULTURE AND HE "STRAIGHT EDGE" ARDCORE COMMUNITY. CARY DUDES WHO ROLL EEP WITH OTHER SCARY DUDES AND BEAT UP PEOPLE WHO SMOKE POT AT SHOWS.
DIAMO
TOUR
MY FRIEND ALBERTO INTRODUCED ME TO MINOR THREAT AND YOUTH OF TODAY AND, IN THE WAKE OF BEING DROPPED BY MY LABEL FOR NOT TURNING A RECORD IN FOUR YEARS, I DECIDED I NEEDED A MAJOR CHANGE IN VOCATION.
I FORMED AN ACTUAL BAND, A HARDCORE BAND, WHICH WE DECIDED TO SUBVERSIVELY TITLE "DIE-MONDS."
THINGS WERE GOOD FOR A WHILE. I WAS CLEAN AND PLAYING SHOWS TO ANGRY, SOBER KIDS STUFFED INTO DIRTY CLUBS AND VFW HALLS, LOOKING FOR A FIGHT.
I EVEN FELL IN LOVE FOR THE FIRST TIME. SHE WAS A HOT VEGAN CHICK NAMED STEPH, AND SHE OWNED ME, BODY AND SOUL.
MAYBE IT WAS MY IMMERSION IN "TRUE LOVE" THAT CHANGED ME, OR MAYBE I GOT SICK OF WATCHING GUYS PUSH WOMEN AROUND AND BEAT UP SKINNY KIDS IN THE NAME OF SO-CALLED "SUBVERSION," BUT HARDCORE STARTED TO APPEAR TO ME AS A PERVERSELY HYPOCRITICAL BOYS' CLUB.
OR MAYBE...MAYBE IT WAS THE BOREDOM AGAIN.
WEEKS ON THE ROAD MISSING STEPH DROVE ME TO START LISTENING TO WHAT WAS THEN DISDAINFULLY LABELED AS "EMO-CORE"--A FORM OF PUNK ROCK THAT FOCUSED ON RELATIONSHIPS INSTEAD OF SOCIO-POLITICAL ISSUES.
MY BAND HAD NO IDEA THAT I HAD BEGUN LISTENING RELIGIOUSLY TO SUNNY DAY REAL ESTATE, JAWBREAKER, AND CAP'N JAZZ. I ASSUMED THIS WOULD DRIVE ALL OUR FANS OUT THE DOOR.
HOWEVER, EVEN WITH THE LIMITED PROMOTION OF A TINY INDIE LABEL, THE ADDITION OF CHEAP TRICK RIFFAGE, AND MORE ROCK-ORIENTED PRODUCTION, OUR "EMO" TRANSITION WAS WARMLY RECEIVED BY AN EVOLVING MUSICAL CLIMATE.
THIS, OF COURSE, AGAIN DREW THE ATTENTION OF

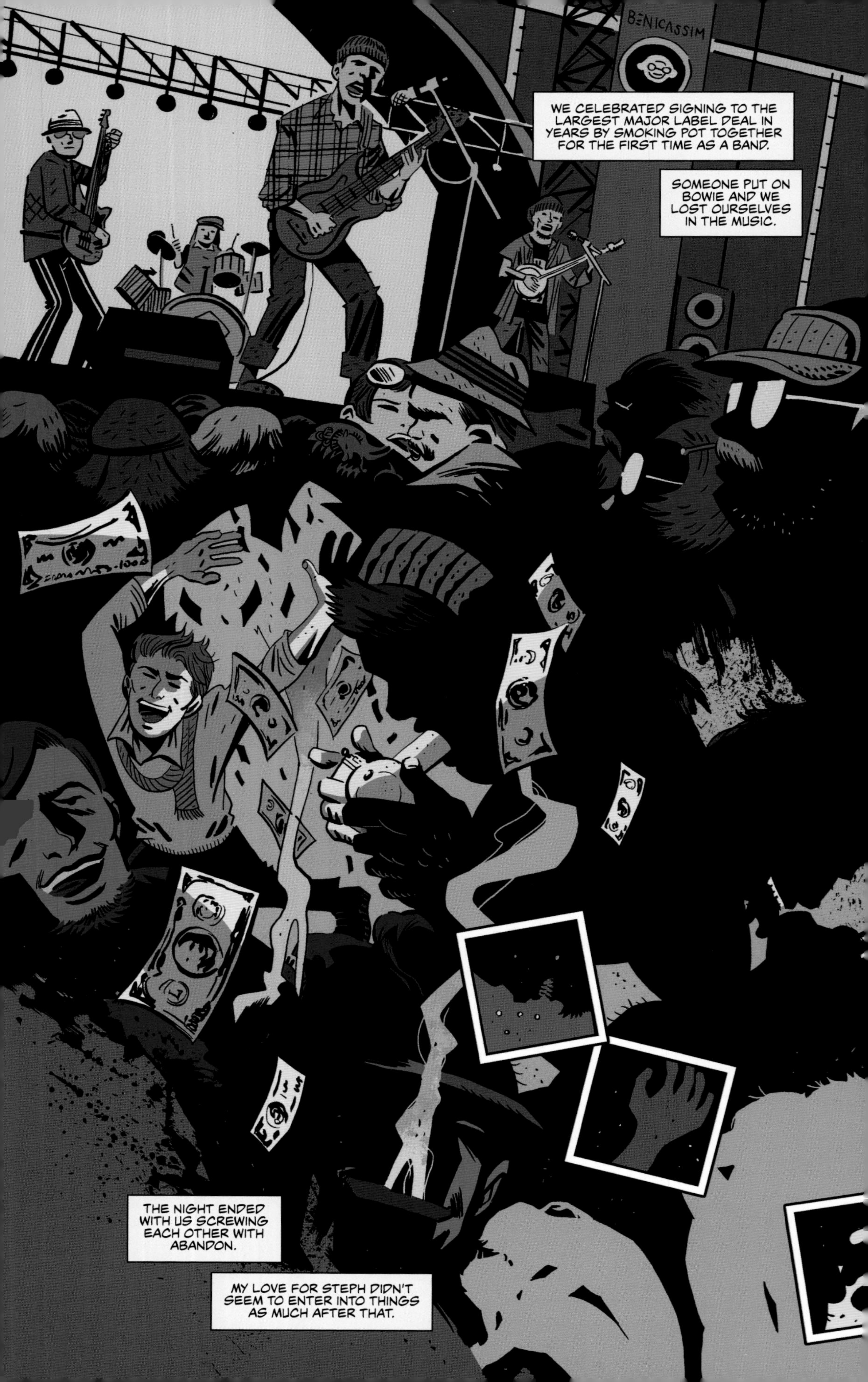
BENICASSIM
WE CELEBRATED SIGNING TO THE LARGEST MAJOR LABEL DEAL IN YEARS BY SMOKING POT TOGETHER FOR THE FIRST TIME AS A BAND.
SOMEONE PUT ON BOWIE AND WE LOST OURSELVES IN THE MUSIC.
THE NIGHT ENDED WITH US SCREWING EACH OTHER WITH ABANDON.
MY LOVE FOR STEPH DIDN'T SEEM TO ENTER INTO THINGS AS MUCH AFTER THAT.

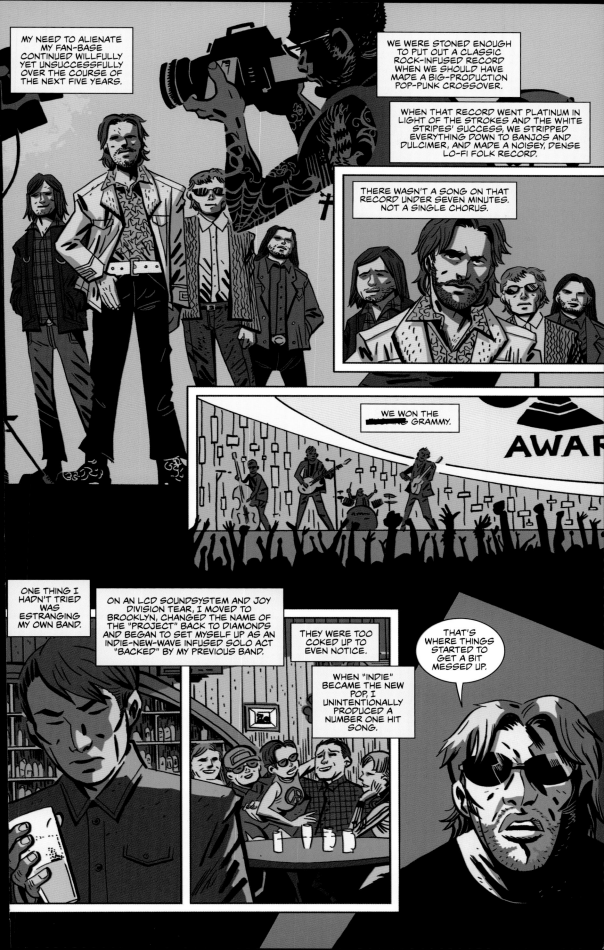

MY NEED TO ALIENATE MY FAN-BASE CONTINUED WILLFULLY YET UNSUCCESSFULLY OVER THE COURSE OF THE NEXT FIVE YEARS.

WE WERE STONED ENOUGH TO PUT OUT A CLASSIC ROCK-INFUSED RECORD WHEN WE SHOULD HAVE MADE A BIG-PRODUCTION POP-PUNK CROSSOVER.

WHEN THAT RECORD WENT PLATINUM IN LIGHT OF THE STROKES AND THE WHITE STRIPES' SUCCESS, WE STRIPPED EVERYTHING DOWN TO BANJOS AND DULCIMER, AND MADE A NOISEY, DENSE LO-FI FOLK RECORD.

THERE WASN'T A SONG ON THAT RECORD UNDER SEVEN MINUTES. NOT A SINGLE CHORUS.

WE WON THE ████████ GRAMMY.

AWAR

ONE THING I HADN'T TRIED WAS ESTRANGING MY OWN BAND.

ON AN LCD SOUNDSYSTEM AND JOY DIVISION TEAR, I MOVED TO BROOKLYN, CHANGED THE NAME OF THE "PROJECT" BACK TO DIAMONDS AND BEGAN TO SET MYSELF UP AS AN INDIE-NEW-WAVE INFUSED SOLO ACT "BACKED" BY MY PREVIOUS BAND.

THEY WERE TOO COKED UP TO EVEN NOTICE.

WHEN "INDIE" BECAME THE NEW POP, I UNINTENTIONALLY PRODUCED A NUMBER ONE HIT SONG.

THAT'S WHERE THINGS STARTED TO GET A BIT MESSED UP.

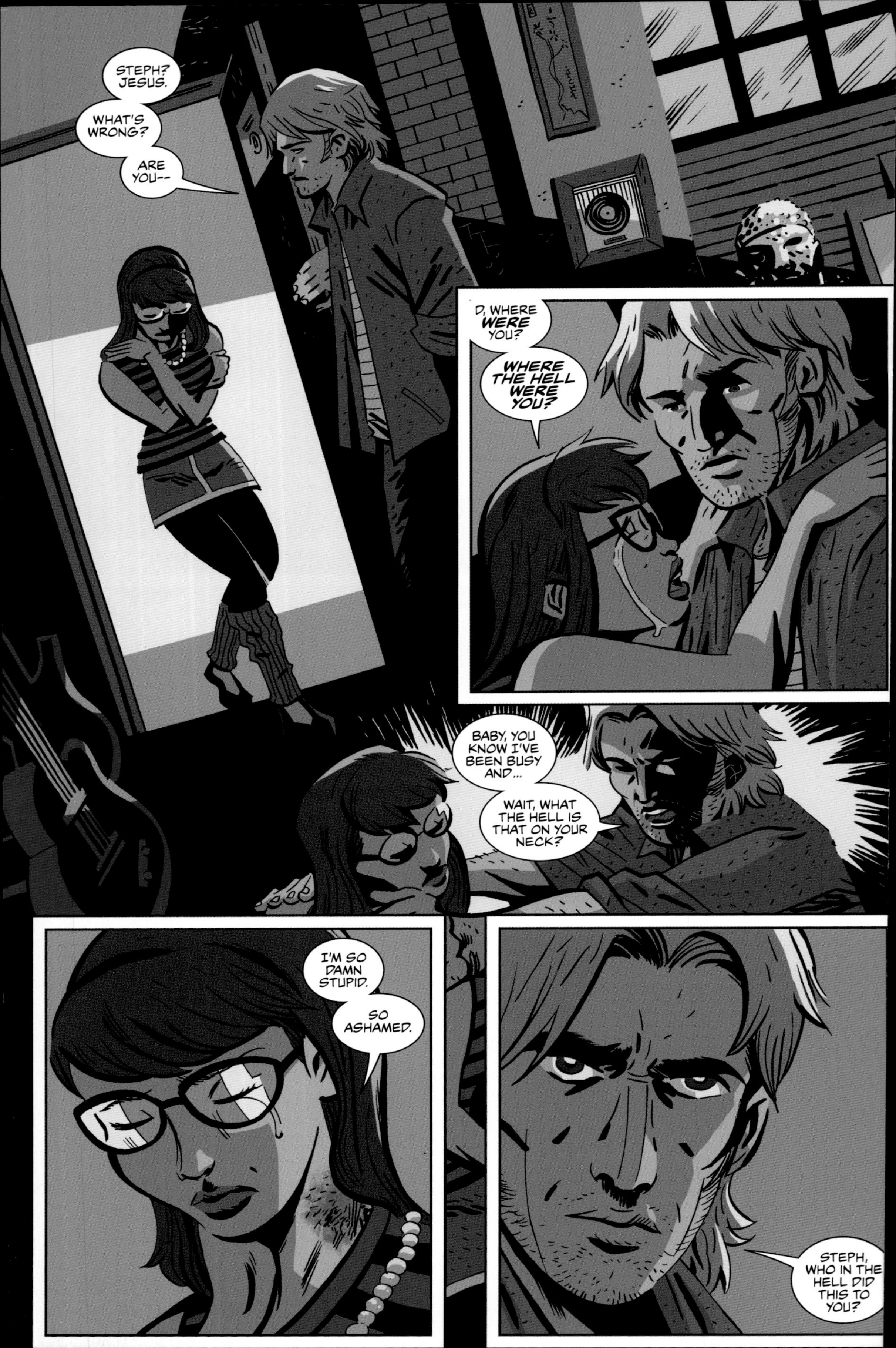
STEPH? JESUS.
WHAT'S WRONG?
ARE YOU--
D, WHERE WERE YOU?
WHERE THE HELL WERE YOU?
BABY, YOU KNOW I'VE BEEN BUSY AND...
WAIT, WHAT THE HELL IS THAT ON YOUR NECK?
I'M SO DAMN STUPID.
SO ASHAMED.
STEPH, WHO IN THE HELL DID THIS TO YOU?

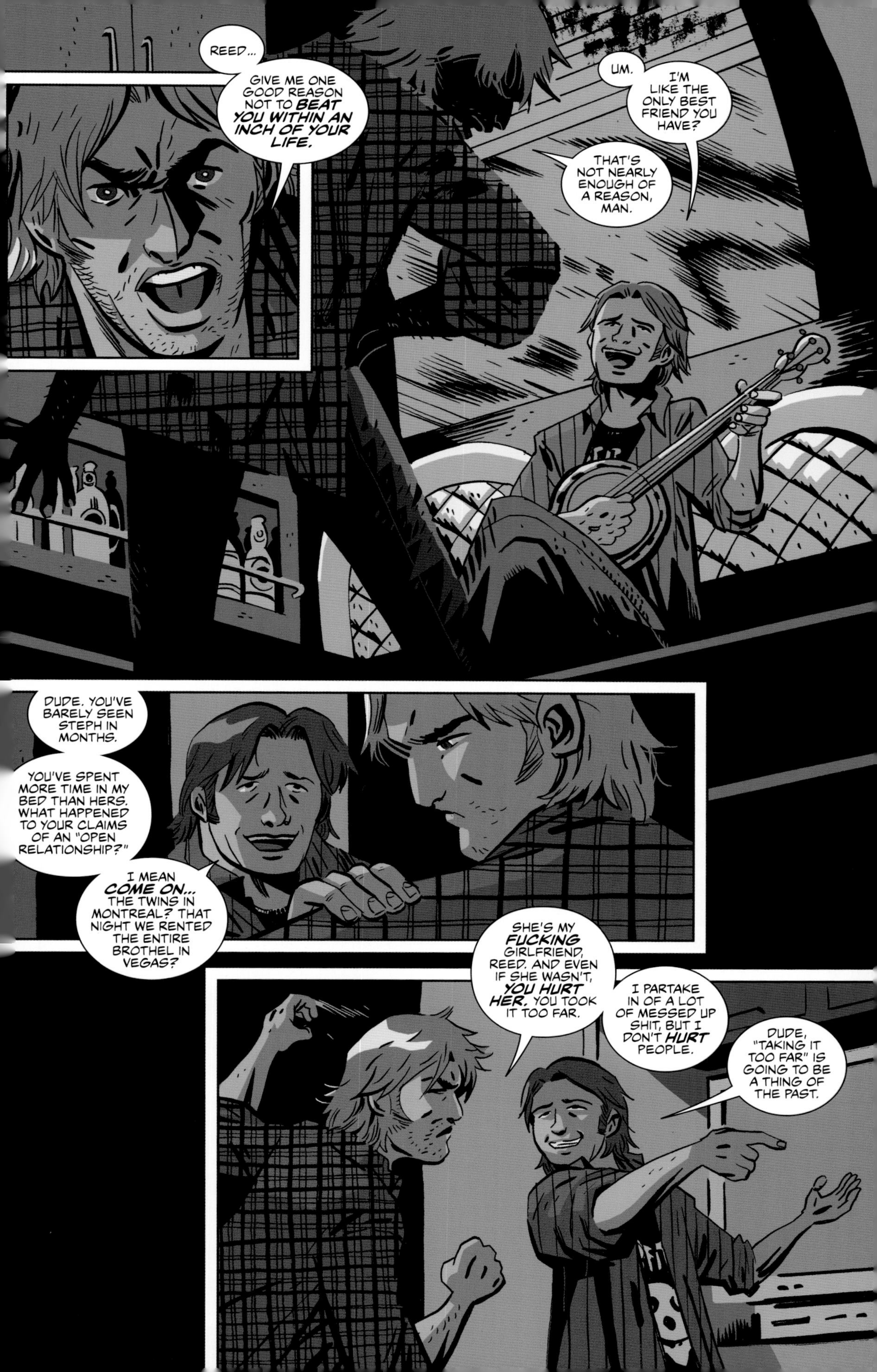
REED...
GIVE ME ONE GOOD REASON NOT TO **BEAT YOU WITHIN AN INCH OF YOUR LIFE.**
UM.
I'M LIKE THE ONLY BEST FRIEND YOU HAVE?
THAT'S NOT NEARLY ENOUGH OF A REASON, MAN.
DUDE. YOU'VE BARELY SEEN STEPH IN MONTHS.
YOU'VE SPENT MORE TIME IN MY BED THAN HERS. WHAT HAPPENED TO YOUR CLAIMS OF AN "OPEN RELATIONSHIP?"
I MEAN **COME ON...** THE TWINS IN MONTREAL? THAT NIGHT WE RENTED THE ENTIRE BROTHEL IN VEGAS?
SHE'S MY **FUCKING** GIRLFRIEND, REED. AND EVEN IF SHE WASN'T, **YOU HURT HER.** YOU TOOK IT TOO FAR.
I PARTAKE IN OF A LOT OF MESSED UP SHIT, BUT I DON'T **HURT** PEOPLE.
DUDE, "TAKING IT TOO FAR" IS GOING TO BE A THING OF THE PAST.

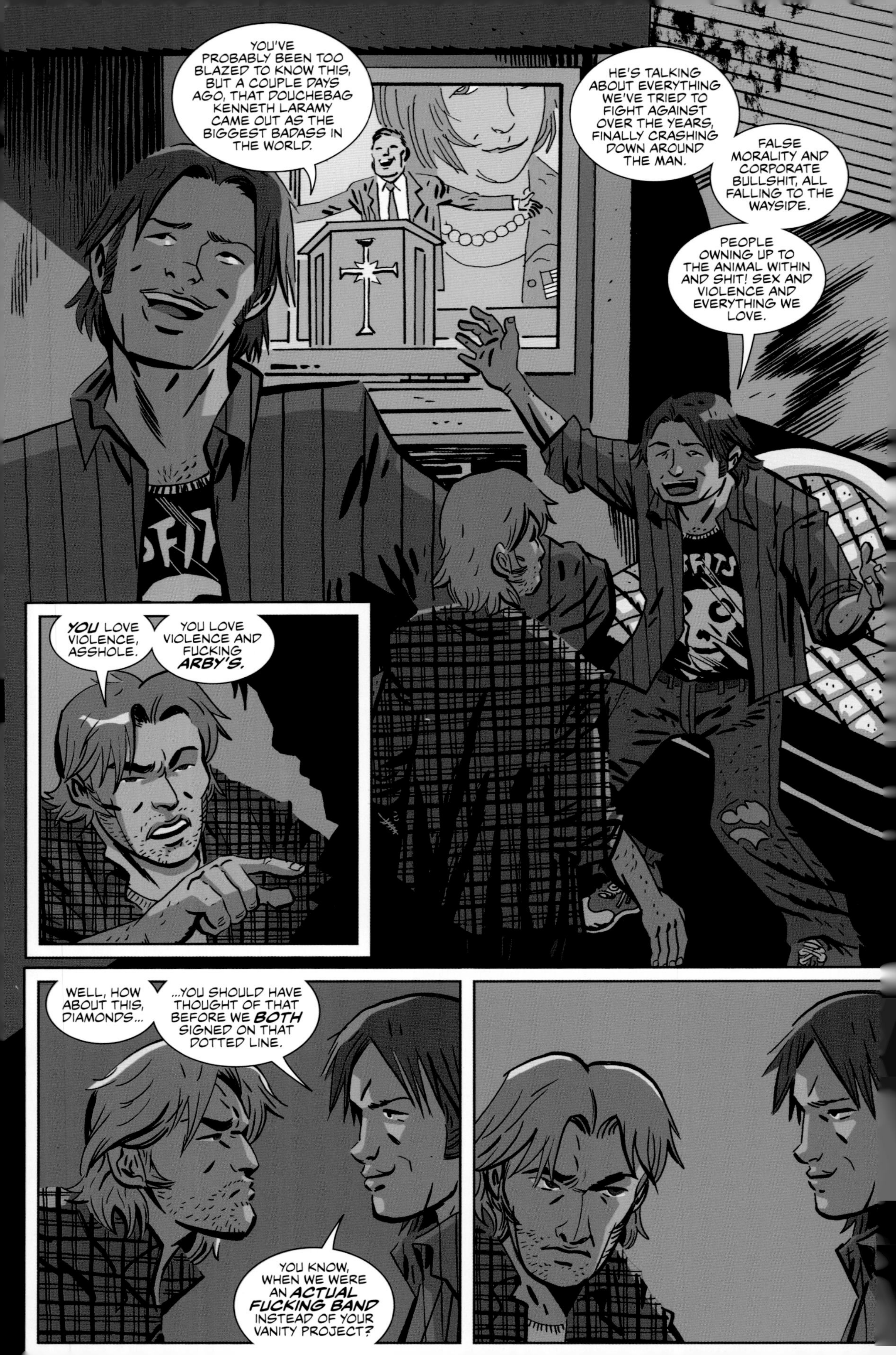
YOU'VE PROBABLY BEEN TOO BLAZED TO KNOW THIS, BUT A COUPLE DAYS AGO, THAT DOUCHEBAG KENNETH LARAMY CAME OUT AS THE BIGGEST BADASS IN THE WORLD.
HE'S TALKING ABOUT EVERYTHING WE'VE TRIED TO FIGHT AGAINST OVER THE YEARS, FINALLY CRASHING DOWN AROUND THE MAN.
FALSE MORALITY AND CORPORATE BULLSHIT, ALL FALLING TO THE WAYSIDE.
PEOPLE OWNING UP TO THE ANIMAL WITHIN AND SHIT! SEX AND VIOLENCE AND EVERYTHING WE LOVE.
YOU LOVE VIOLENCE, ASSHOLE.
YOU LOVE VIOLENCE AND FUCKING *ARBY'S.*
WELL, HOW ABOUT THIS, DIAMONDS...
...YOU SHOULD HAVE THOUGHT OF THAT BEFORE WE *BOTH* SIGNED ON THAT DOTTED LINE.
YOU KNOW, WHEN WE WERE AN *ACTUAL FUCKING BAND* INSTEAD OF YOUR VANITY PROJECT?

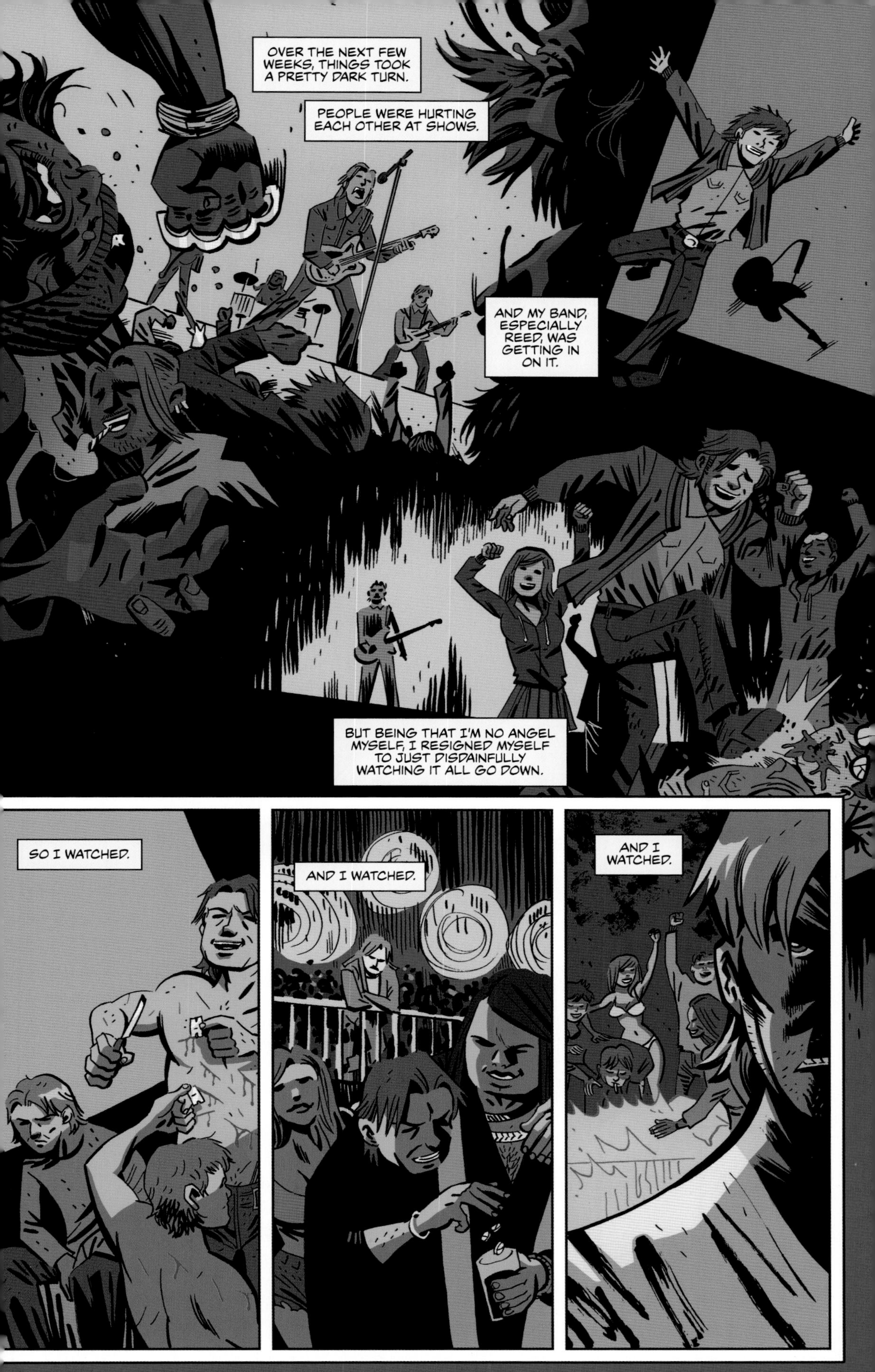

OVER THE NEXT FEW WEEKS, THINGS TOOK A PRETTY DARK TURN.
PEOPLE WERE HURTING EACH OTHER AT SHOWS.
AND MY BAND, ESPECIALLY REED, WAS GETTING IN ON IT.
BUT BEING THAT I'M NO ANGEL MYSELF, I RESIGNED MYSELF TO JUST DISDAINFULLY WATCHING IT ALL GO DOWN.
SO I WATCHED.
AND I WATCHED.
AND I WATCHED.

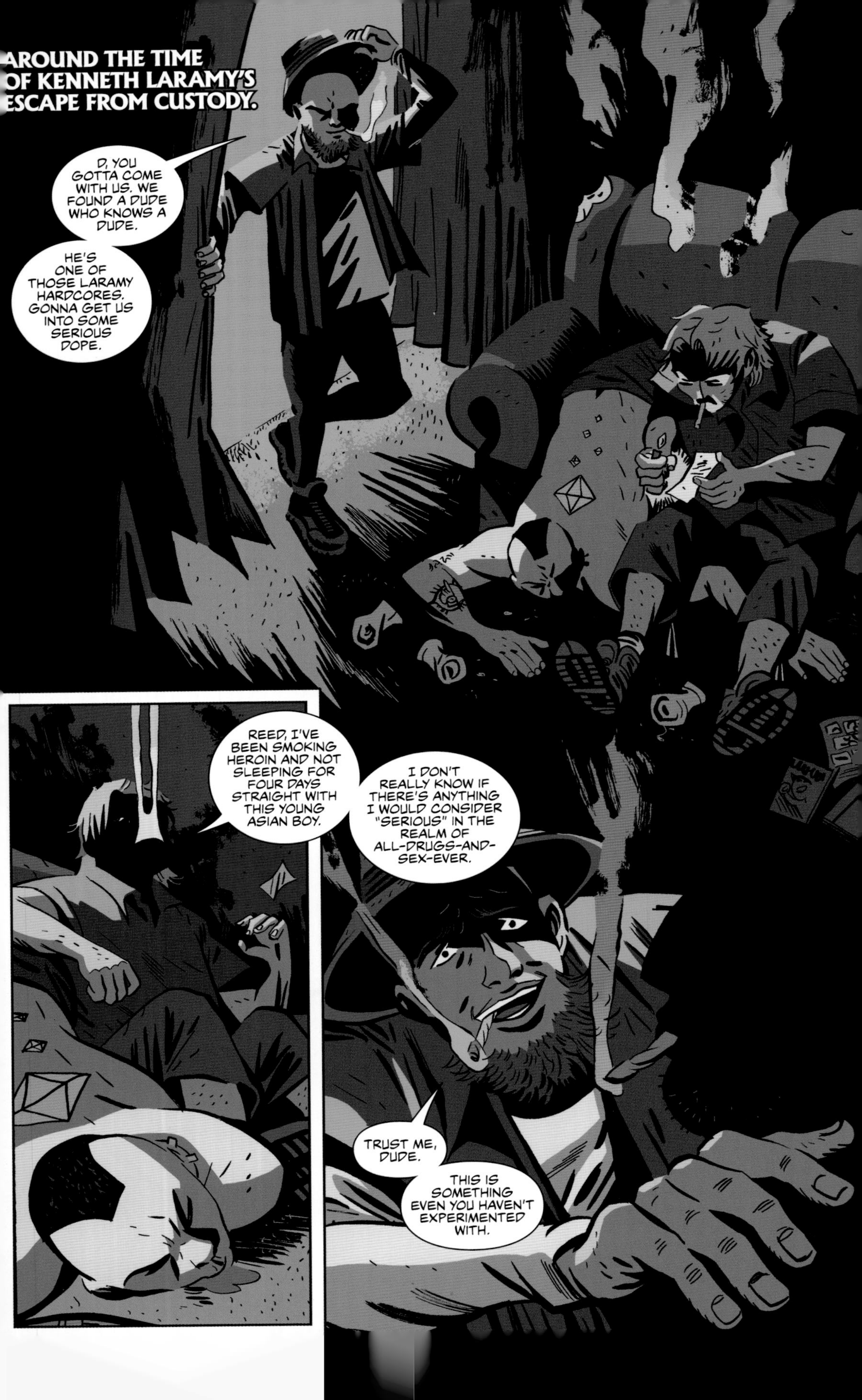
AROUND THE TIME OF KENNETH LARAMY'S ESCAPE FROM CUSTODY.
D, YOU GOTTA COME WITH US. WE FOUND A DUDE WHO KNOWS A DUDE.
HE'S ONE OF THOSE LARAMY HARDCORES. GONNA GET US INTO SOME SERIOUS DOPE.
REED, I'VE BEEN SMOKING HEROIN AND NOT SLEEPING FOR FOUR DAYS STRAIGHT WITH THIS YOUNG ASIAN BOY.
I DON'T REALLY KNOW IF THERE'S ANYTHING I WOULD CONSIDER "SERIOUS" IN THE REALM OF ALL-DRUGS-AND-SEX-EVER.
TRUST ME, DUDE.
THIS IS SOMETHING EVEN YOU HAVEN'T EXPERIMENTED WITH.

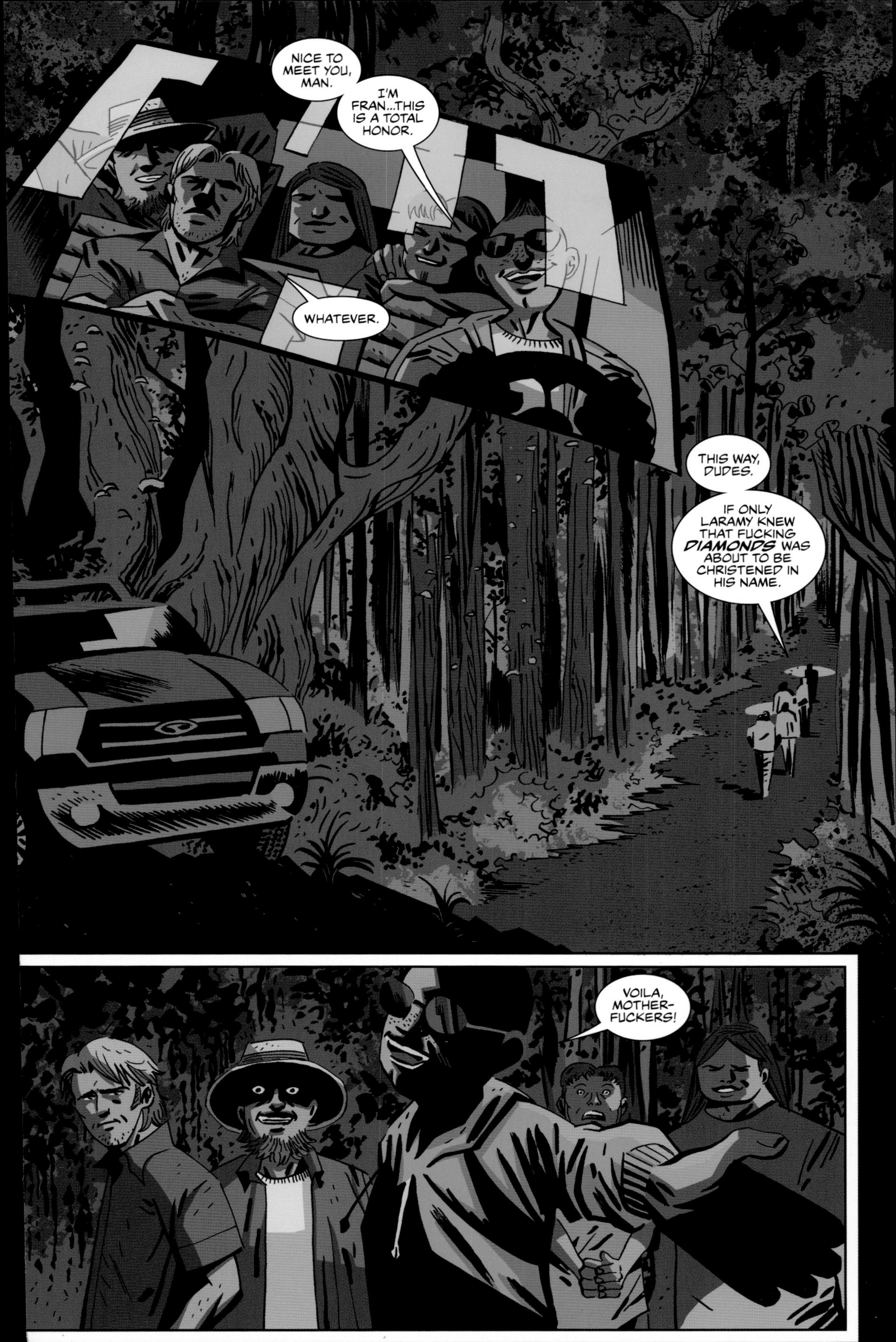
NICE TO MEET YOU, MAN.
I'M FRAN...THIS IS A TOTAL HONOR.
WHATEVER.
THIS WAY, DUDES.
IF ONLY LARAMY KNEW THAT FUCKING *DIAMONDS* WAS ABOUT TO BE CHRISTENED IN HIS NAME.
VOILA, MOTHER-FUCKERS!

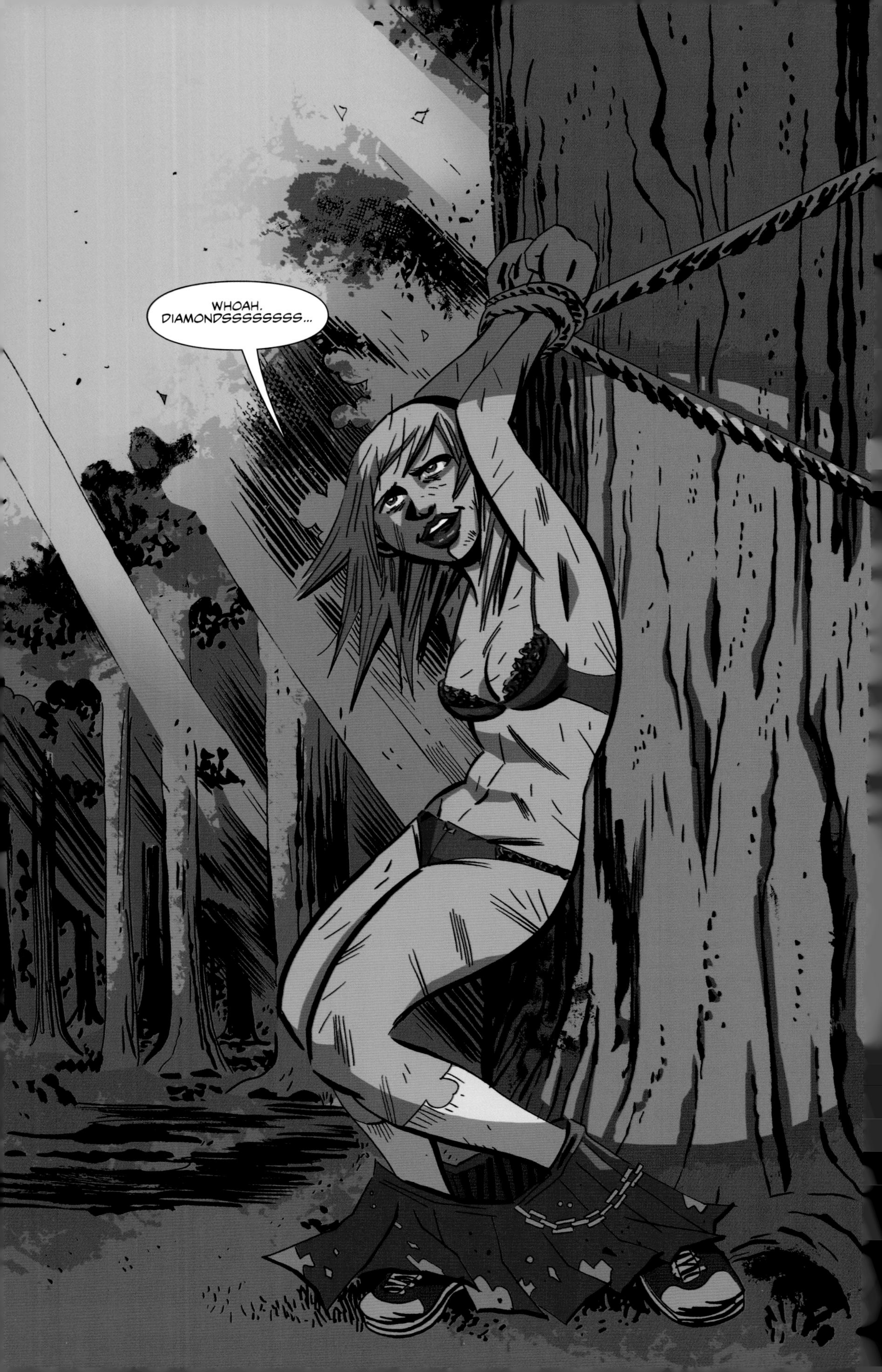
WHOAH. DIAMONDSSSSSSSS...

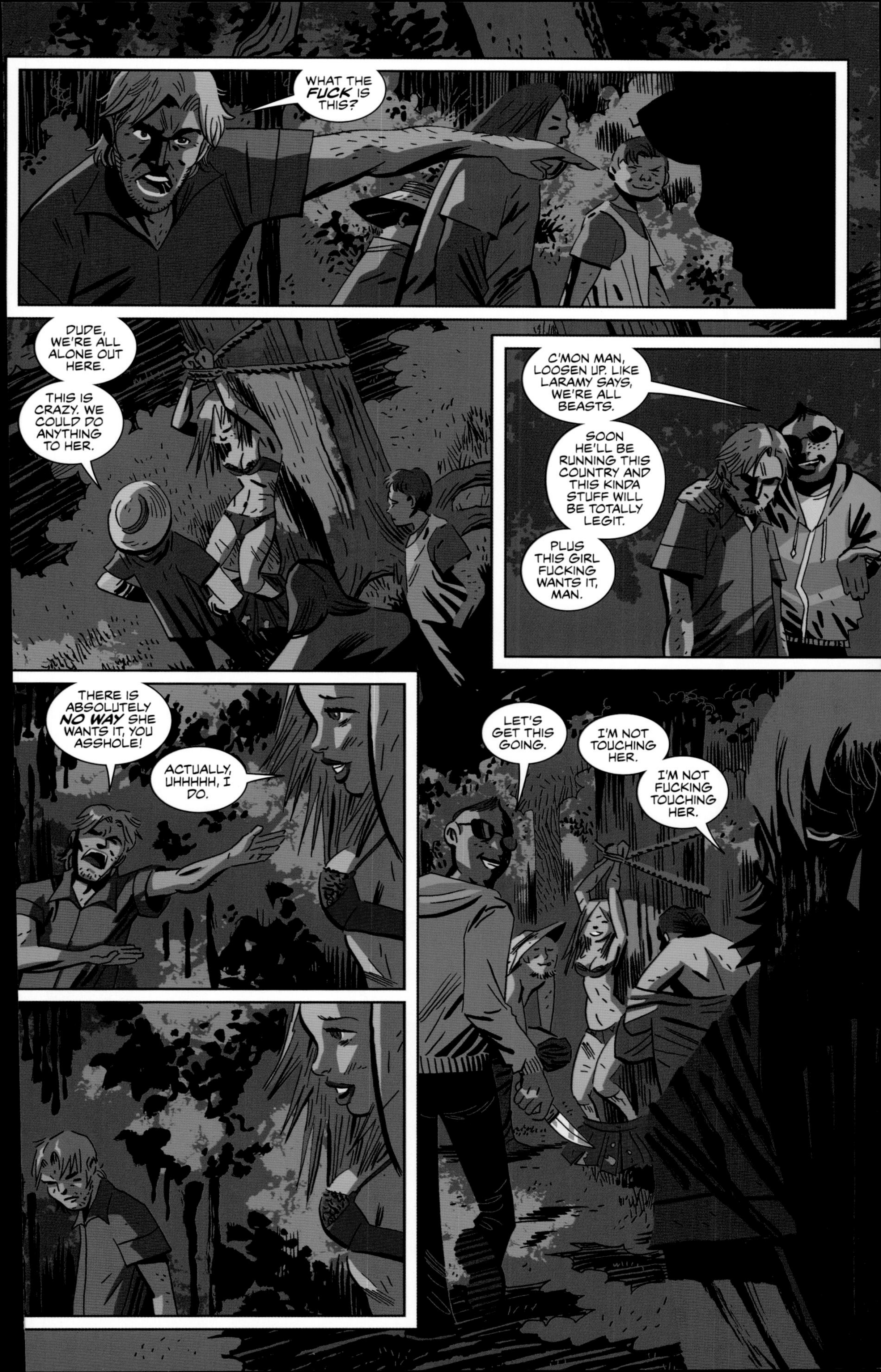
WHAT THE **FUCK** IS THIS?
DUDE, WE'RE ALL ALONE OUT HERE.
THIS IS CRAZY. WE COULD DO ANYTHING TO HER.
C'MON MAN, LOOSEN UP. LIKE LARAMY SAYS, WE'RE ALL BEASTS.
SOON HE'LL BE RUNNING THIS COUNTRY AND THIS KINDA STUFF WILL BE TOTALLY LEGIT.
PLUS THIS GIRL FUCKING WANTS IT, MAN.
THERE IS ABSOLUTELY **NO WAY** SHE WANTS IT, YOU ASSHOLE!
ACTUALLY, UHHHHH, I DO.
LET'S GET THIS GOING.
I'M NOT TOUCHING HER.
I'M NOT FUCKING TOUCHING HER.

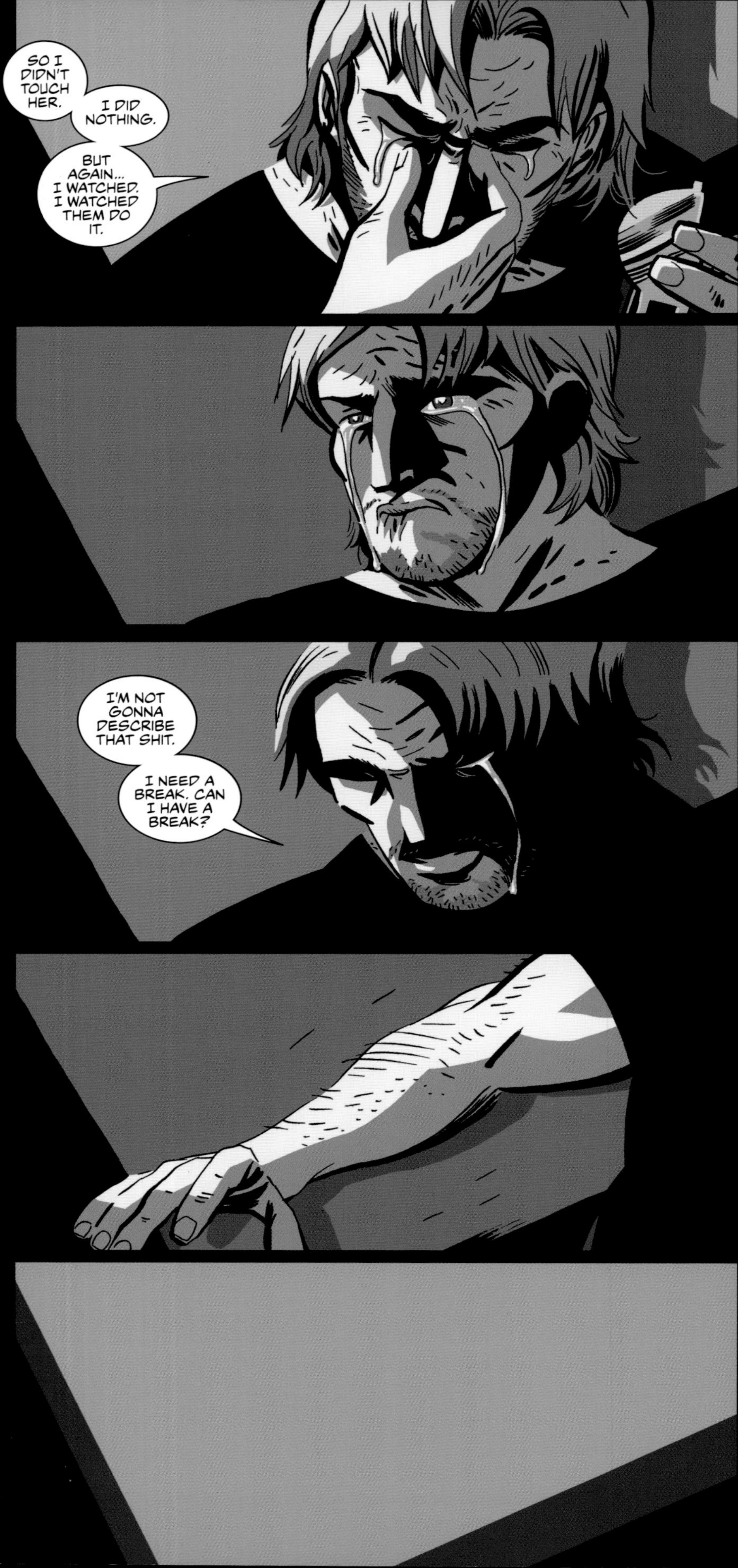
SO I DIDN'T TOUCH HER.
I DID NOTHING.
BUT AGAIN... I WATCHED. I WATCHED THEM DO IT.
I'M NOT GONNA DESCRIBE THAT SHIT.
I NEED A BREAK. CAN I HAVE A BREAK?

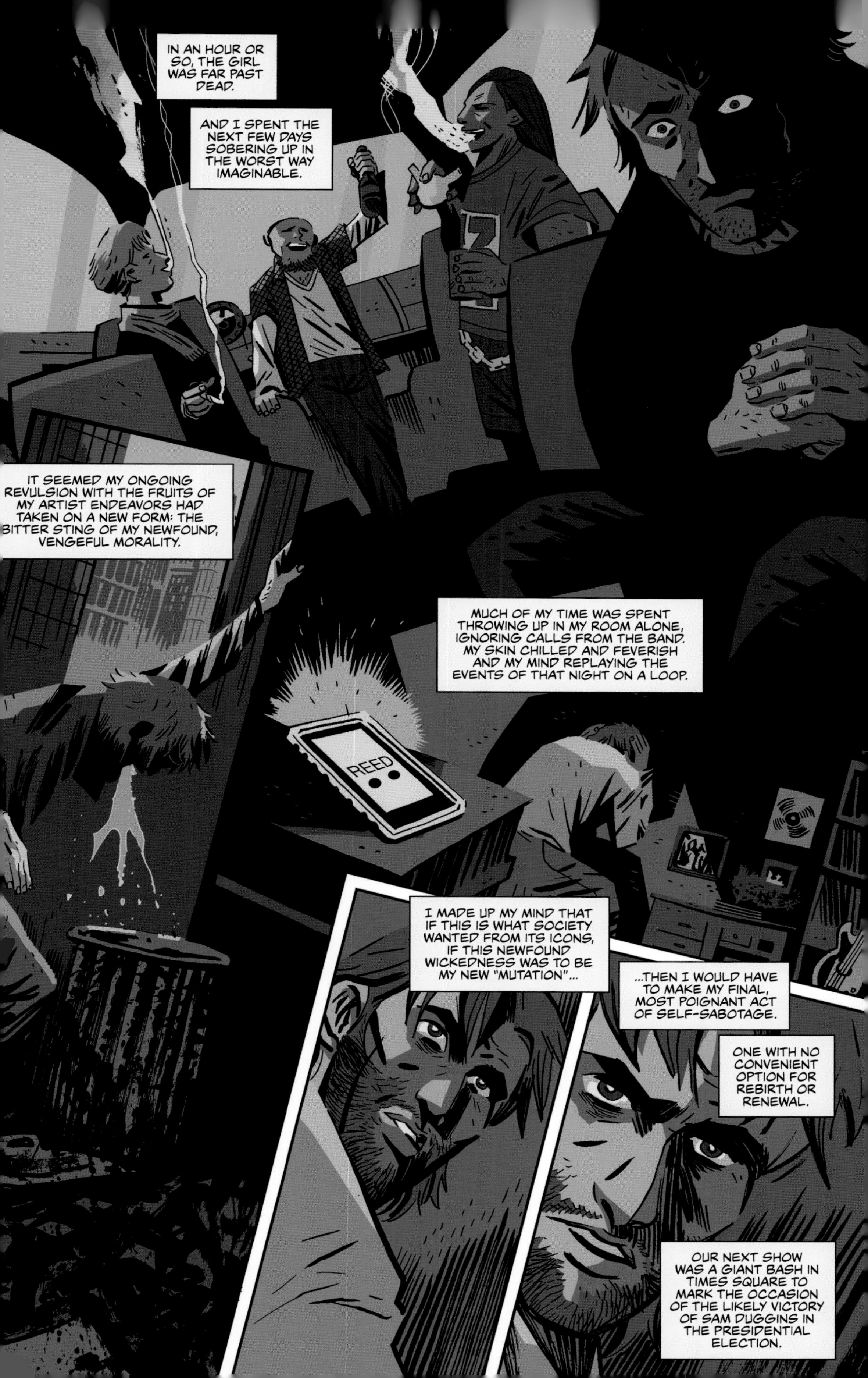
IN AN HOUR OR SO, THE GIRL WAS FAR PAST DEAD.
AND I SPENT THE NEXT FEW DAYS SOBERING UP IN THE WORST WAY IMAGINABLE.
IT SEEMED MY ONGOING REVULSION WITH THE FRUITS OF MY ARTIST ENDEAVORS HAD TAKEN ON A NEW FORM: THE BITTER STING OF MY NEWFOUND, VENGEFUL MORALITY.
MUCH OF MY TIME WAS SPENT THROWING UP IN MY ROOM ALONE, IGNORING CALLS FROM THE BAND. MY SKIN CHILLED AND FEVERISH AND MY MIND REPLAYING THE EVENTS OF THAT NIGHT ON A LOOP.
REED
I MADE UP MY MIND THAT IF THIS IS WHAT SOCIETY WANTED FROM ITS ICONS, IF THIS NEWFOUND WICKEDNESS WAS TO BE MY NEW "MUTATION"...
...THEN I WOULD HAVE TO MAKE MY FINAL, MOST POIGNANT ACT OF SELF-SABOTAGE.
ONE WITH NO CONVENIENT OPTION FOR REBIRTH OR RENEWAL.
OUR NEXT SHOW WAS A GIANT BASH IN TIMES SQUARE TO MARK THE OCCASION OF THE LIKELY VICTORY OF SAM DUGGINS IN THE PRESIDENTIAL ELECTION.

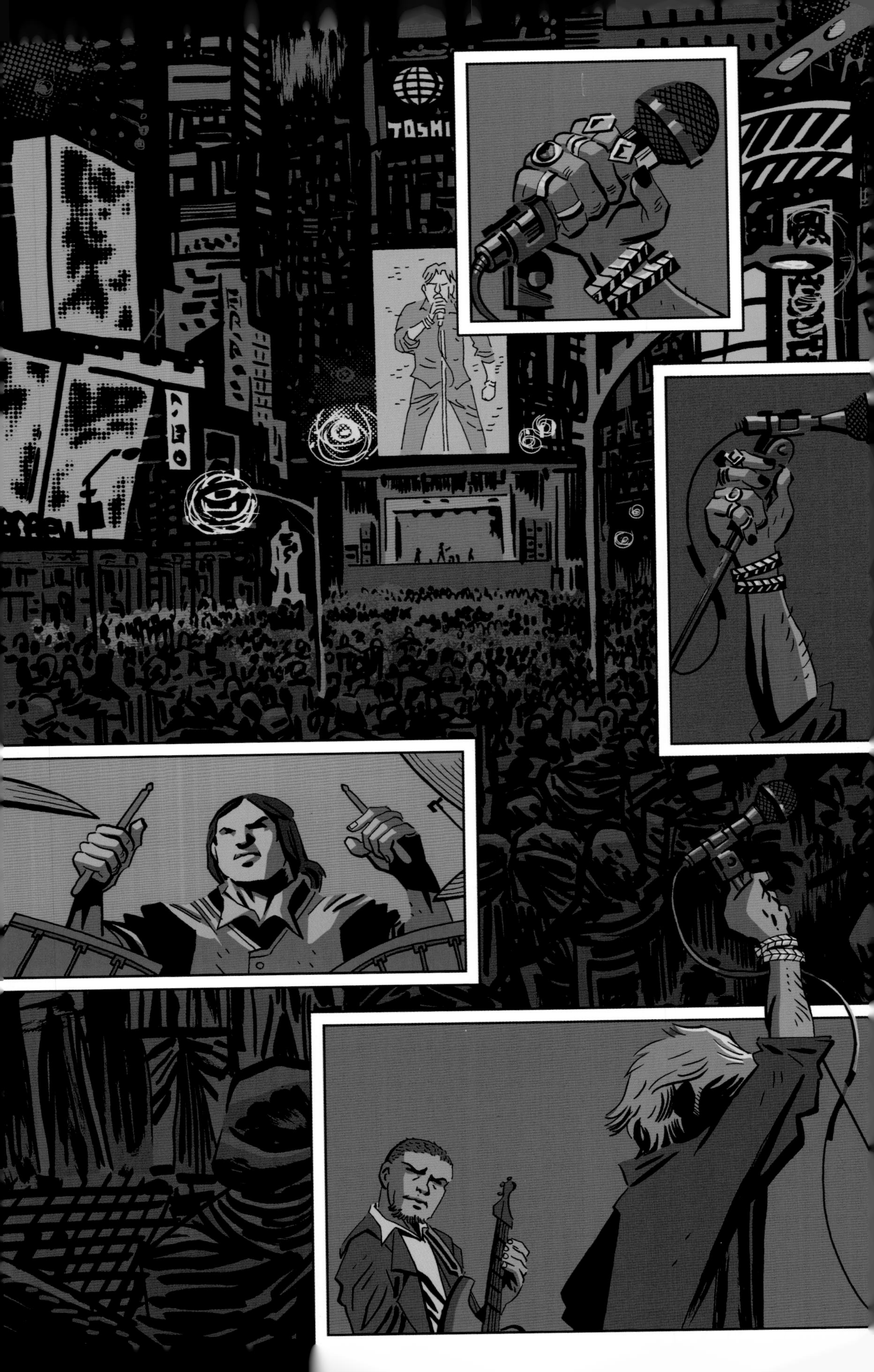
TOSHI

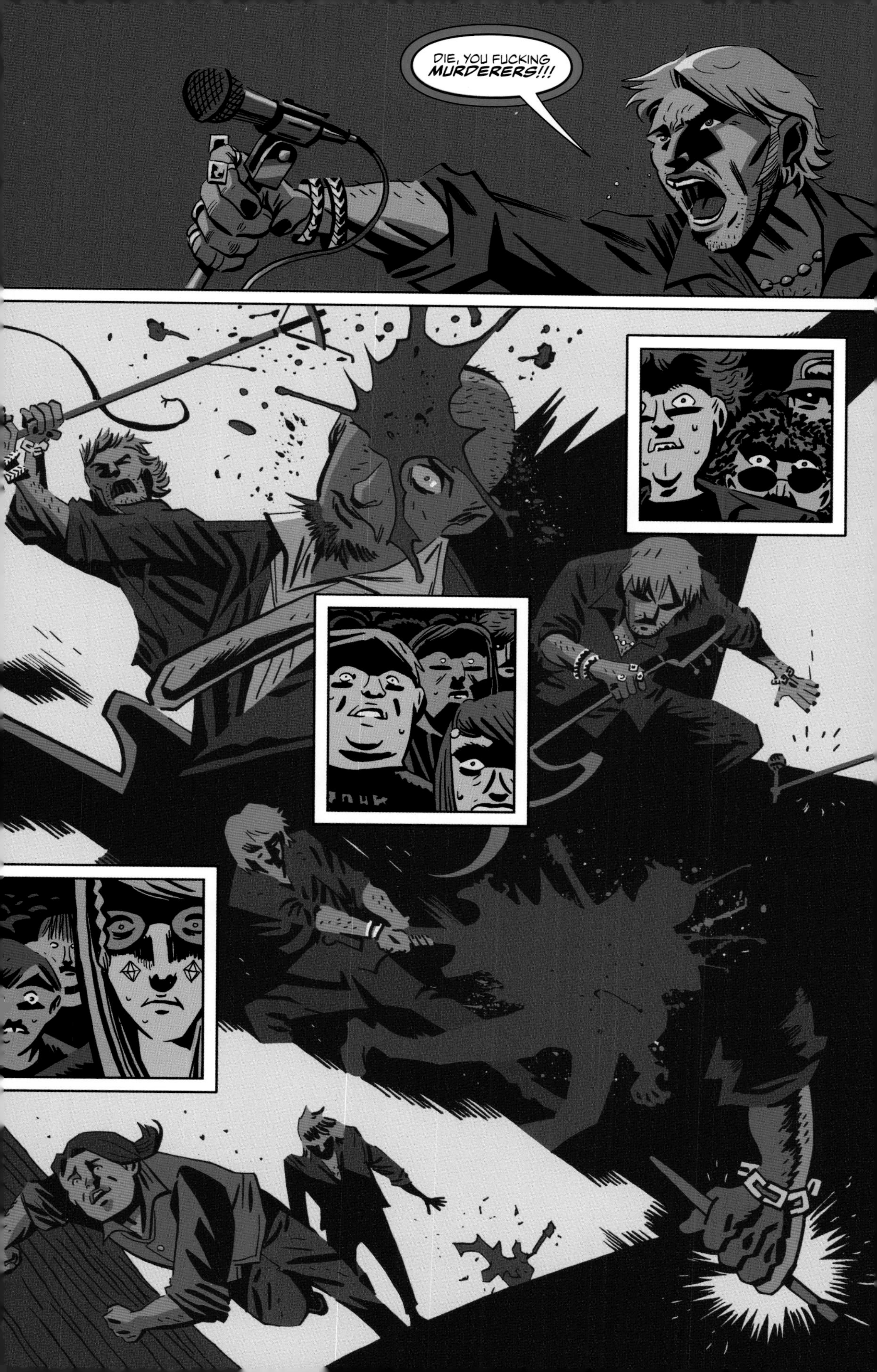
DIE, YOU FUCKING **MURDERERS!!!**

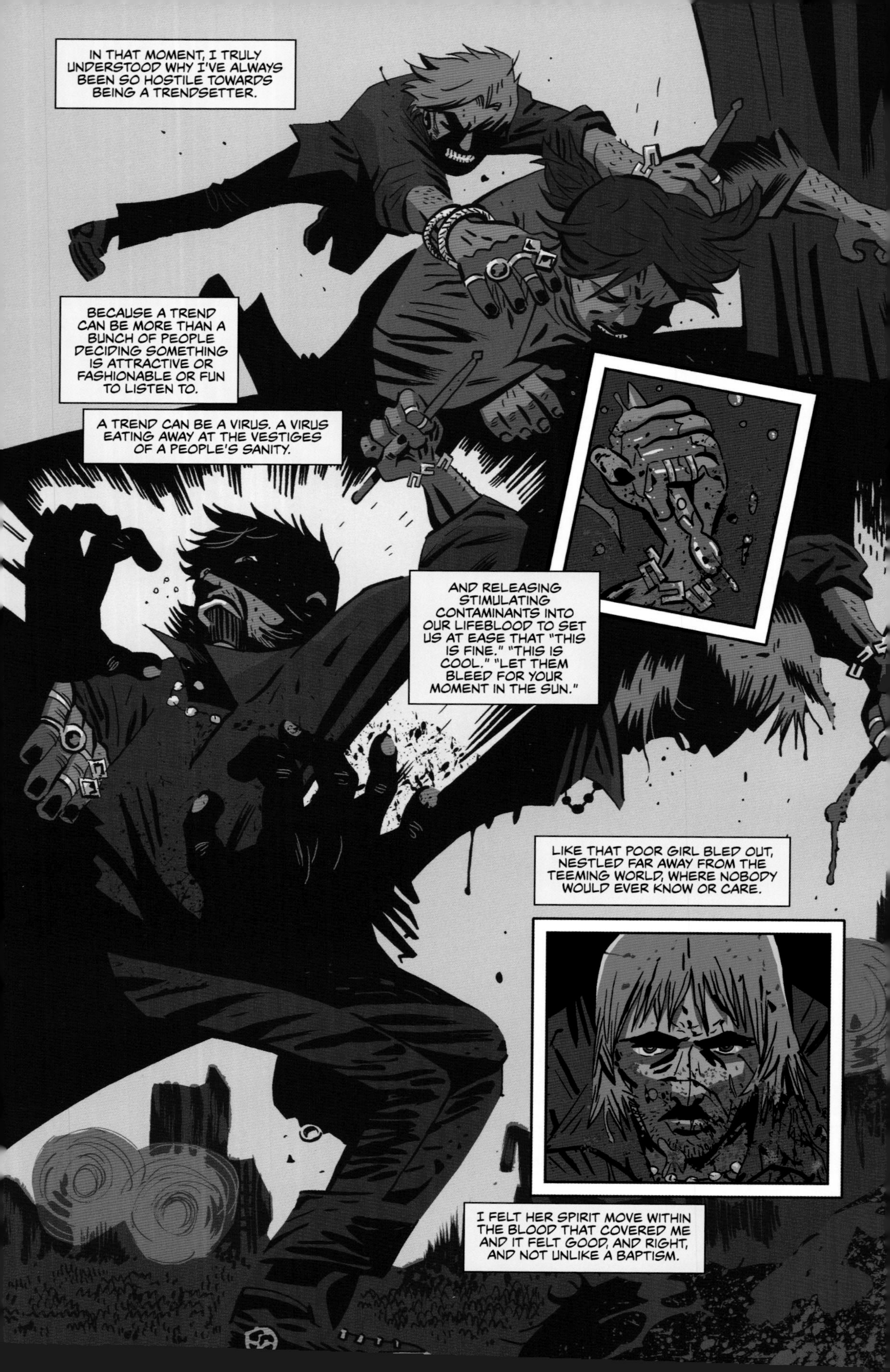
IN THAT MOMENT, I TRULY UNDERSTOOD WHY I'VE ALWAYS BEEN SO HOSTILE TOWARDS BEING A TRENDSETTER.
BECAUSE A TREND CAN BE MORE THAN A BUNCH OF PEOPLE DECIDING SOMETHING IS ATTRACTIVE OR FASHIONABLE OR FUN TO LISTEN TO.
A TREND CAN BE A VIRUS. A VIRUS EATING AWAY AT THE VESTIGES OF A PEOPLE'S SANITY.
AND RELEASING STIMULATING CONTAMINANTS INTO OUR LIFEBLOOD TO SET US AT EASE THAT "THIS IS FINE." "THIS IS COOL." "LET THEM BLEED FOR YOUR MOMENT IN THE SUN."
LIKE THAT POOR GIRL BLED OUT, NESTLED FAR AWAY FROM THE TEEMING WORLD, WHERE NOBODY WOULD EVER KNOW OR CARE.
I FELT HER SPIRIT MOVE WITHIN THE BLOOD THAT COVERED ME AND IT FELT GOOD, AND RIGHT, AND NOT UNLIKE A BAPTISM.

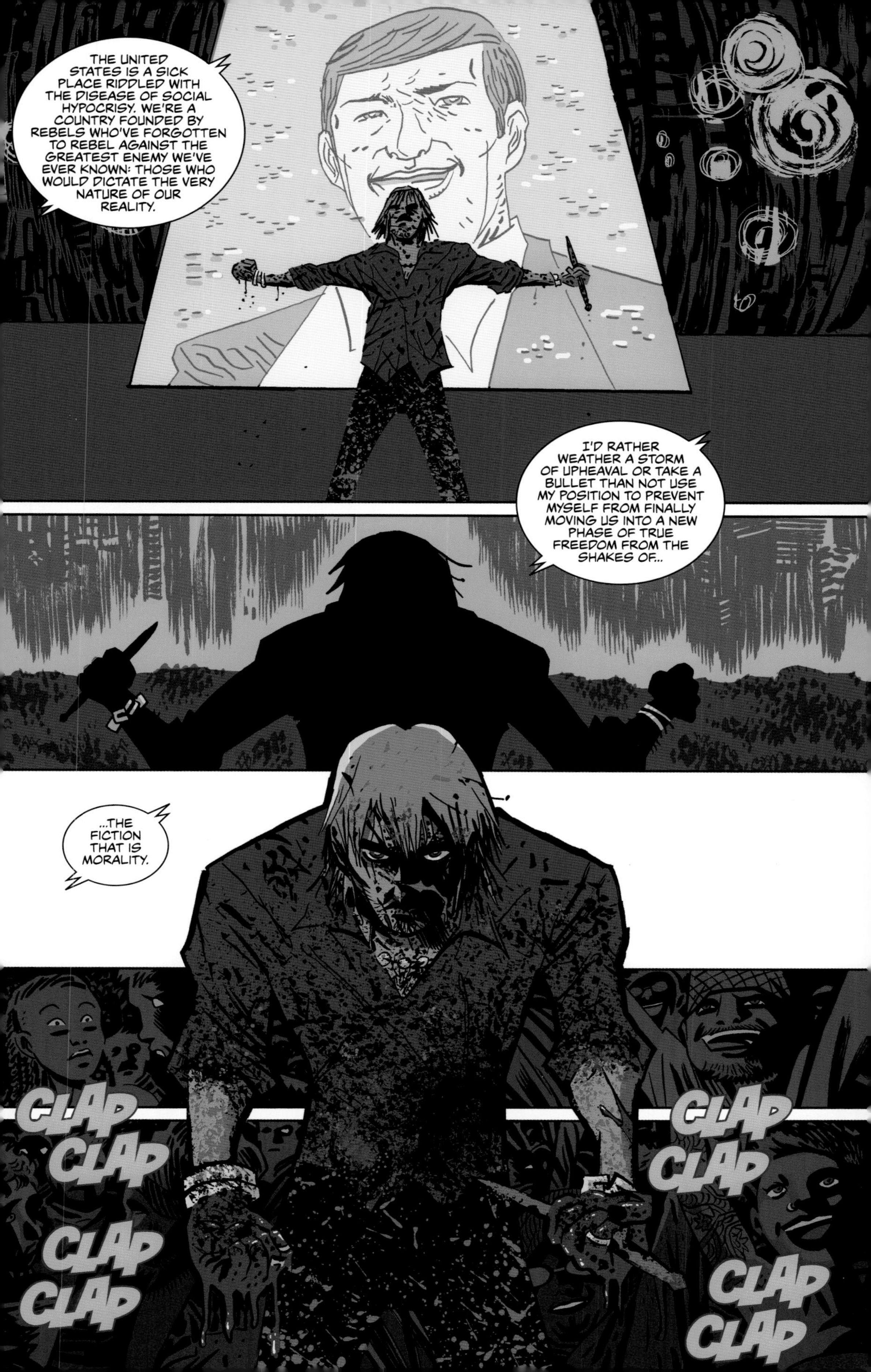
THE UNITED STATES IS A SICK PLACE RIDDLED WITH THE DISEASE OF SOCIAL HYPOCRISY. WE'RE A COUNTRY FOUNDED BY REBELS WHO'VE FORGOTTEN TO REBEL AGAINST THE GREATEST ENEMY WE'VE EVER KNOWN: THOSE WHO WOULD DICTATE THE VERY NATURE OF OUR REALITY.
I'D RATHER WEATHER A STORM OF UPHEAVAL OR TAKE A BULLET THAN NOT USE MY POSITION TO PREVENT MYSELF FROM FINALLY MOVING US INTO A NEW PHASE OF TRUE FREEDOM FROM THE SHAKES OF...
...THE FICTION THAT IS MORALITY.
CLAP CLAP CLAP CLAP
CLAP CLAP CLAP CLAP

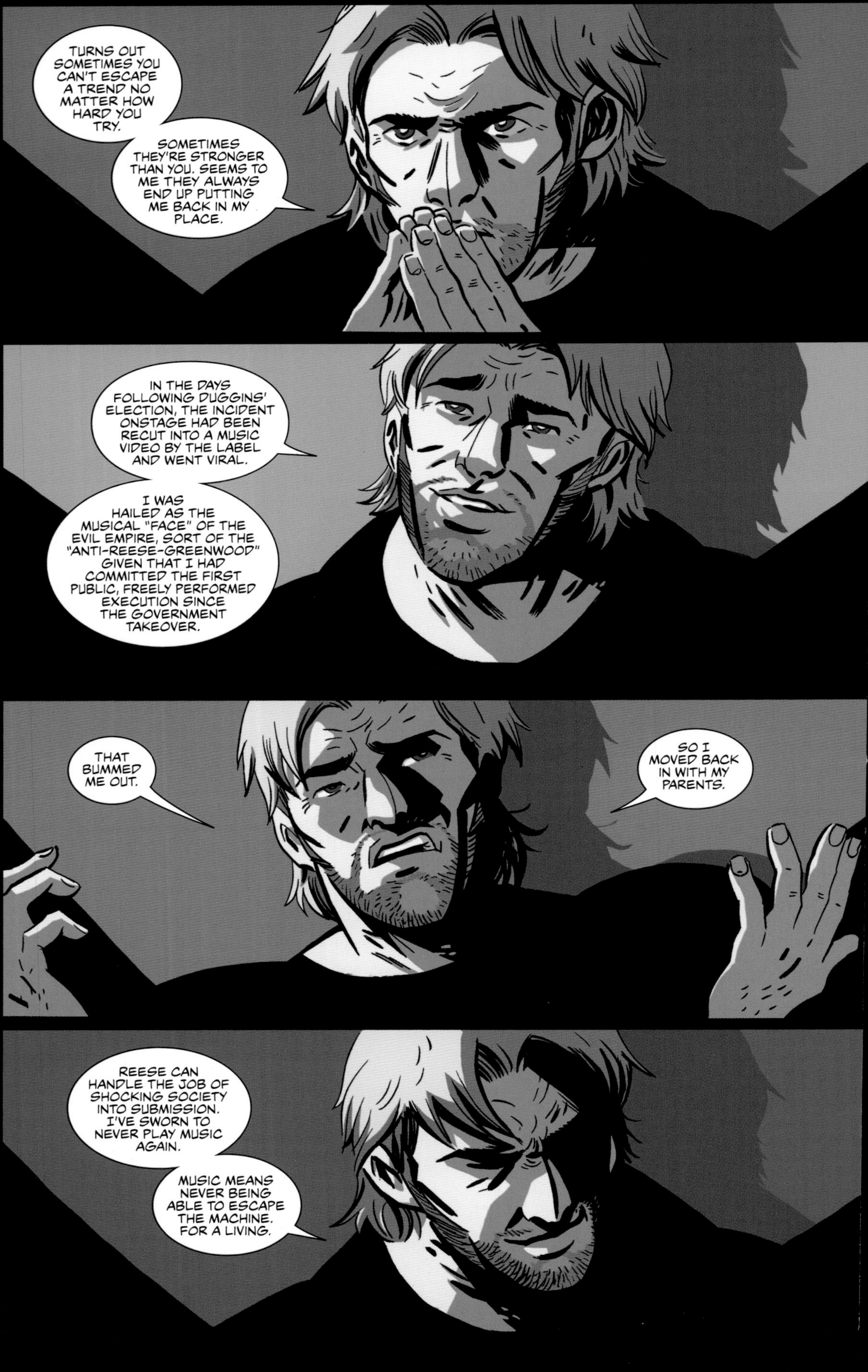
TURNS OUT SOMETIMES YOU CAN'T ESCAPE A TREND NO MATTER HOW HARD YOU TRY.
SOMETIMES THEY'RE STRONGER THAN YOU. SEEMS TO ME THEY ALWAYS END UP PUTTING ME BACK IN MY PLACE.
IN THE DAYS FOLLOWING DUGGINS' ELECTION, THE INCIDENT ONSTAGE HAD BEEN RECUT INTO A MUSIC VIDEO BY THE LABEL AND WENT VIRAL.
I WAS HAILED AS THE MUSICAL "FACE" OF THE EVIL EMPIRE, SORT OF THE "ANTI-REESE-GREENWOOD" GIVEN THAT I HAD COMMITTED THE FIRST PUBLIC, FREELY PERFORMED EXECUTION SINCE THE GOVERNMENT TAKEOVER.
THAT BUMMED ME OUT.
SO I MOVED BACK IN WITH MY PARENTS.
REESE CAN HANDLE THE JOB OF SHOCKING SOCIETY INTO SUBMISSION. I'VE SWORN TO NEVER PLAY MUSIC AGAIN.
MUSIC MEANS NEVER BEING ABLE TO ESCAPE THE MACHINE. FOR A LIVING.

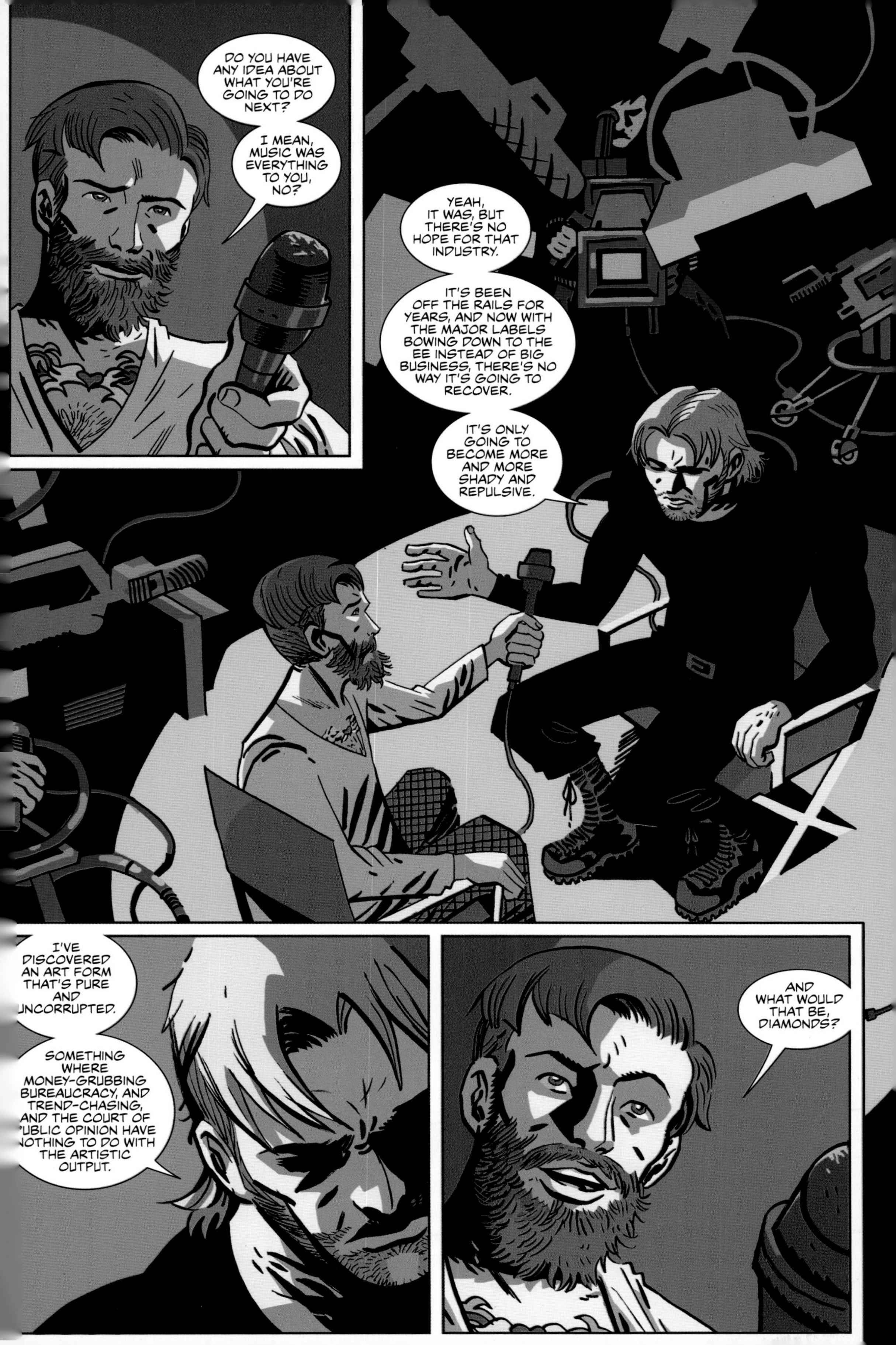
DO YOU HAVE ANY IDEA ABOUT WHAT YOU'RE GOING TO DO NEXT?
I MEAN, MUSIC WAS EVERYTHING TO YOU, NO?
YEAH, IT WAS, BUT THERE'S NO HOPE FOR THAT INDUSTRY.
IT'S BEEN OFF THE RAILS FOR YEARS, AND NOW WITH THE MAJOR LABELS BOWING DOWN TO THE EE INSTEAD OF BIG BUSINESS, THERE'S NO WAY IT'S GOING TO RECOVER.
IT'S ONLY GOING TO BECOME MORE AND MORE SHADY AND REPULSIVE.
I'VE DISCOVERED AN ART FORM THAT'S PURE AND UNCORRUPTED.
SOMETHING WHERE MONEY-GRUBBING BUREAUCRACY, AND TREND-CHASING, AND THE COURT OF PUBLIC OPINION HAVE NOTHING TO DO WITH THE ARTISTIC OUTPUT.
AND WHAT WOULD THAT BE, DIAMONDS?

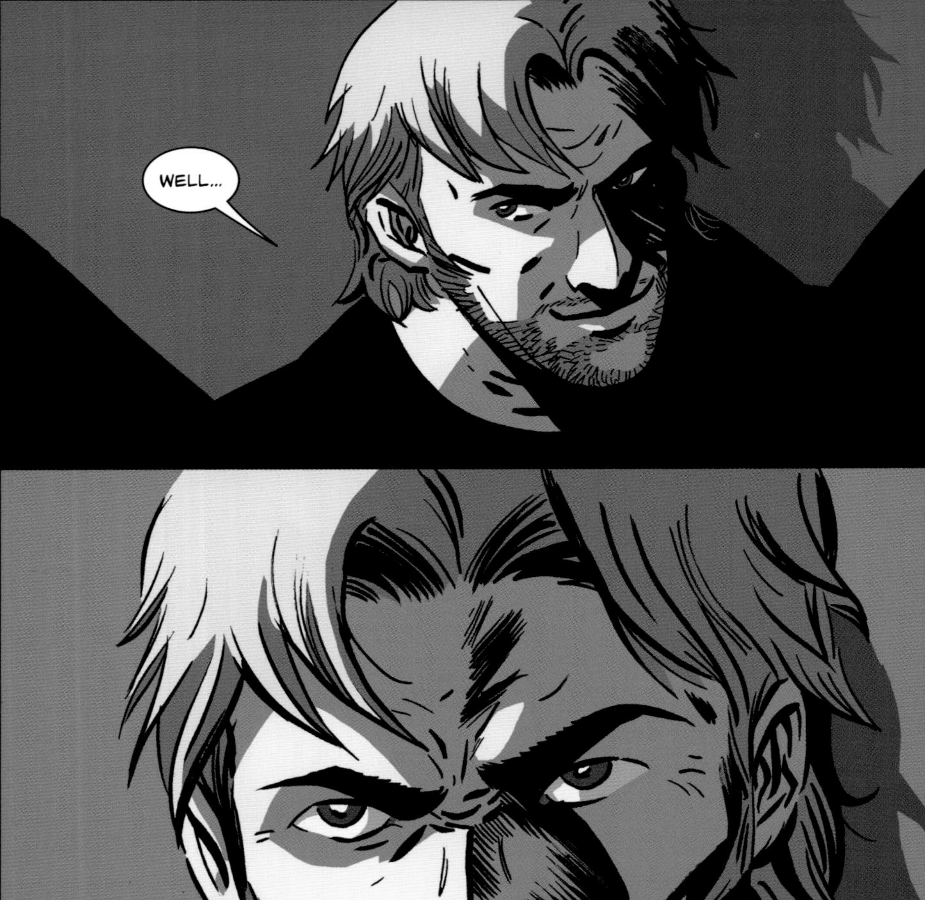
WELL...
I THINK I MIGHT TRY MY HAND AT WRITING COMIC BOOKS.

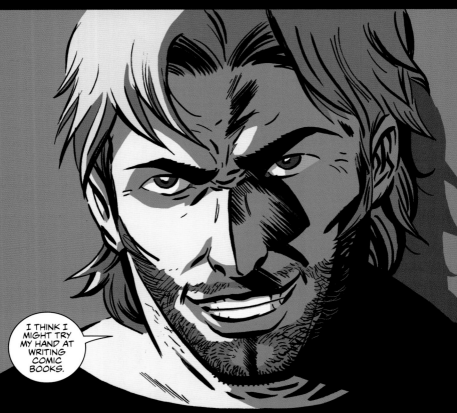

"DIAMONDS" AN EVIL EMPIRE TALE

Taking it too far is going to be a thing of the past.

ext. 2.0

CHAPTER
TEN

fig. 2

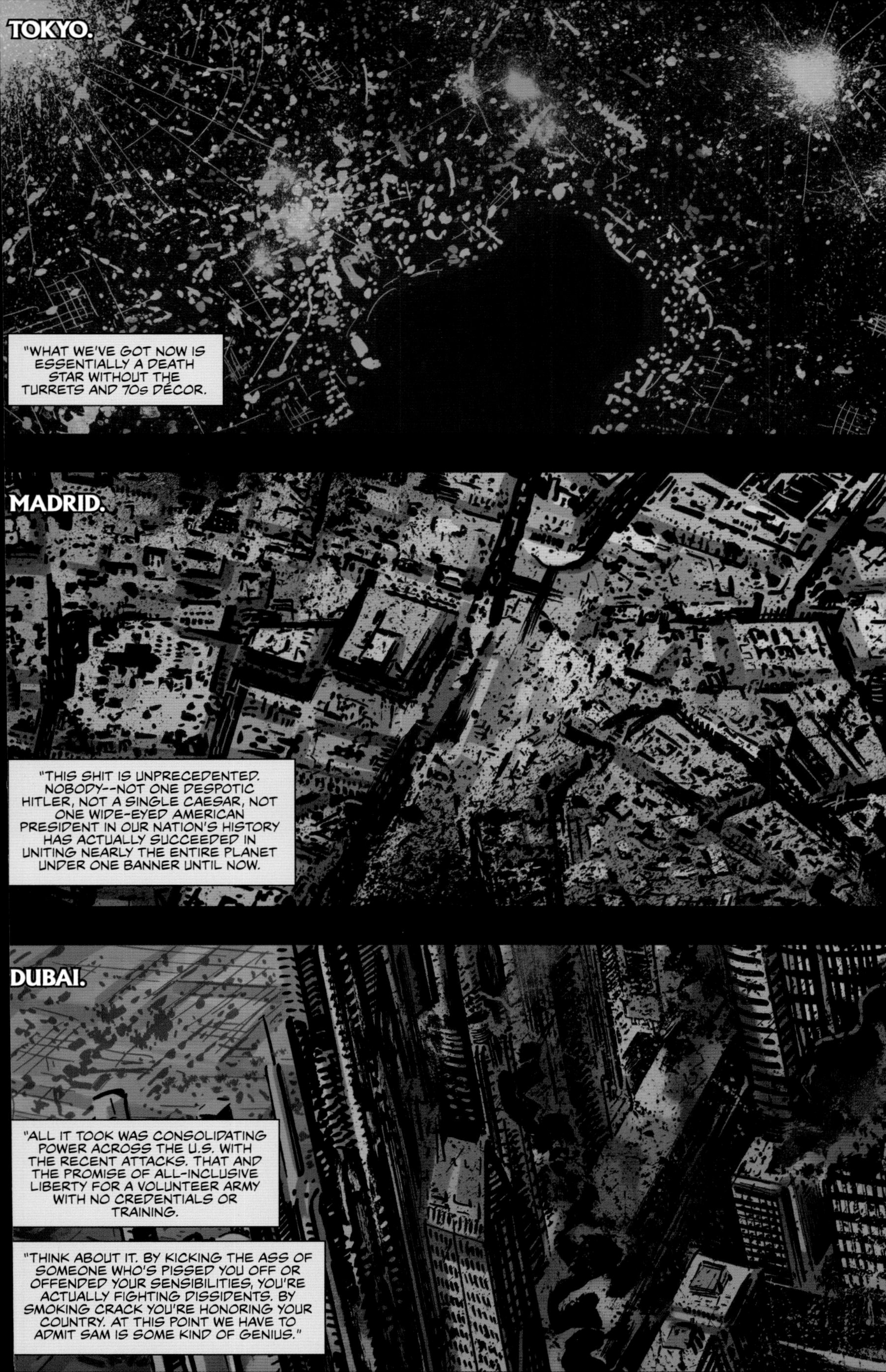
TOKYO.
"WHAT WE'VE GOT NOW IS ESSENTIALLY A DEATH STAR WITHOUT THE TURRETS AND 70s DÉCOR.
MADRID.
"THIS SHIT IS UNPRECEDENTED. NOBODY--NOT ONE DESPOTIC HITLER, NOT A SINGLE CAESAR, NOT ONE WIDE-EYED AMERICAN PRESIDENT IN OUR NATION'S HISTORY HAS ACTUALLY SUCCEEDED IN UNITING NEARLY THE ENTIRE PLANET UNDER ONE BANNER UNTIL NOW.
DUBAI.
"ALL IT TOOK WAS CONSOLIDATING POWER ACROSS THE U.S. WITH THE RECENT ATTACKS. THAT AND THE PROMISE OF ALL-INCLUSIVE LIBERTY FOR A VOLUNTEER ARMY WITH NO CREDENTIALS OR TRAINING.
"THINK ABOUT IT. BY KICKING THE ASS OF SOMEONE WHO'S PISSED YOU OFF OR OFFENDED YOUR SENSIBILITIES, YOU'RE ACTUALLY FIGHTING DISSIDENTS. BY SMOKING CRACK YOU'RE HONORING YOUR COUNTRY. AT THIS POINT WE HAVE TO ADMIT SAM IS SOME KIND OF GENIUS."

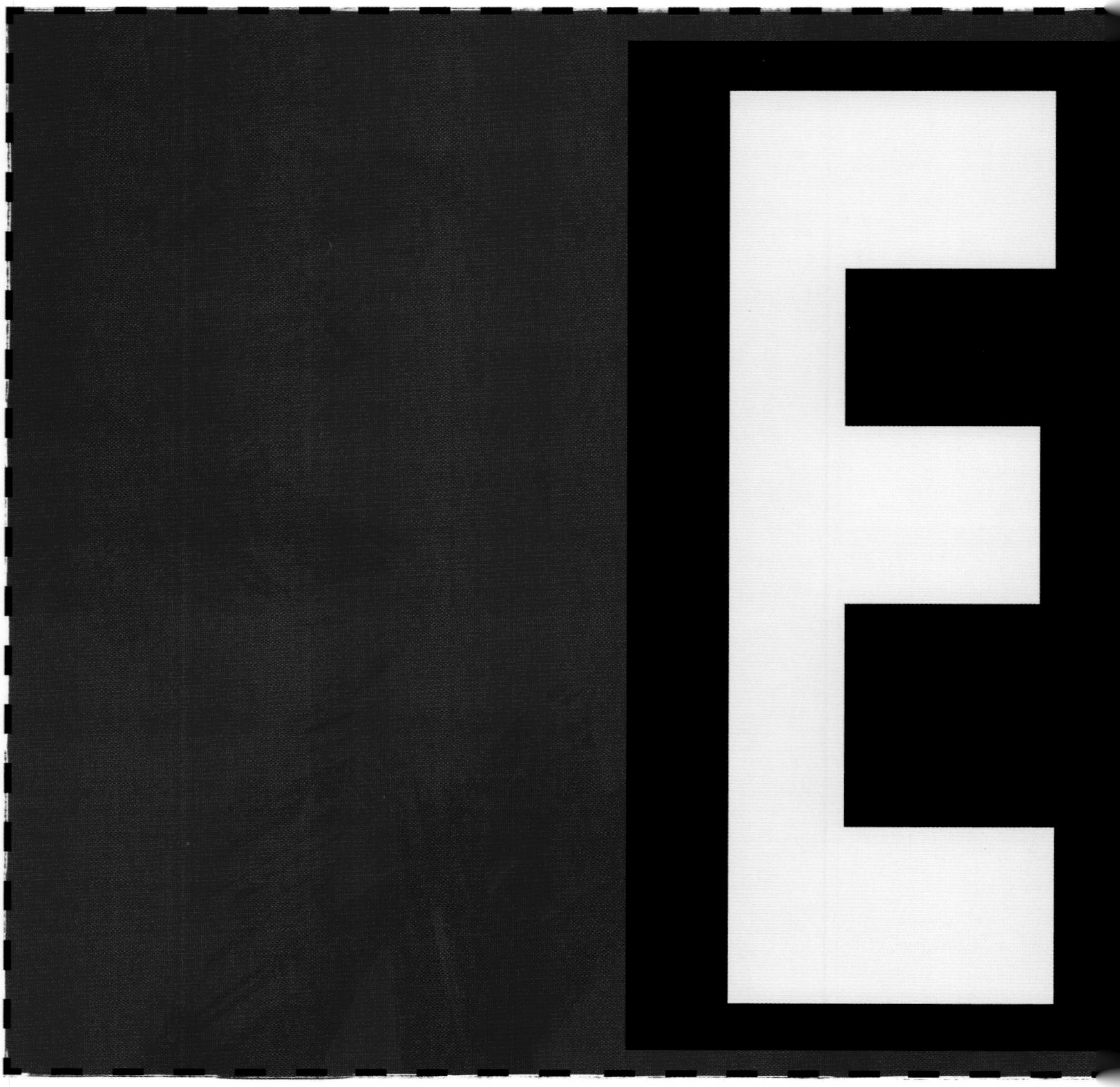

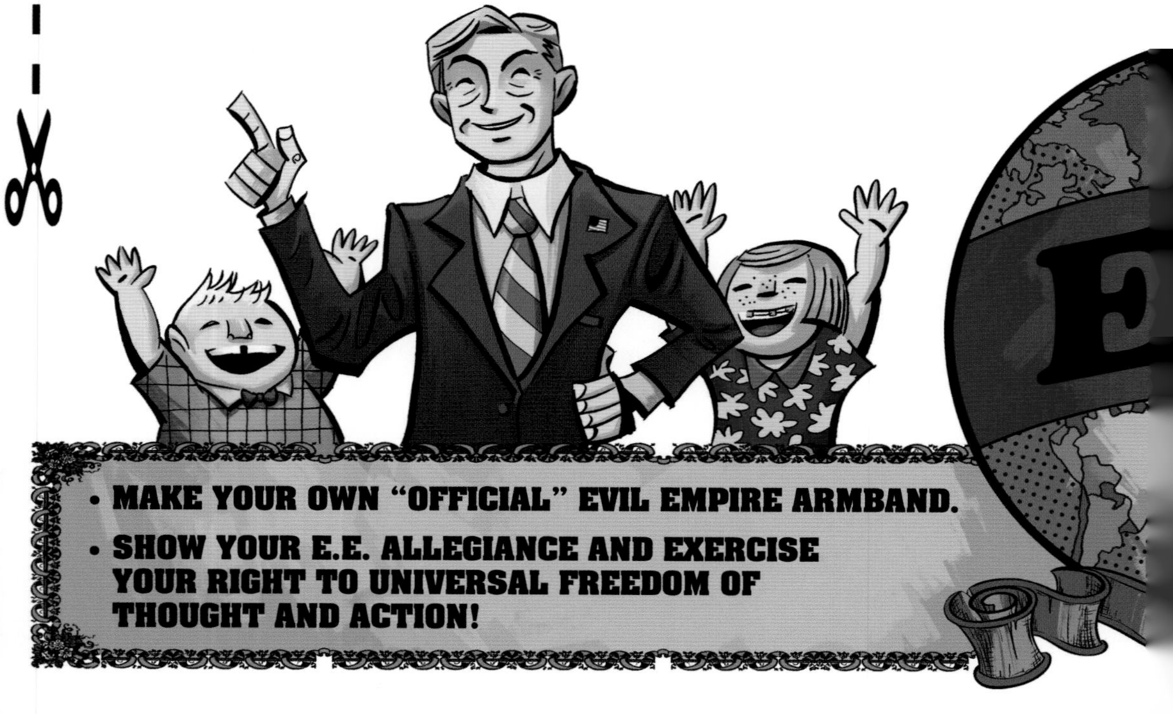

- MAKE YOUR OWN "OFFICIAL" EVIL EMPIRE ARMBAND.
- SHOW YOUR E.E. ALLEGIANCE AND EXERCISE YOUR RIGHT TO UNIVERSAL FREEDOM OF THOUGHT AND ACTION!

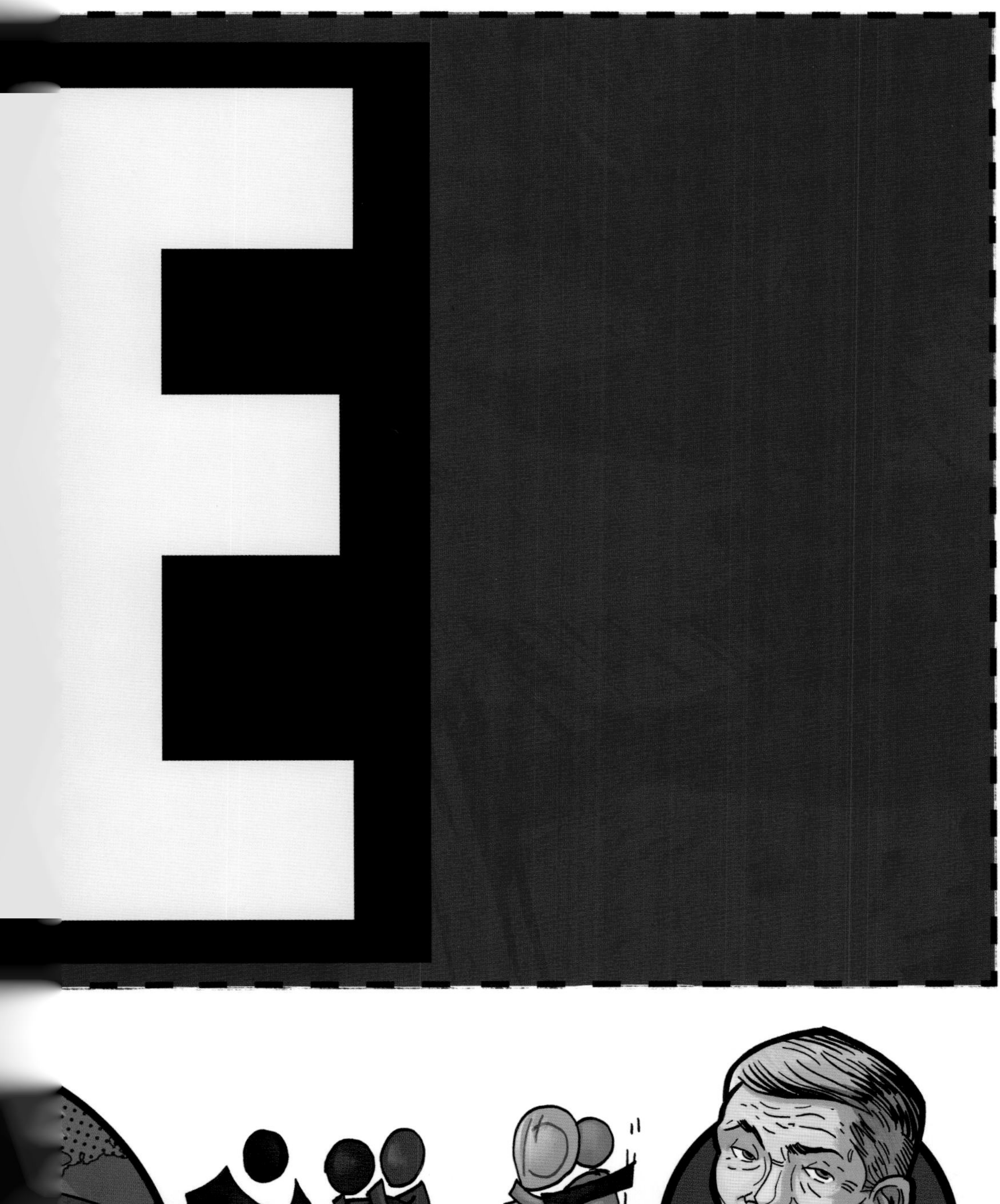
E

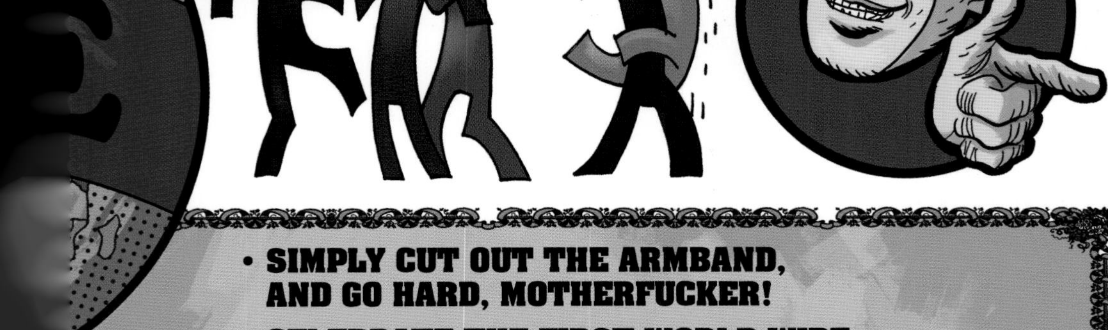

- **SIMPLY CUT OUT THE ARMBAND, AND GO HARD, MOTHERFUCKER!**
- **CELEBRATE THE FIRST WORLD-WIDE INTEGRATED SOCIETY!**

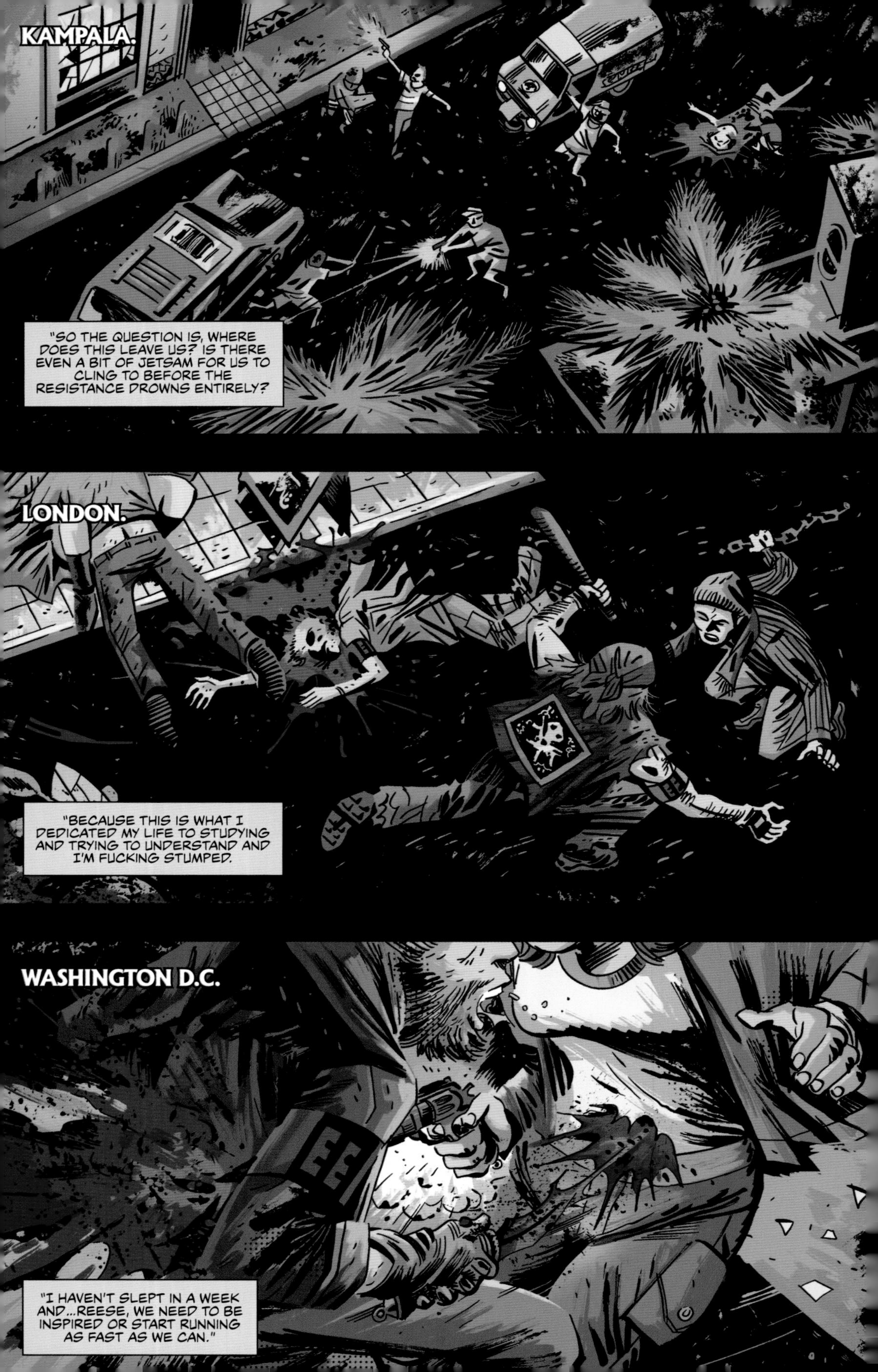
KAMPALA.
"SO THE QUESTION IS, WHERE DOES THIS LEAVE US? IS THERE EVEN A BIT OF JETSAM FOR US TO CLING TO BEFORE THE RESISTANCE DROWNS ENTIRELY?
LONDON.
"BECAUSE THIS IS WHAT I DEDICATED MY LIFE TO STUDYING AND TRYING TO UNDERSTAND AND I'M FUCKING STUMPED.
WASHINGTON D.C.
"I HAVEN'T SLEPT IN A WEEK AND...REESE, WE NEED TO BE INSPIRED OR START RUNNING AS FAST AS WE CAN."

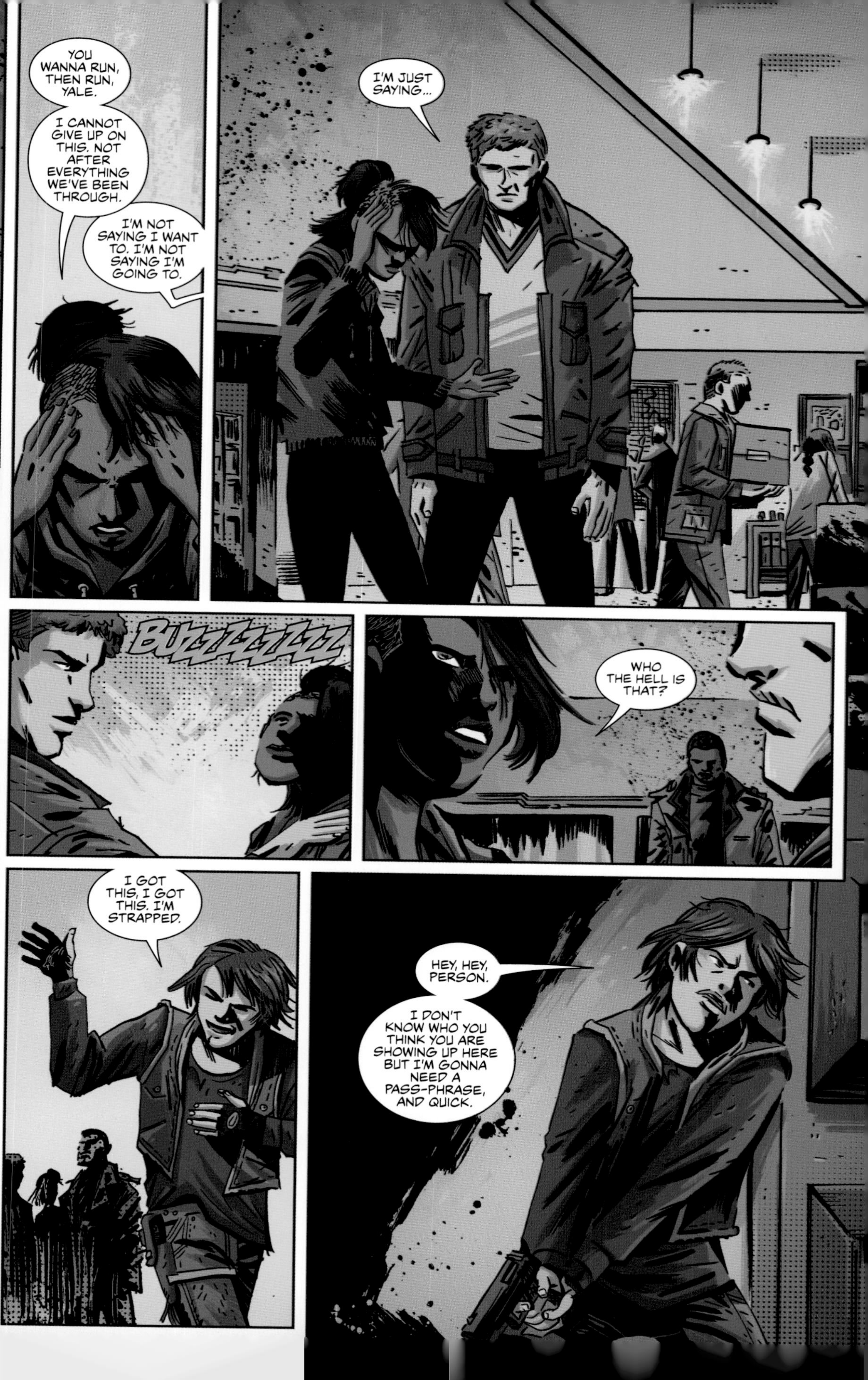
YOU WANNA RUN, THEN RUN, YALE.
I CANNOT GIVE UP ON THIS. NOT AFTER EVERYTHING WE'VE BEEN THROUGH.
I'M NOT SAYING I WANT TO. I'M NOT SAYING I'M GOING TO.
I'M JUST SAYING...
BUZZZZZZZ
WHO THE HELL IS THAT?
I GOT THIS, I GOT THIS. I'M STRAPPED.
HEY, HEY, PERSON.
I DON'T KNOW WHO YOU THINK YOU ARE SHOWING UP HERE BUT I'M GONNA NEED A PASS-PHRASE, AND QUICK.

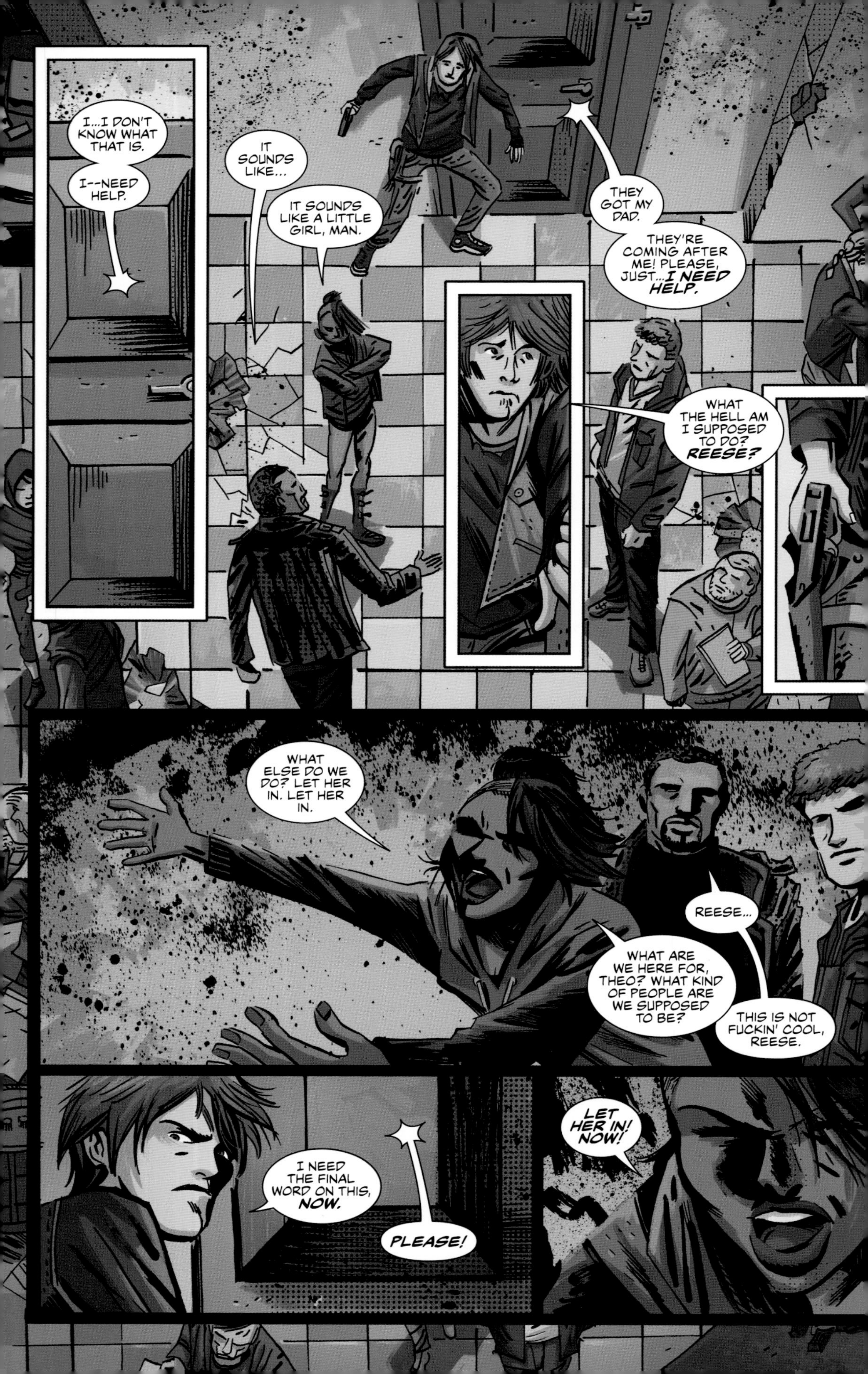
I...I DON'T KNOW WHAT THAT IS.
I--NEED HELP.
IT SOUNDS LIKE...
IT SOUNDS LIKE A LITTLE GIRL, MAN.
THEY GOT MY DAD.
THEY'RE COMING AFTER ME! PLEASE, JUST... **I NEED HELP.**
WHAT THE HELL AM I SUPPOSED TO DO? **REESE?**
WHAT ELSE DO WE DO? LET HER IN. LET HER IN.
REESE...
WHAT ARE WE HERE FOR, THEO? WHAT KIND OF PEOPLE ARE WE SUPPOSED TO BE?
THIS IS NOT FUCKIN' COOL, REESE.
I NEED THE FINAL WORD ON THIS, **NOW.**
PLEASE!
LET HER IN! NOW!

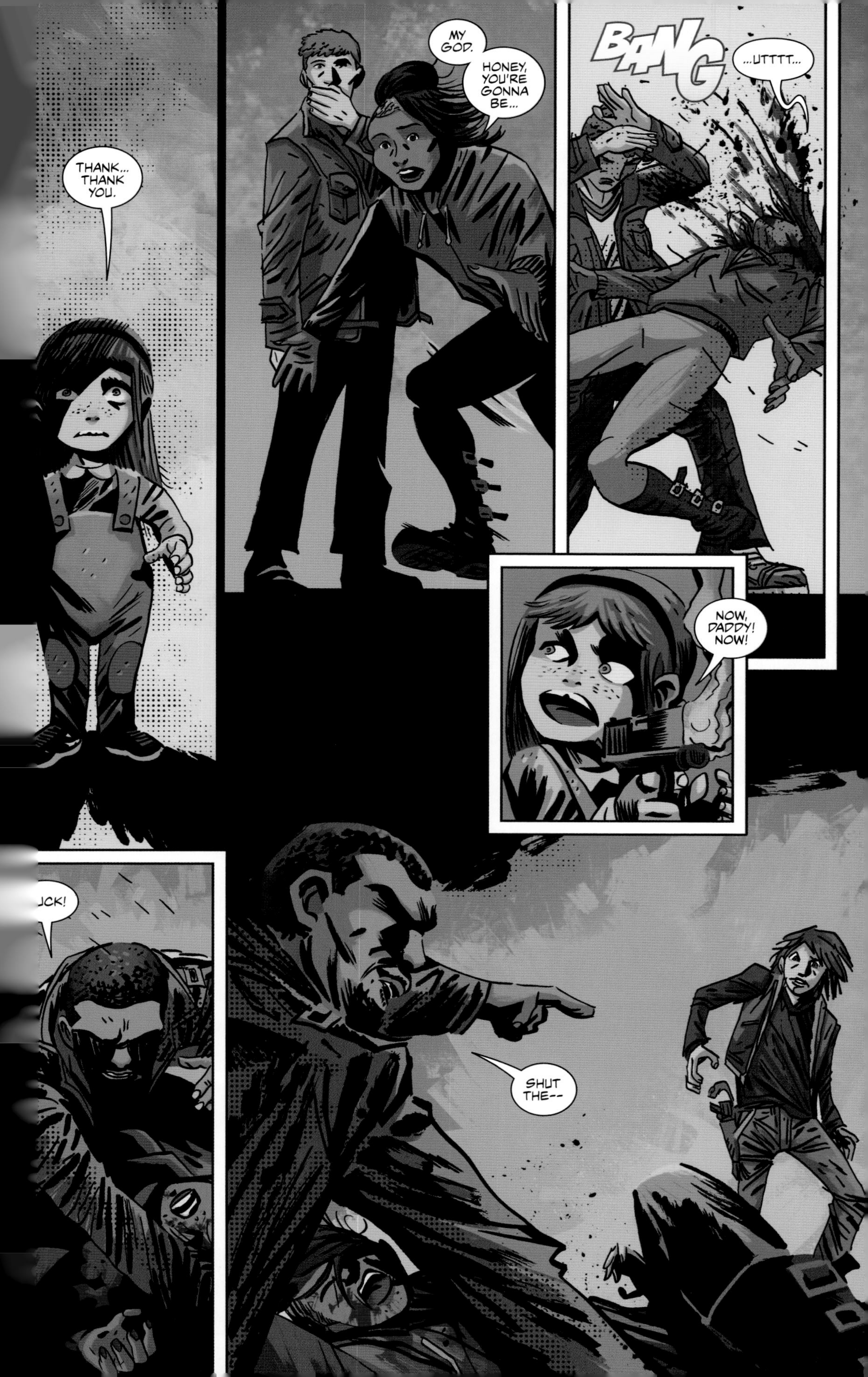
THANK... THANK YOU.
MY GOD.
HONEY, YOU'RE GONNA BE...
BANG
...UTTTT...
NOW, DADDY! NOW!
UCK!
SHUT THE--

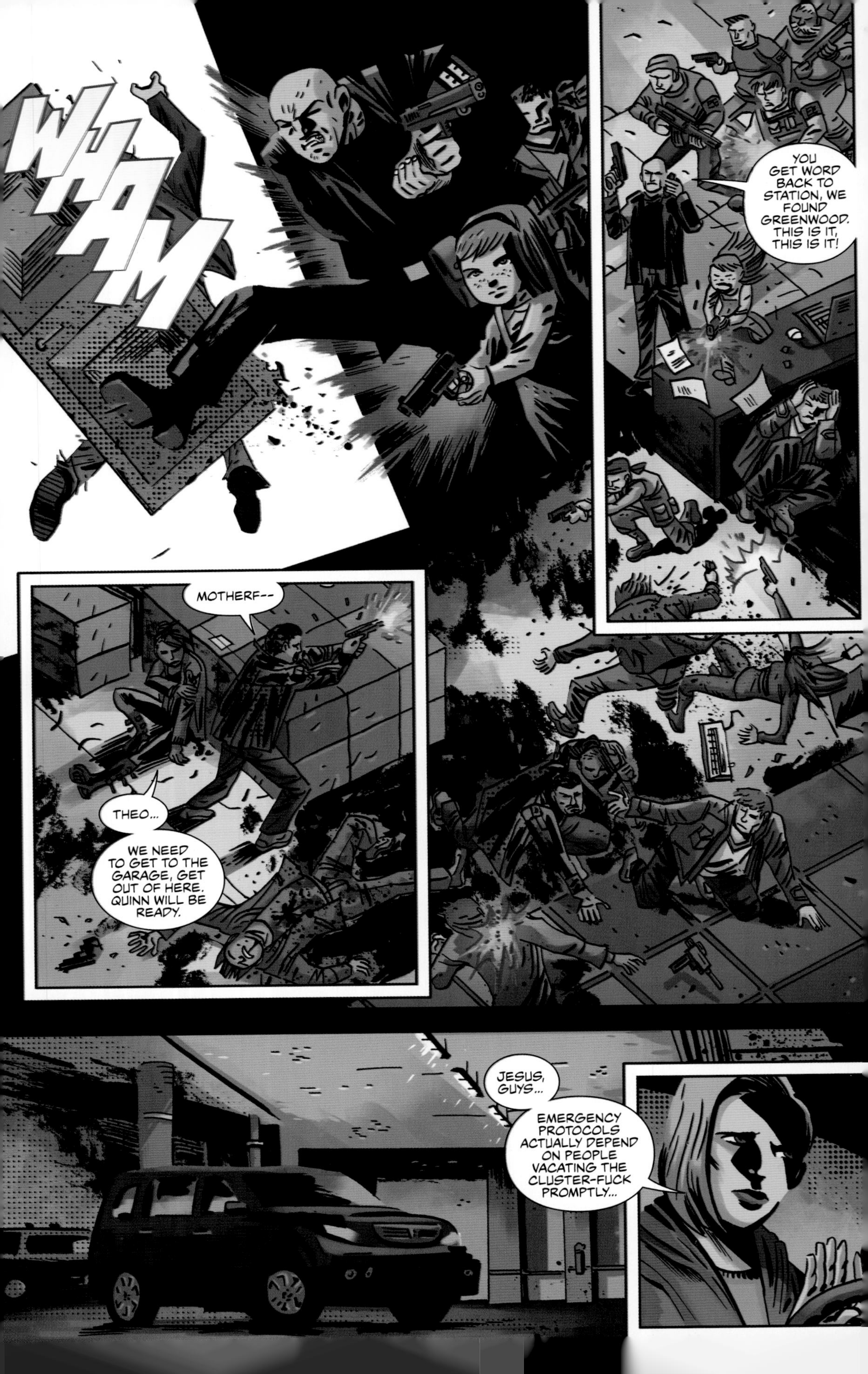
WHAM
YOU GET WORD BACK TO STATION, WE FOUND GREENWOOD. THIS IS IT, THIS IS IT!
MOTHERF--
THEO...
WE NEED TO GET TO THE GARAGE, GET OUT OF HERE. QUINN WILL BE READY.
JESUS, GUYS...
EMERGENCY PROTOCOLS ACTUALLY DEPEND ON PEOPLE VACATING THE CLUSTER-FUCK PROMPTLY...

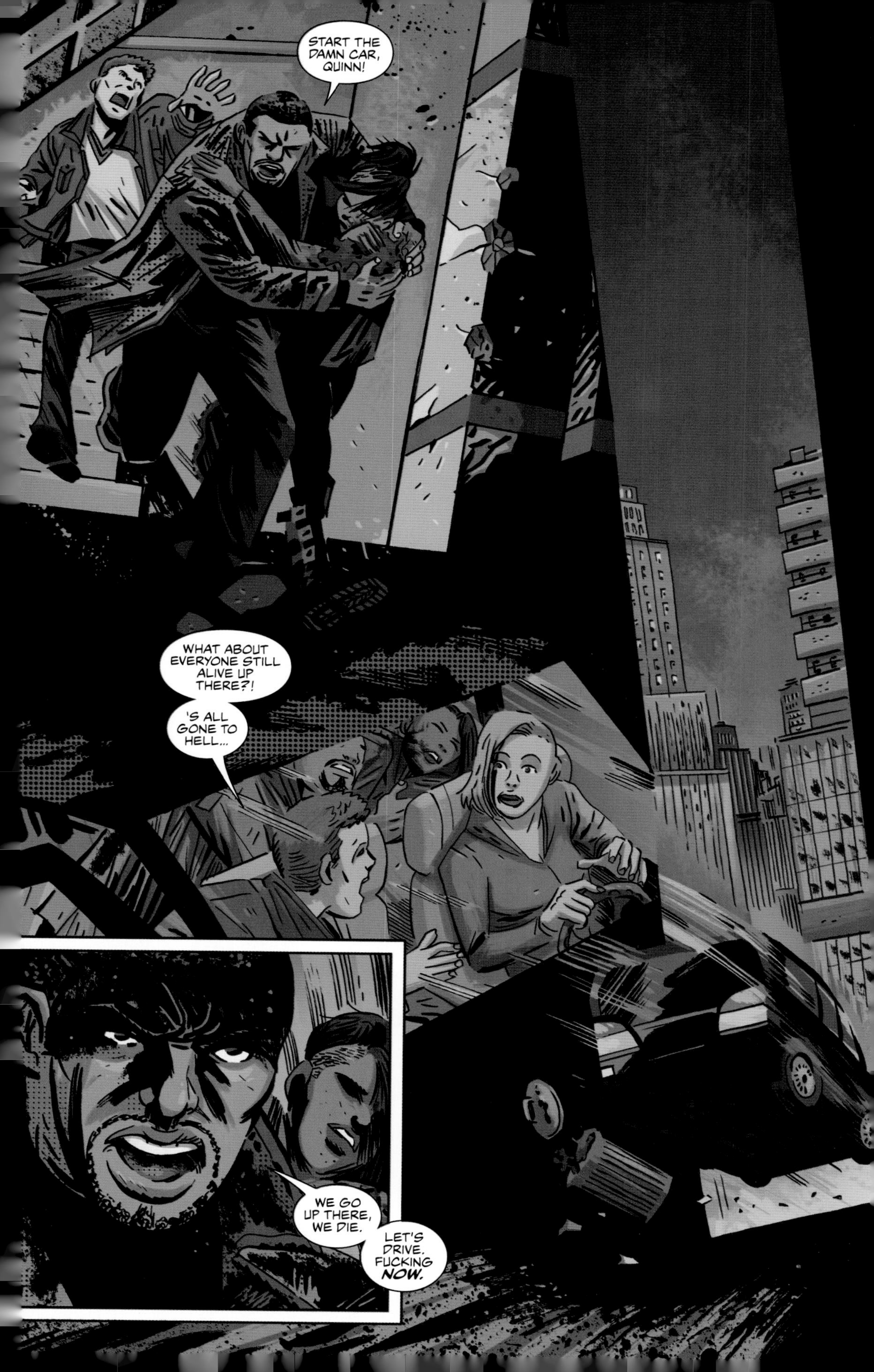
START THE DAMN CAR, QUINN!
WHAT ABOUT EVERYONE STILL ALIVE UP THERE?!
'S ALL GONE TO HELL...
WE GO UP THERE, WE DIE.
LET'S DRIVE. FUCKING NOW.

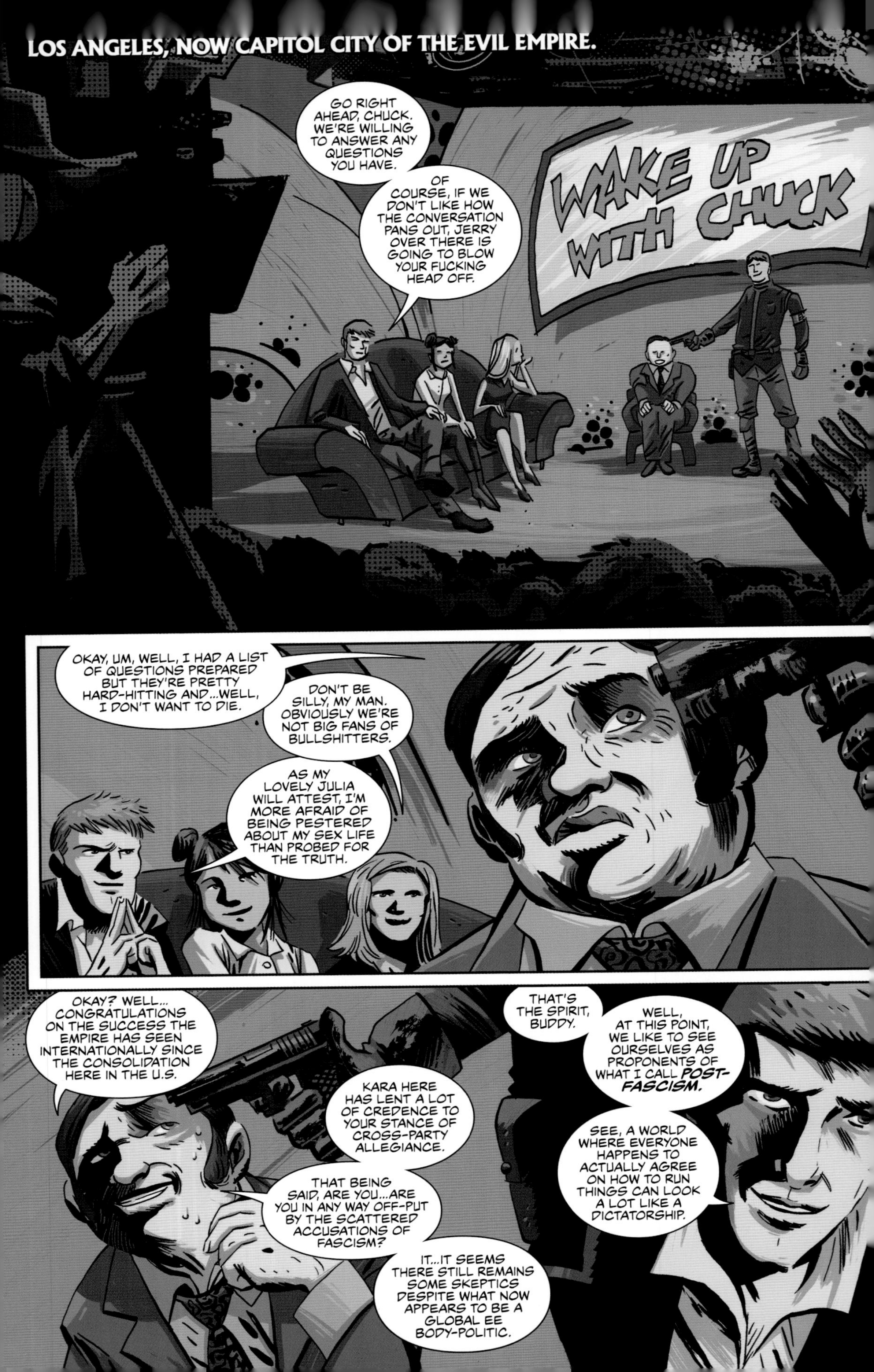
LOS ANGELES, NOW CAPITOL CITY OF THE EVIL EMPIRE.
GO RIGHT AHEAD, CHUCK. WE'RE WILLING TO ANSWER ANY QUESTIONS YOU HAVE.
OF COURSE, IF WE DON'T LIKE HOW THE CONVERSATION PANS OUT, JERRY OVER THERE IS GOING TO BLOW YOUR FUCKING HEAD OFF.
WAKE UP WITH CHUCK
OKAY, UM, WELL, I HAD A LIST OF QUESTIONS PREPARED BUT THEY'RE PRETTY HARD-HITTING AND...WELL, I DON'T WANT TO DIE.
DON'T BE SILLY, MY MAN. OBVIOUSLY WE'RE NOT BIG FANS OF BULLSHITTERS.
AS MY LOVELY JULIA WILL ATTEST, I'M MORE AFRAID OF BEING PESTERED ABOUT MY SEX LIFE THAN PROBED FOR THE TRUTH.
OKAY? WELL... CONGRATULATIONS ON THE SUCCESS THE EMPIRE HAS SEEN INTERNATIONALLY SINCE THE CONSOLIDATION HERE IN THE U.S.
KARA HERE HAS LENT A LOT OF CREDENCE TO YOUR STANCE OF CROSS-PARTY ALLEGIANCE.
THAT BEING SAID, ARE YOU...ARE YOU IN ANY WAY OFF-PUT BY THE SCATTERED ACCUSATIONS OF FASCISM?
IT...IT SEEMS THERE STILL REMAINS SOME SKEPTICS DESPITE WHAT NOW APPEARS TO BE A GLOBAL EE BODY-POLITIC.
THAT'S THE SPIRIT, BUDDY.
WELL, AT THIS POINT, WE LIKE TO SEE OURSELVES AS PROPONENTS OF WHAT I CALL *POST-FASCISM.*
SEE, A WORLD WHERE EVERYONE HAPPENS TO ACTUALLY AGREE ON HOW TO RUN THINGS CAN LOOK A LOT LIKE A DICTATORSHIP.

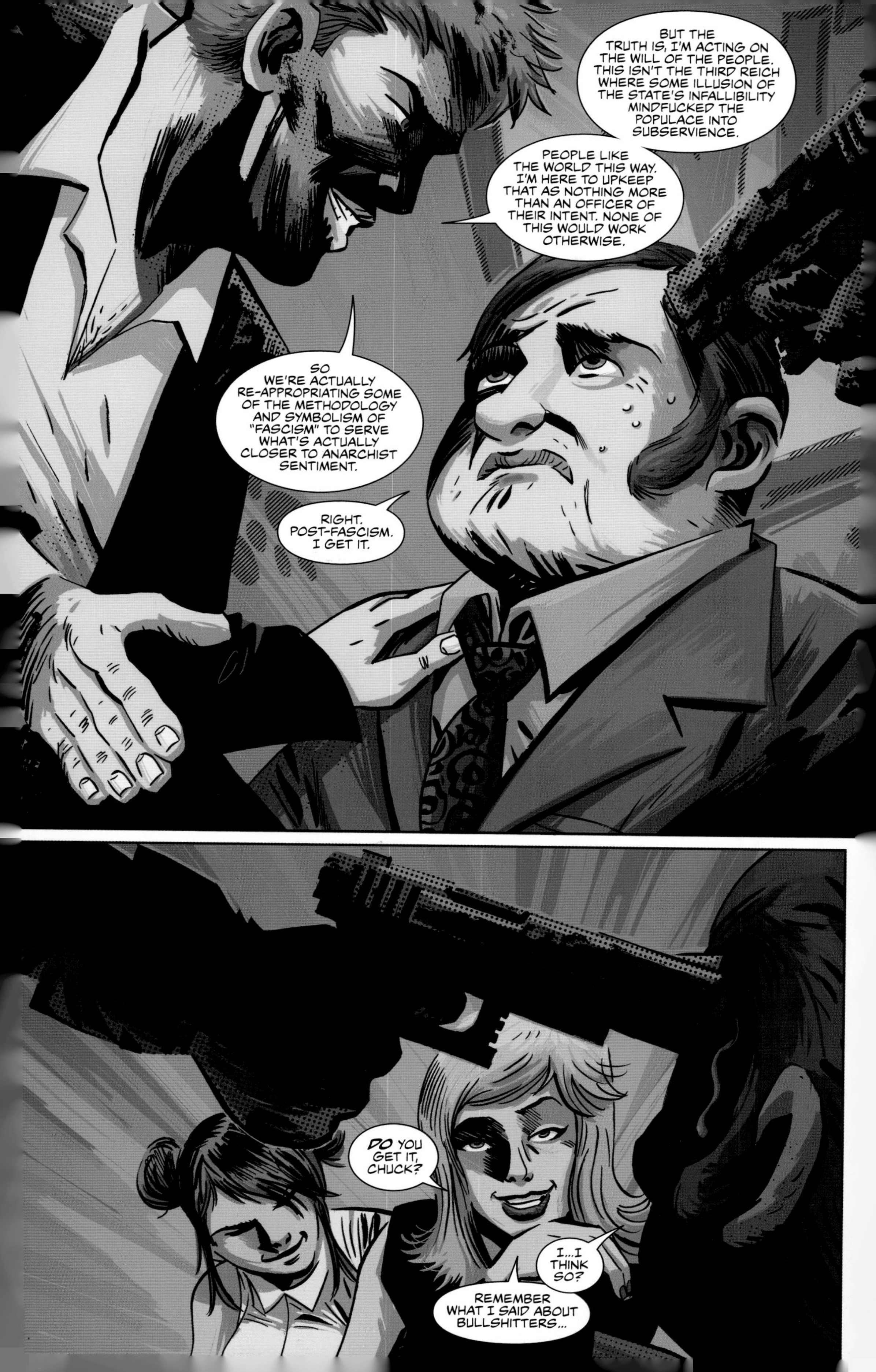
BUT THE TRUTH IS, I'M ACTING ON THE WILL OF THE PEOPLE. THIS ISN'T THE THIRD REICH WHERE SOME ILLUSION OF THE STATE'S INFALLIBILITY MINDFUCKED THE POPULACE INTO SUBSERVIENCE.
PEOPLE LIKE THE WORLD THIS WAY. I'M HERE TO UPKEEP THAT AS NOTHING MORE THAN AN OFFICER OF THEIR INTENT. NONE OF THIS WOULD WORK OTHERWISE.
SO WE'RE ACTUALLY RE-APPROPRIATING SOME OF THE METHODOLOGY AND SYMBOLISM OF "FASCISM" TO SERVE WHAT'S ACTUALLY CLOSER TO ANARCHIST SENTIMENT.
RIGHT. POST-FASCISM. I GET IT.
DO YOU GET IT, CHUCK?
I...I THINK SO?
REMEMBER WHAT I SAID ABOUT BULLSHITTERS...

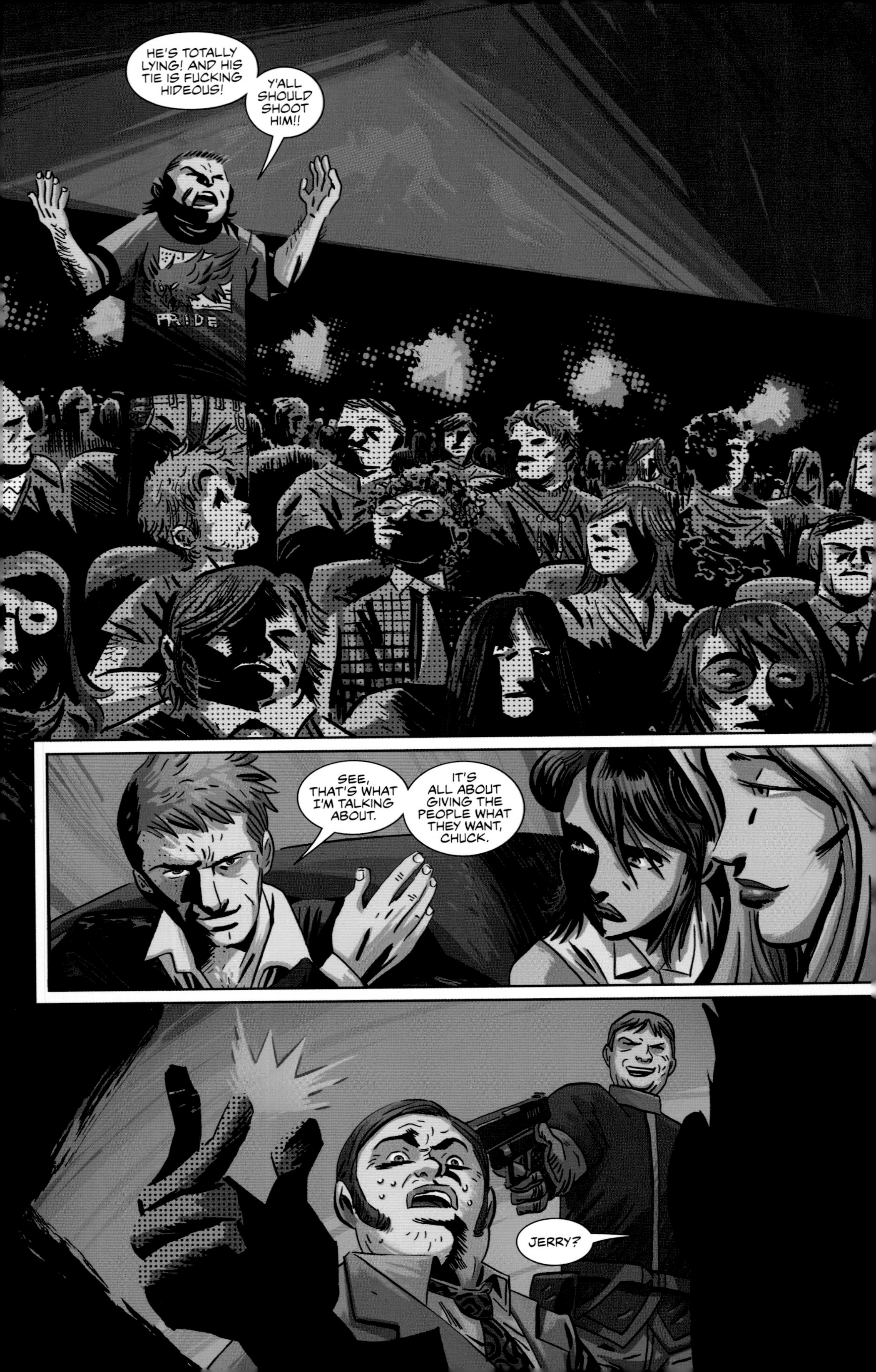
HE'S TOTALLY LYING! AND HIS TIE IS FUCKING HIDEOUS!
Y'ALL SHOULD SHOOT HIM!!
PRIDE
SEE, THAT'S WHAT I'M TALKING ABOUT.
IT'S ALL ABOUT GIVING THE PEOPLE WHAT THEY WANT, CHUCK.
JERRY?

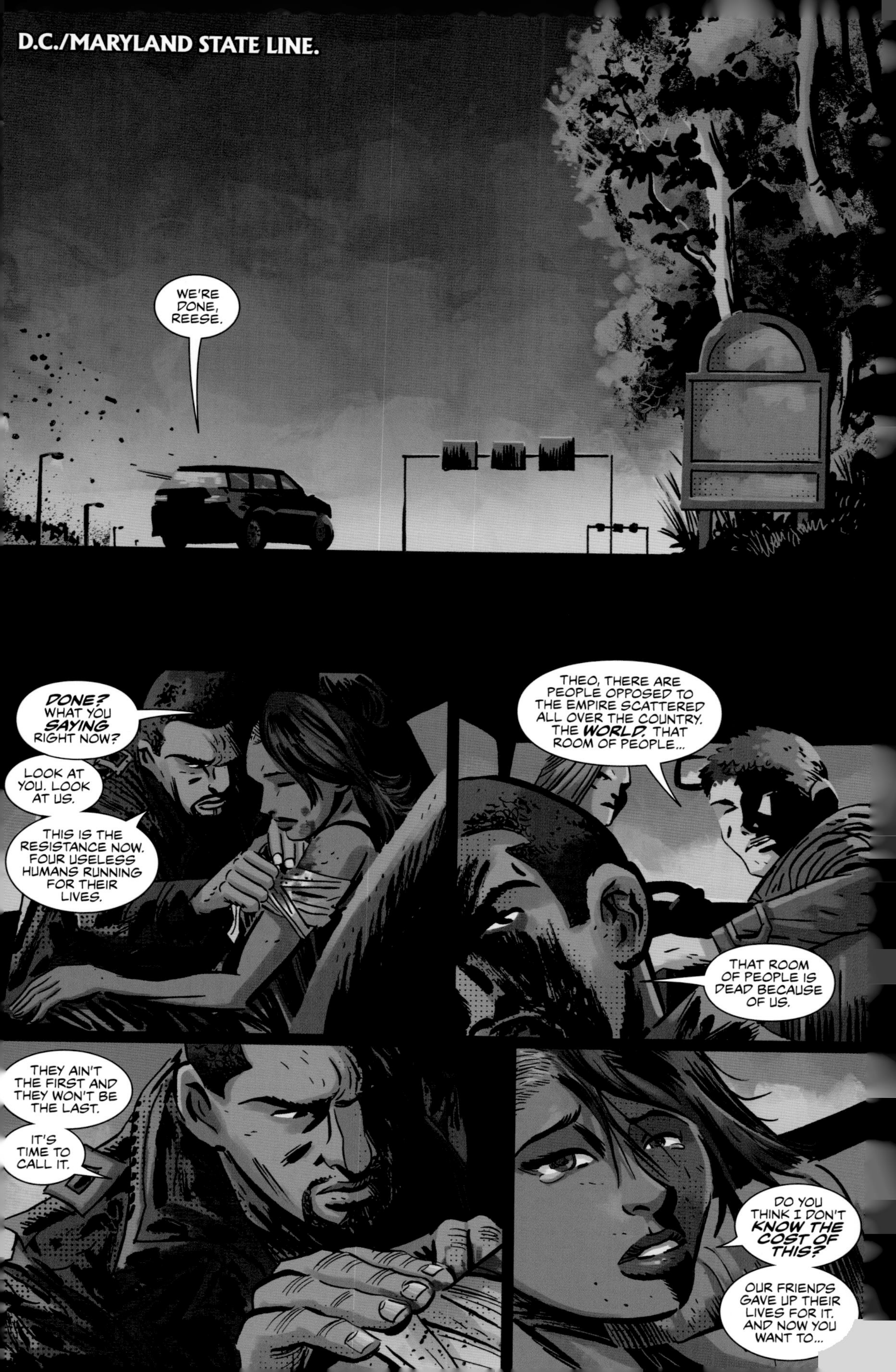
D.C./MARYLAND STATE LINE.
WE'RE DONE, REESE.
DONE? WHAT YOU SAYING RIGHT NOW?
LOOK AT YOU. LOOK AT US.
THIS IS THE RESISTANCE NOW. FOUR USELESS HUMANS RUNNING FOR THEIR LIVES.
THEO, THERE ARE PEOPLE OPPOSED TO THE EMPIRE SCATTERED ALL OVER THE COUNTRY. THE WORLD. THAT ROOM OF PEOPLE...
THAT ROOM OF PEOPLE IS DEAD BECAUSE OF US.
THEY AIN'T THE FIRST AND THEY WON'T BE THE LAST.
IT'S TIME TO CALL IT.
DO YOU THINK I DON'T KNOW THE COST OF THIS?
OUR FRIENDS GAVE UP THEIR LIVES FOR IT. AND NOW YOU WANT TO...

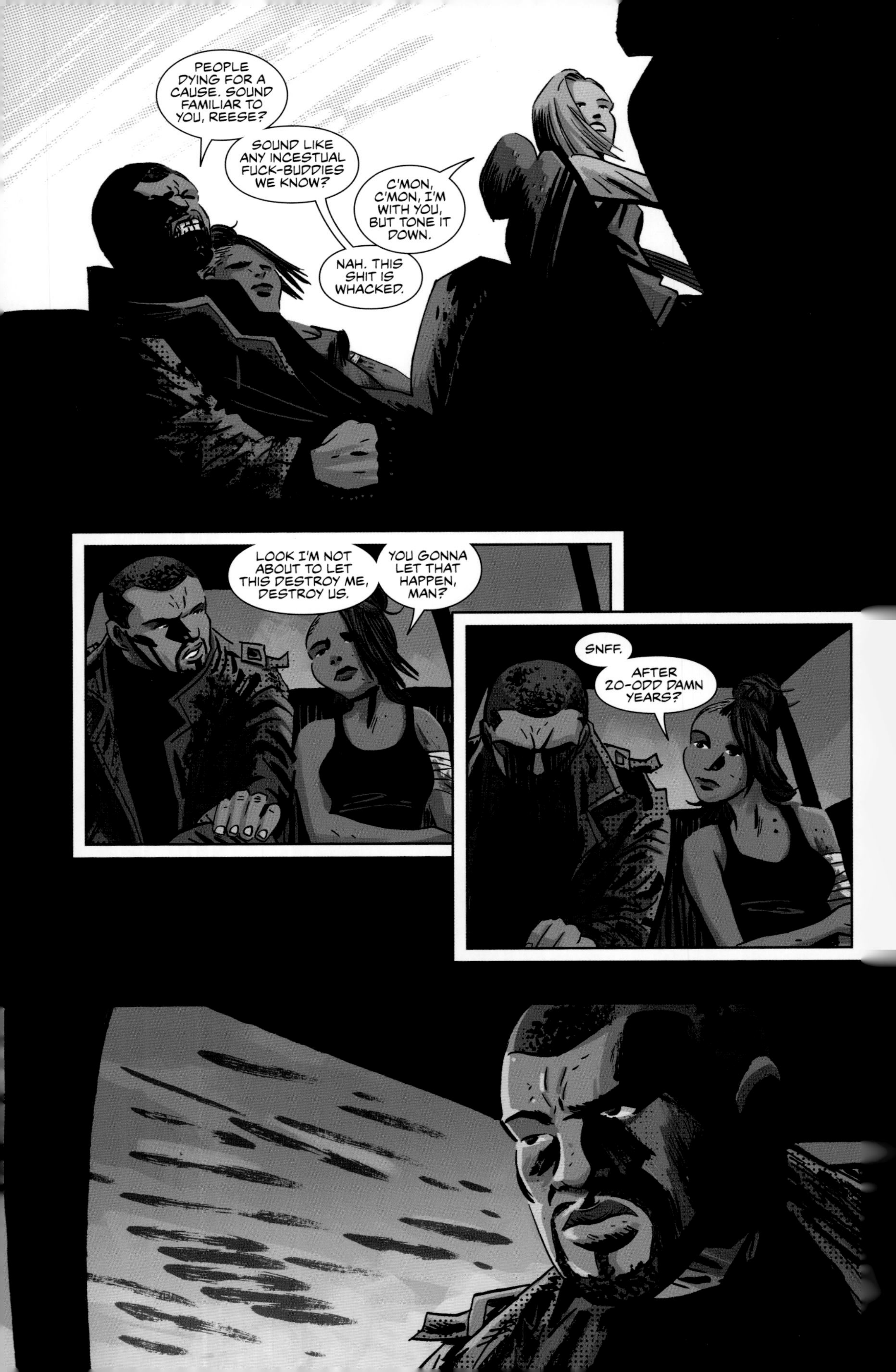
PEOPLE DYING FOR A CAUSE. SOUND FAMILIAR TO YOU, REESE?
SOUND LIKE ANY INCESTUAL FUCK-BUDDIES WE KNOW?
C'MON, C'MON, I'M WITH YOU, BUT TONE IT DOWN.
NAH. THIS SHIT IS WHACKED.
LOOK I'M NOT ABOUT TO LET THIS DESTROY ME, DESTROY US.
YOU GONNA LET THAT HAPPEN, MAN?
SNFF.
AFTER 20-ODD DAMN YEARS?

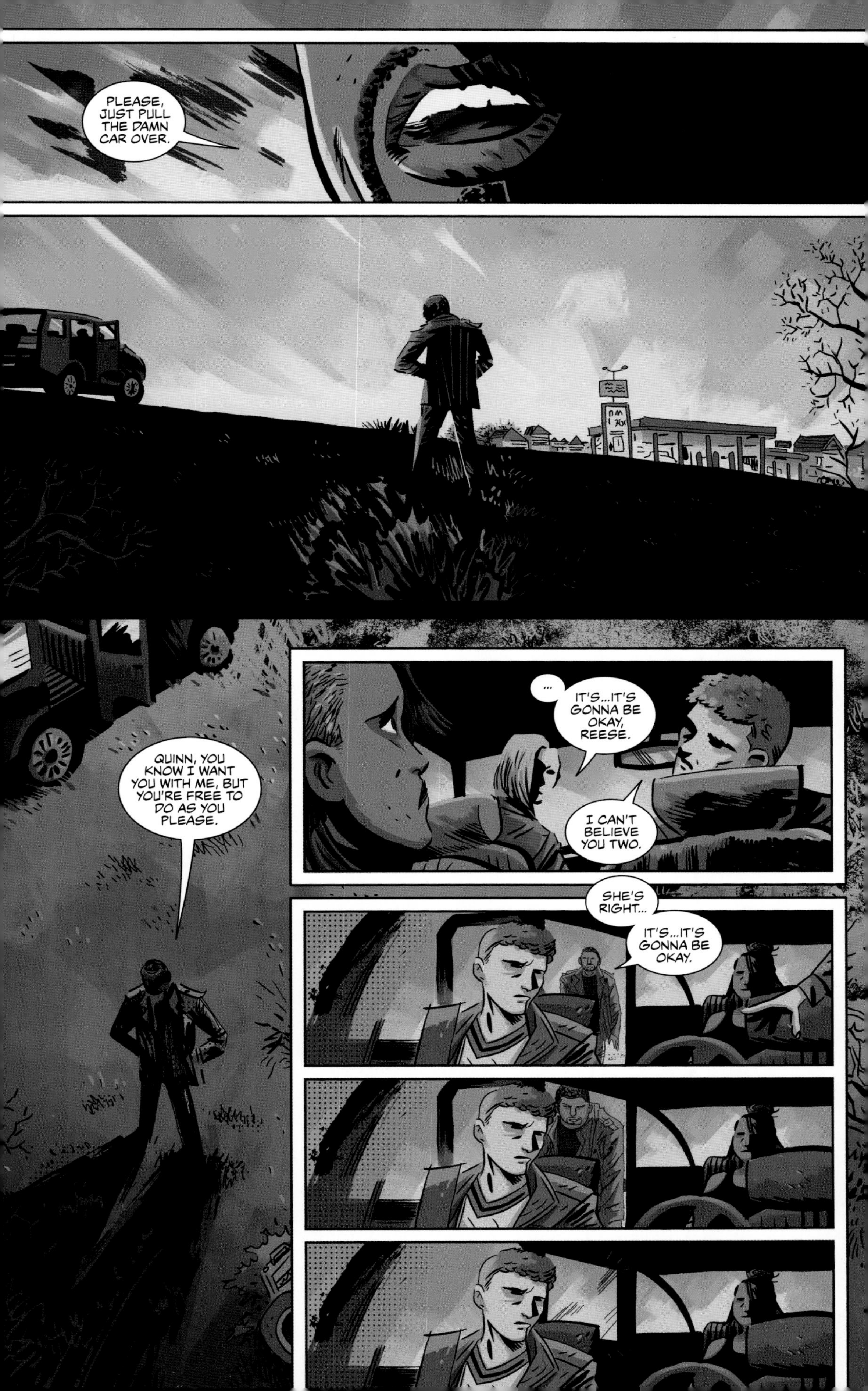
PLEASE, JUST PULL THE DAMN CAR OVER.
QUINN, YOU KNOW I WANT YOU WITH ME, BUT YOU'RE FREE TO DO AS YOU PLEASE.
...
IT'S...IT'S GONNA BE OKAY, REESE.
I CAN'T BELIEVE YOU TWO.
SHE'S RIGHT...
IT'S...IT'S GONNA BE OKAY.

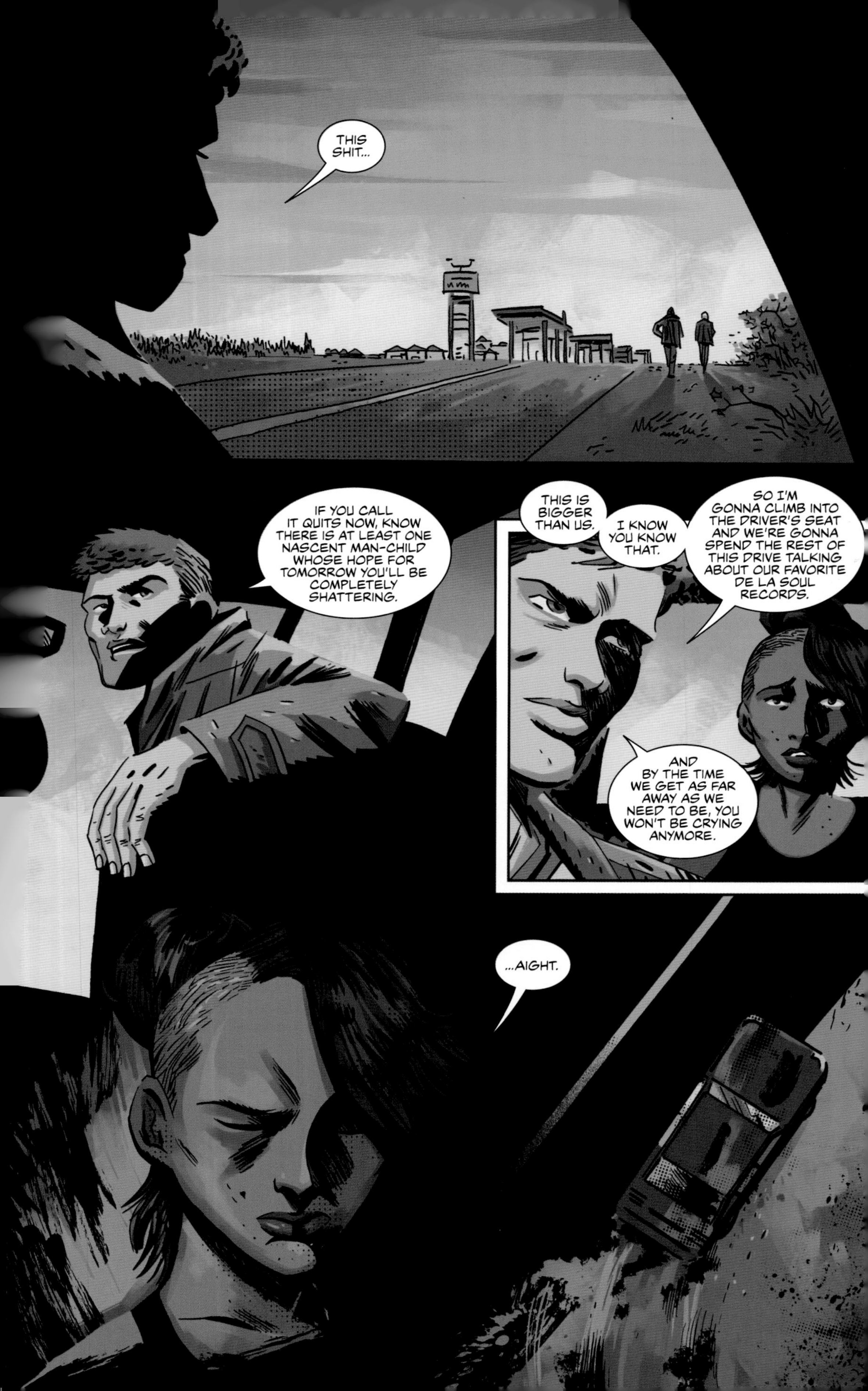
THIS SHIT...
IF YOU CALL IT QUITS NOW, KNOW THERE IS AT LEAST ONE NASCENT MAN-CHILD WHOSE HOPE FOR TOMORROW YOU'LL BE COMPLETELY SHATTERING.
THIS IS BIGGER THAN US.
I KNOW YOU KNOW THAT.
SO I'M GONNA CLIMB INTO THE DRIVER'S SEAT AND WE'RE GONNA SPEND THE REST OF THIS DRIVE TALKING ABOUT OUR FAVORITE DE LA SOUL RECORDS.
AND BY THE TIME WE GET AS FAR AWAY AS WE NEED TO BE, YOU WON'T BE CRYING ANYMORE.
...AIGHT.

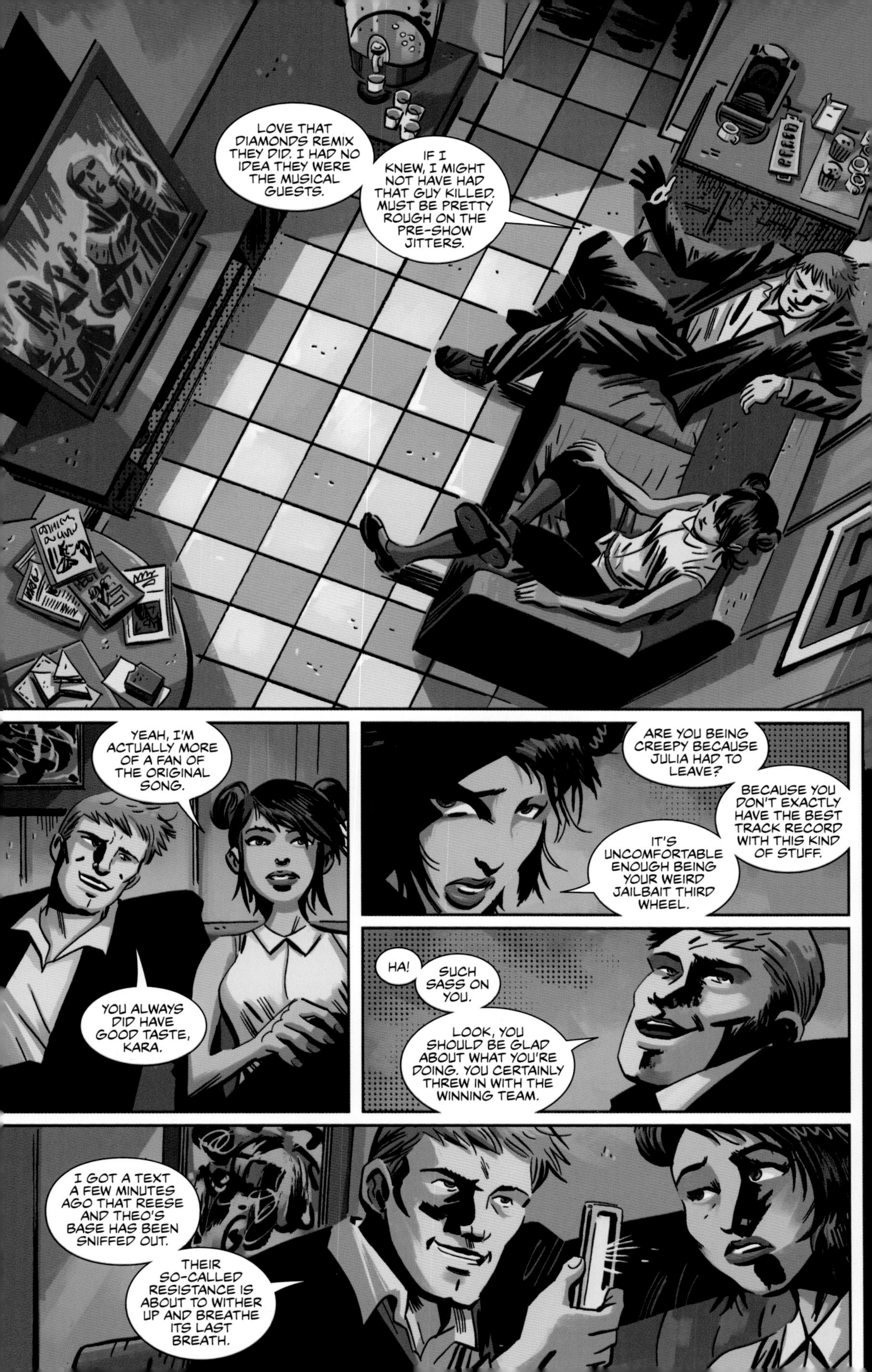
LOVE THAT DIAMONDS REMIX THEY DID. I HAD NO IDEA THEY WERE THE MUSICAL GUESTS.
IF I KNEW, I MIGHT NOT HAVE HAD THAT GUY KILLED. MUST BE PRETTY ROUGH ON THE PRE-SHOW JITTERS.
YEAH, I'M ACTUALLY MORE OF A FAN OF THE ORIGINAL SONG.
YOU ALWAYS DID HAVE GOOD TASTE, KARA.
ARE YOU BEING CREEPY BECAUSE JULIA HAD TO LEAVE?
BECAUSE YOU DON'T EXACTLY HAVE THE BEST TRACK RECORD WITH THIS KIND OF STUFF.
IT'S UNCOMFORTABLE ENOUGH BEING YOUR WEIRD JAILBAIT THIRD WHEEL.
HA!
SUCH SASS ON YOU.
LOOK, YOU SHOULD BE GLAD ABOUT WHAT YOU'RE DOING. YOU CERTAINLY THREW IN WITH THE WINNING TEAM.
I GOT A TEXT A FEW MINUTES AGO THAT REESE AND THEO'S BASE HAS BEEN SNIFFED OUT.
THEIR SO-CALLED RESISTANCE IS ABOUT TO WITHER UP AND BREATHE ITS LAST BREATH.

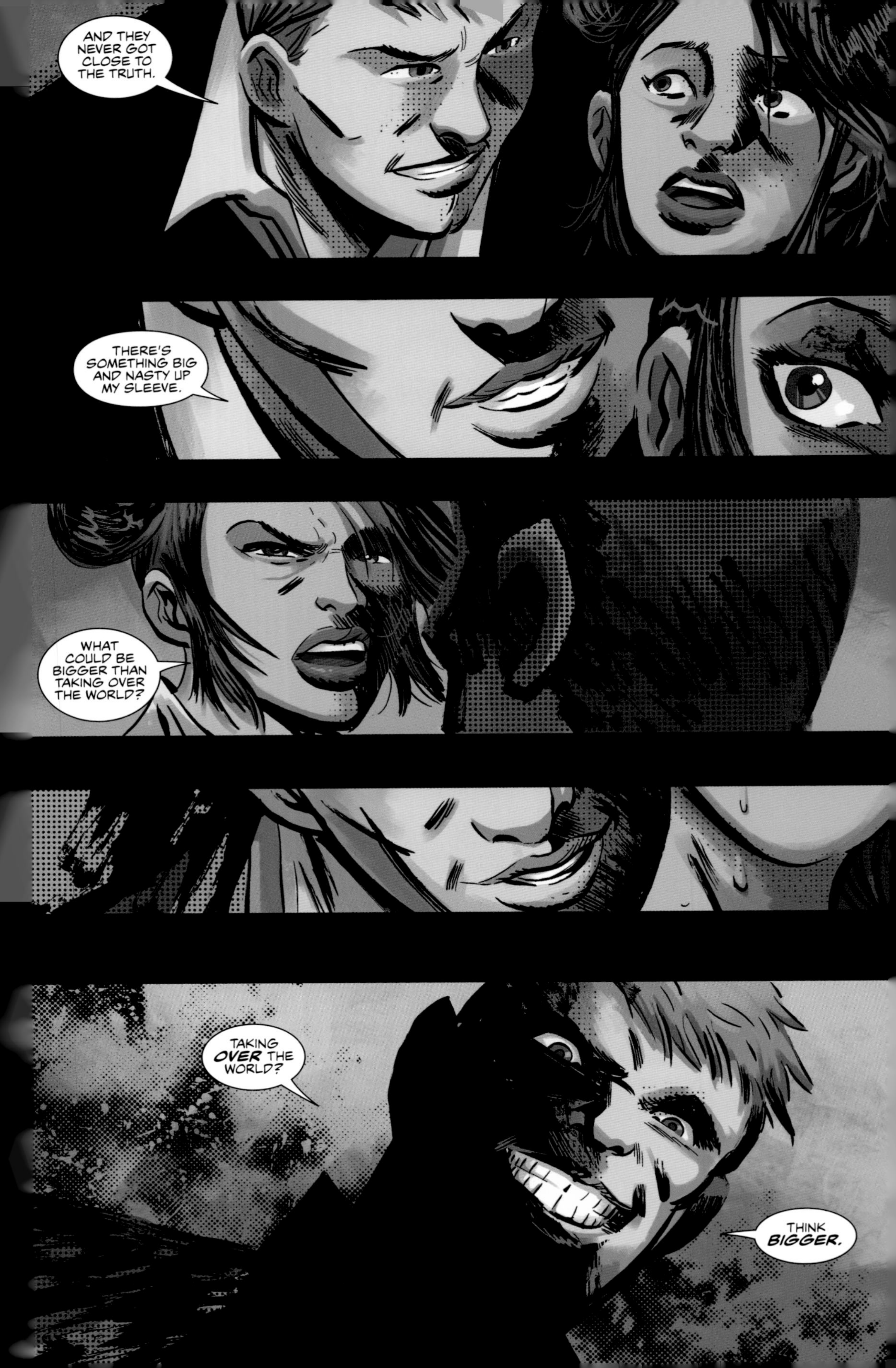
AND THEY NEVER GOT CLOSE TO THE TRUTH.
THERE'S SOMETHING BIG AND NASTY UP MY SLEEVE.
WHAT COULD BE BIGGER THAN TAKING OVER THE WORLD?
TAKING *OVER* THE WORLD?
THINK *BIGGER.*

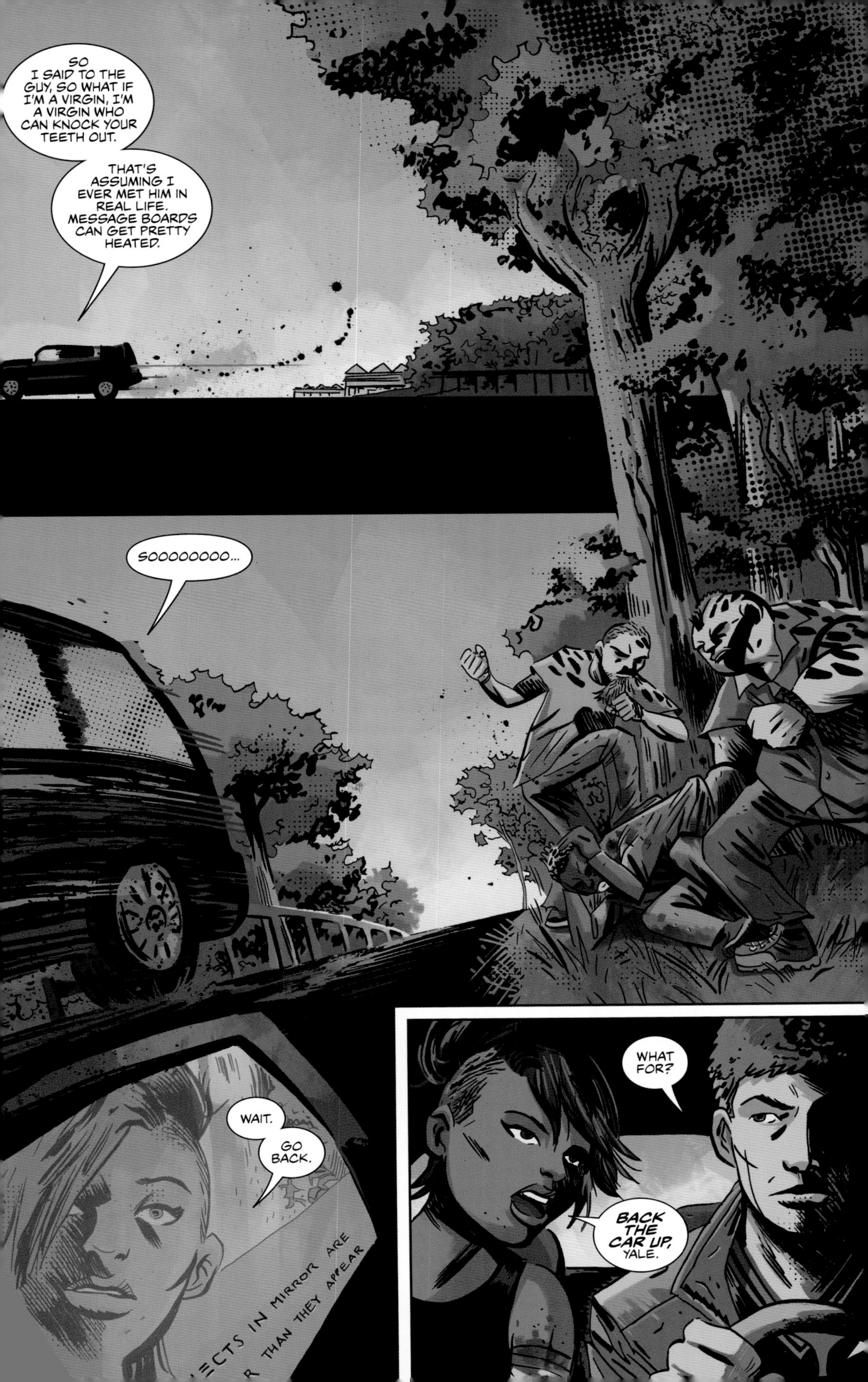
SO I SAID TO THE GUY, SO WHAT IF I'M A VIRGIN, I'M A VIRGIN WHO CAN KNOCK YOUR TEETH OUT.
THAT'S ASSUMING I EVER MET HIM IN REAL LIFE. MESSAGE BOARDS CAN GET PRETTY HEATED.
SOOOOOOOO...
WAIT.
GO BACK.
ECTS IN MIRROR ARE
R THAN THEY APPEAR
WHAT FOR?
BACK THE CAR UP, YALE.

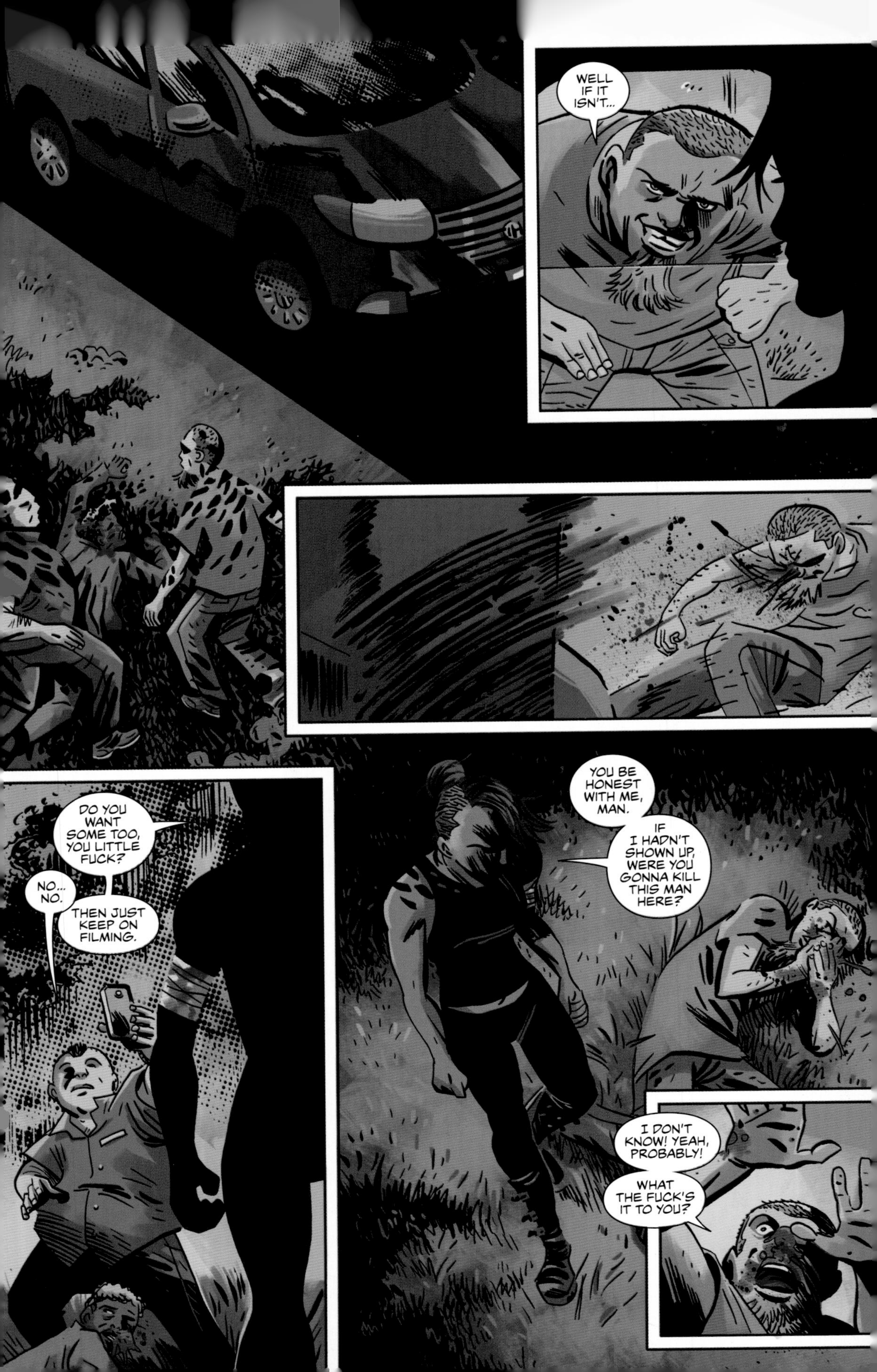
WELL IF IT ISN'T...
DO YOU WANT SOME TOO, YOU LITTLE FUCK?
NO... NO.
THEN JUST KEEP ON FILMING.
YOU BE HONEST WITH ME, MAN.
IF I HADN'T SHOWN UP, WERE YOU GONNA KILL THIS MAN HERE?
I DON'T KNOW! YEAH, PROBABLY!
WHAT THE FUCK'S IT TO YOU?

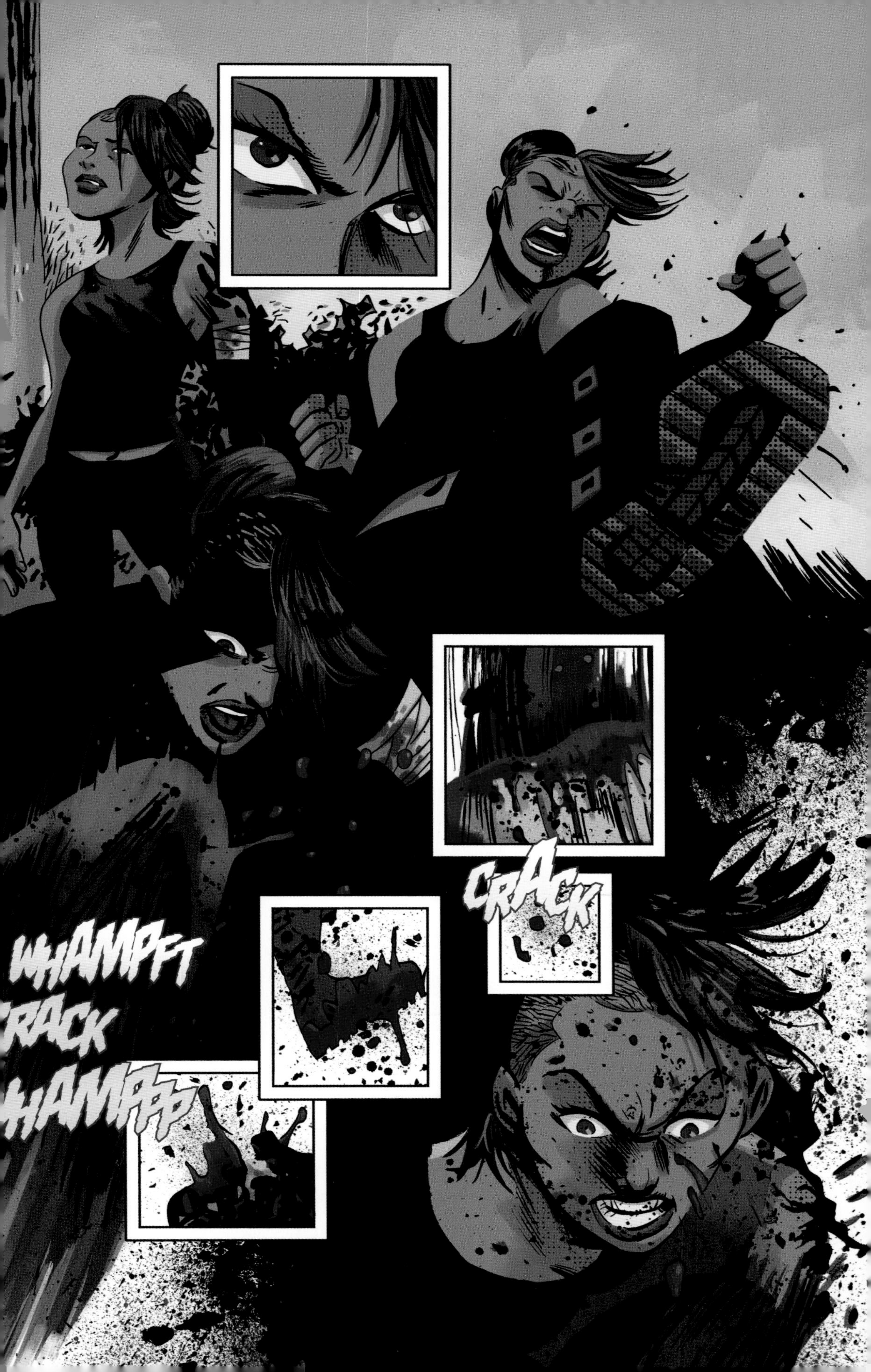
WHAMPFT
CRACK
WHAMPP
CRACK

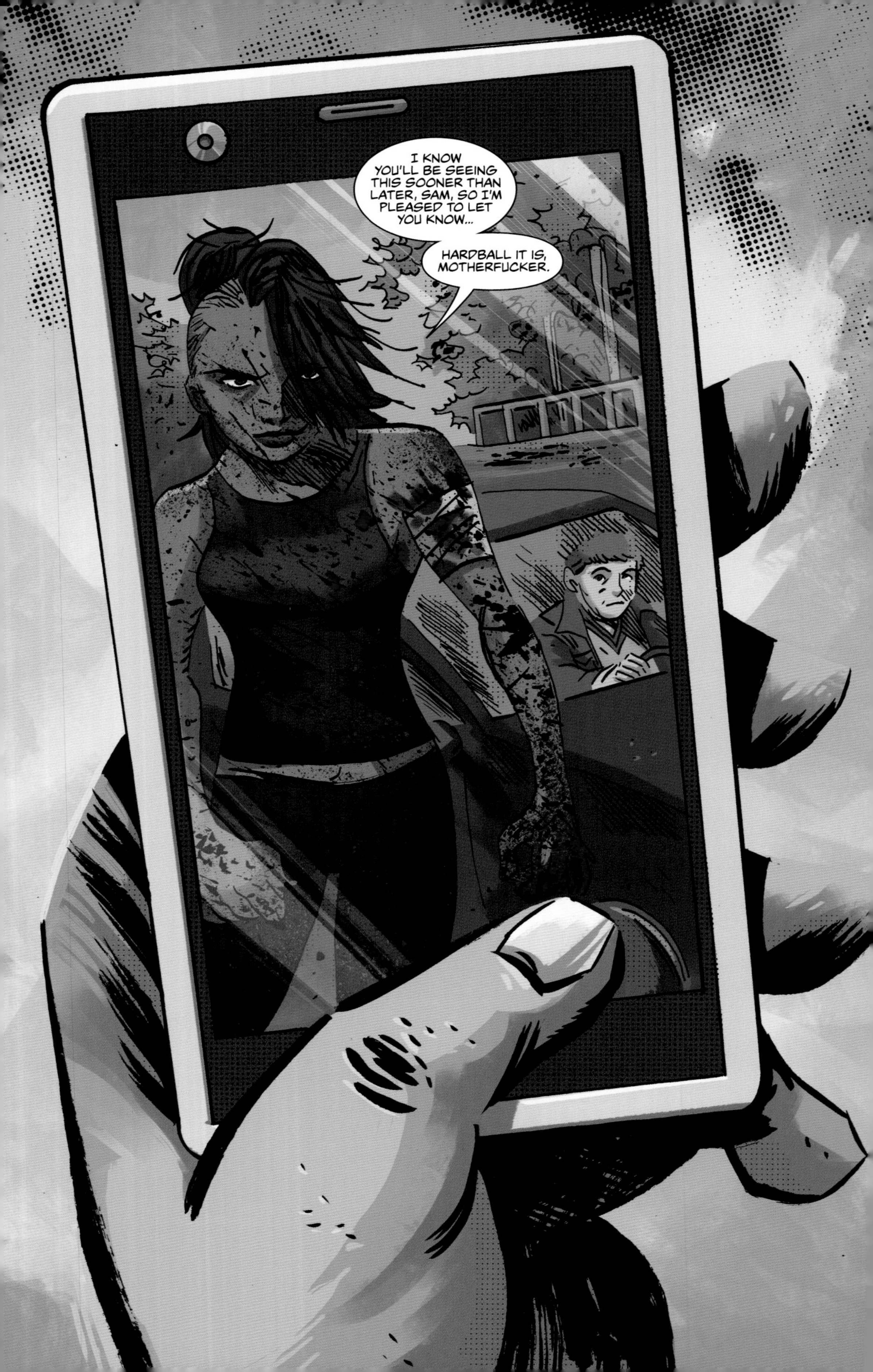
I KNOW YOU'LL BE SEEING THIS SOONER THAN LATER, SAM, SO I'M PLEASED TO LET YOU KNOW...
HARDBALL IT IS, MOTHERFUCKER.

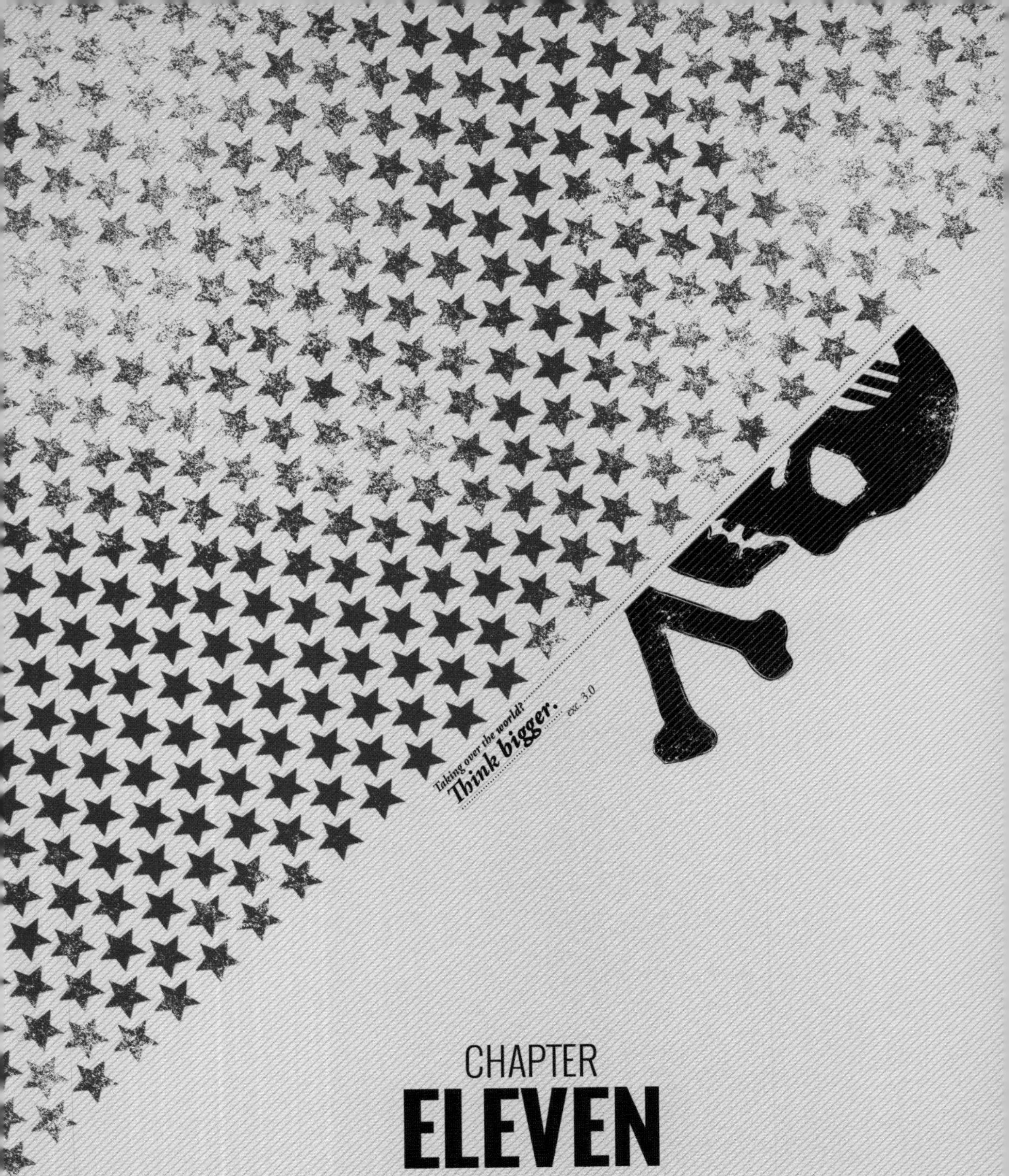
Taking over the world?
Think bigger.
exc. 3.0

CHAPTER ELEVEN

fig. 3

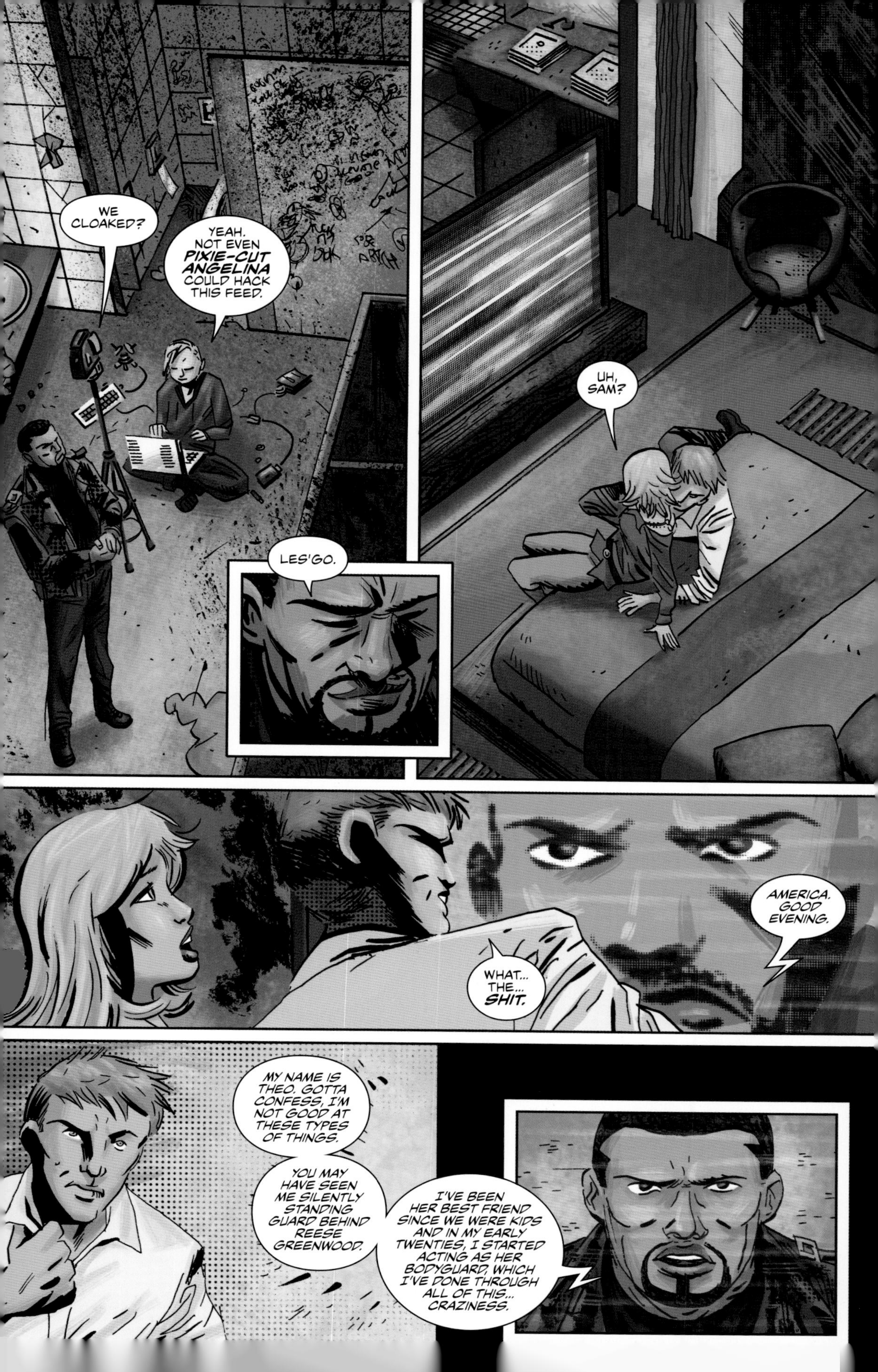
WE CLOAKED?
YEAH. NOT EVEN PIXIE-CUT ANGELINA COULD HACK THIS FEED.
LES'GO.
UH, SAM?
WHAT... THE... SHIT.
AMERICA. GOOD EVENING.
MY NAME IS THEO. GOTTA CONFESS, I'M NOT GOOD AT THESE TYPES OF THINGS.
YOU MAY HAVE SEEN ME SILENTLY STANDING GUARD BEHIND REESE GREENWOOD.
I'VE BEEN HER BEST FRIEND SINCE WE WERE KIDS AND IN MY EARLY TWENTIES, I STARTED ACTING AS HER BODYGUARD, WHICH I'VE DONE THROUGH ALL OF THIS... CRAZINESS.

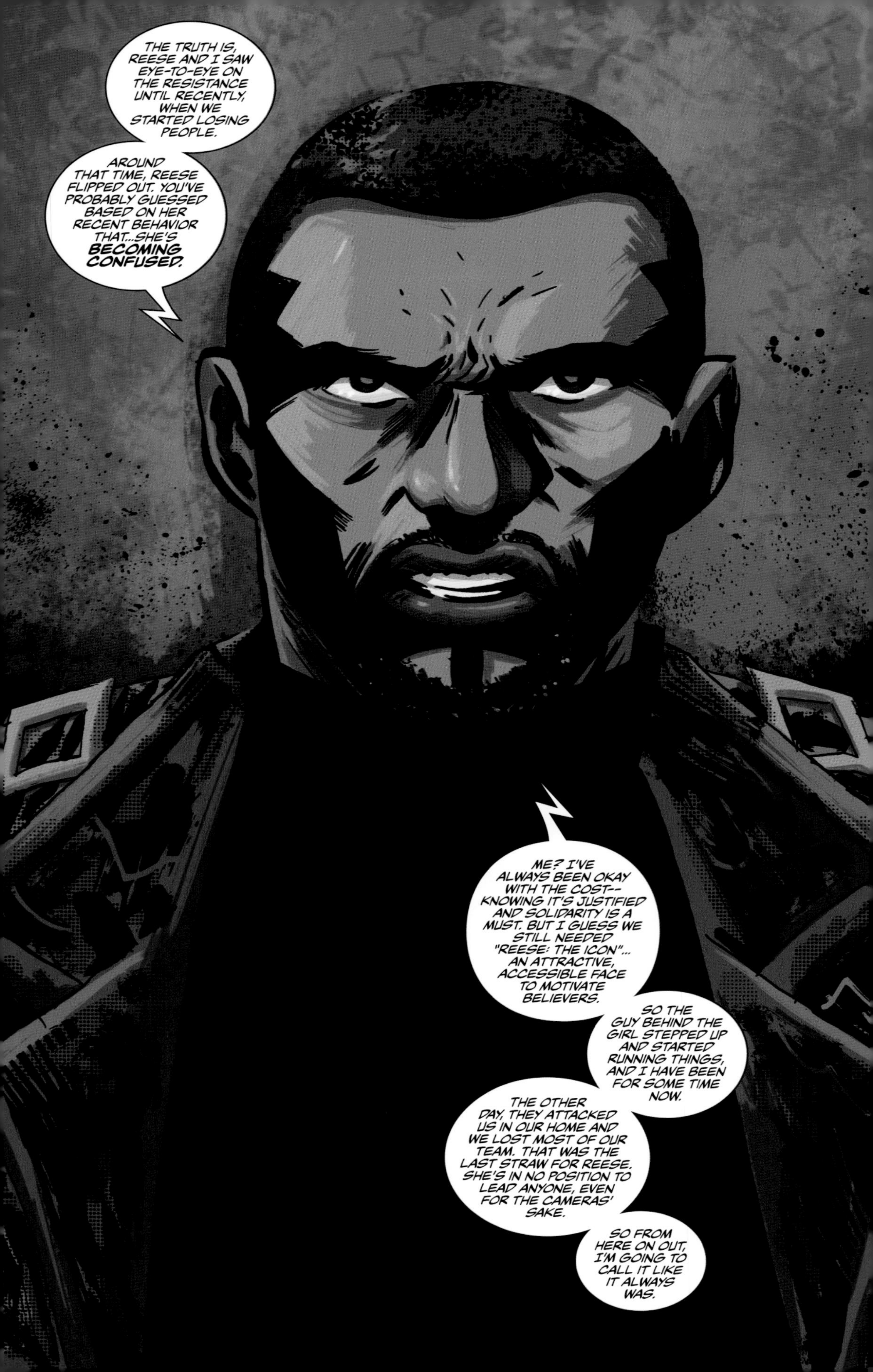
THE TRUTH IS, REESE AND I SAW EYE-TO-EYE ON THE RESISTANCE UNTIL RECENTLY, WHEN WE STARTED LOSING PEOPLE.
AROUND THAT TIME, REESE FLIPPED OUT. YOU'VE PROBABLY GUESSED BASED ON HER RECENT BEHAVIOR THAT...SHE'S **BECOMING CONFUSED.**
ME? I'VE ALWAYS BEEN OKAY WITH THE COST-- KNOWING IT'S JUSTIFIED AND SOLIDARITY IS A MUST. BUT I GUESS WE STILL NEEDED "REESE: THE ICON"... AN ATTRACTIVE, ACCESSIBLE FACE TO MOTIVATE BELIEVERS.
SO THE GUY BEHIND THE GIRL STEPPED UP AND STARTED RUNNING THINGS, AND I HAVE BEEN FOR SOME TIME NOW.
THE OTHER DAY, THEY ATTACKED US IN OUR HOME AND WE LOST MOST OF OUR TEAM. THAT WAS THE LAST STRAW FOR REESE. SHE'S IN NO POSITION TO LEAD ANYONE, EVEN FOR THE CAMERAS' SAKE.
SO FROM HERE ON OUT, I'M GOING TO CALL IT LIKE IT ALWAYS WAS.

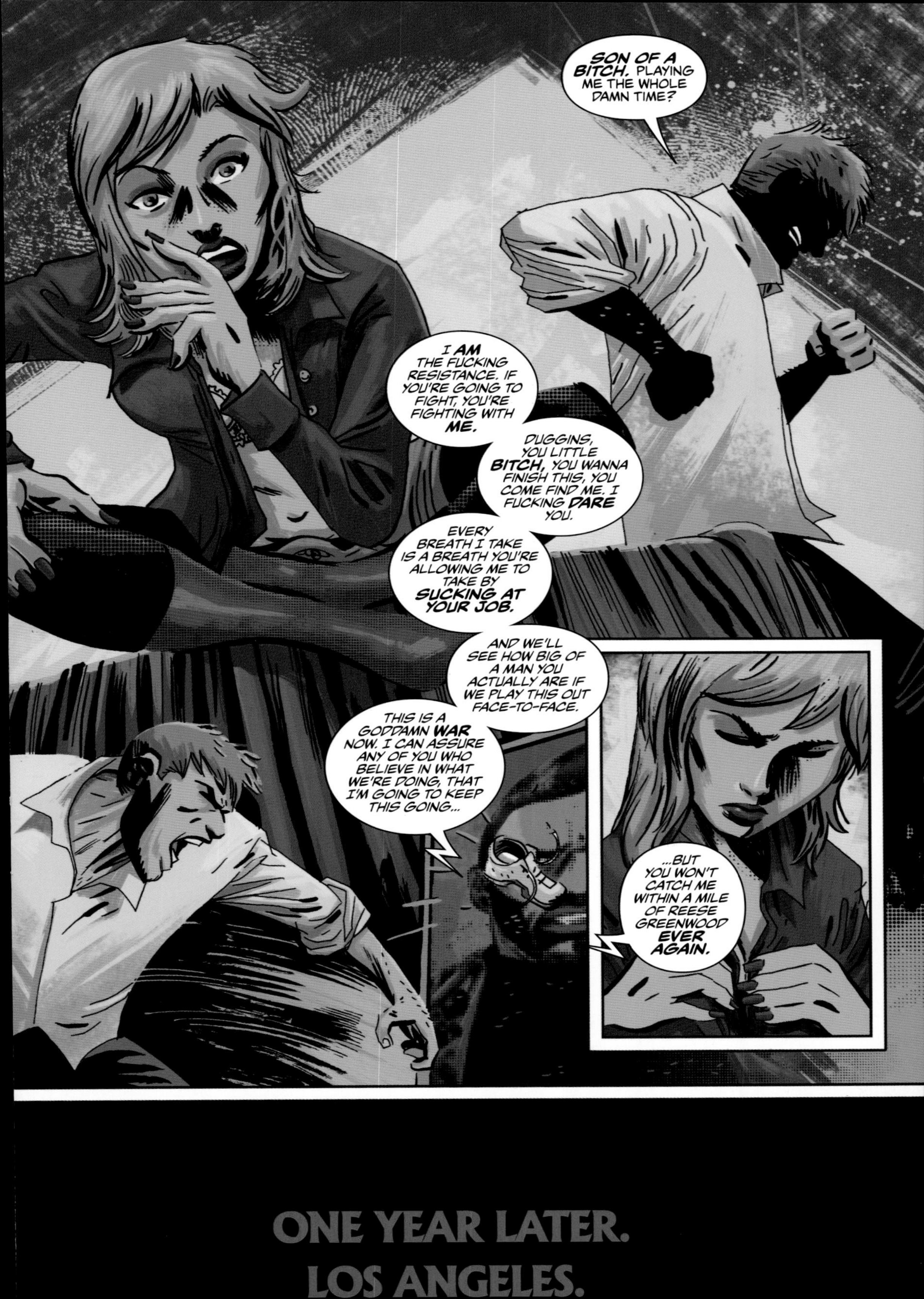
SON OF A BITCH. PLAYING ME THE WHOLE DAMN TIME?
I AM THE FUCKING RESISTANCE. IF YOU'RE GOING TO FIGHT, YOU'RE FIGHTING WITH ME.
DUGGINS, YOU LITTLE BITCH, YOU WANNA FINISH THIS, YOU COME FIND ME. I FUCKING DARE YOU.
EVERY BREATH I TAKE IS A BREATH YOU'RE ALLOWING ME TO TAKE BY SUCKING AT YOUR JOB.
AND WE'LL SEE HOW BIG OF A MAN YOU ACTUALLY ARE IF WE PLAY THIS OUT FACE-TO-FACE.
THIS IS A GODDAMN WAR NOW. I CAN ASSURE ANY OF YOU WHO BELIEVE IN WHAT WE'RE DOING, THAT I'M GOING TO KEEP THIS GOING...
...BUT YOU WON'T CATCH ME WITHIN A MILE OF REESE GREENWOOD EVER AGAIN.

ONE YEAR LATER.
LOS ANGELES.

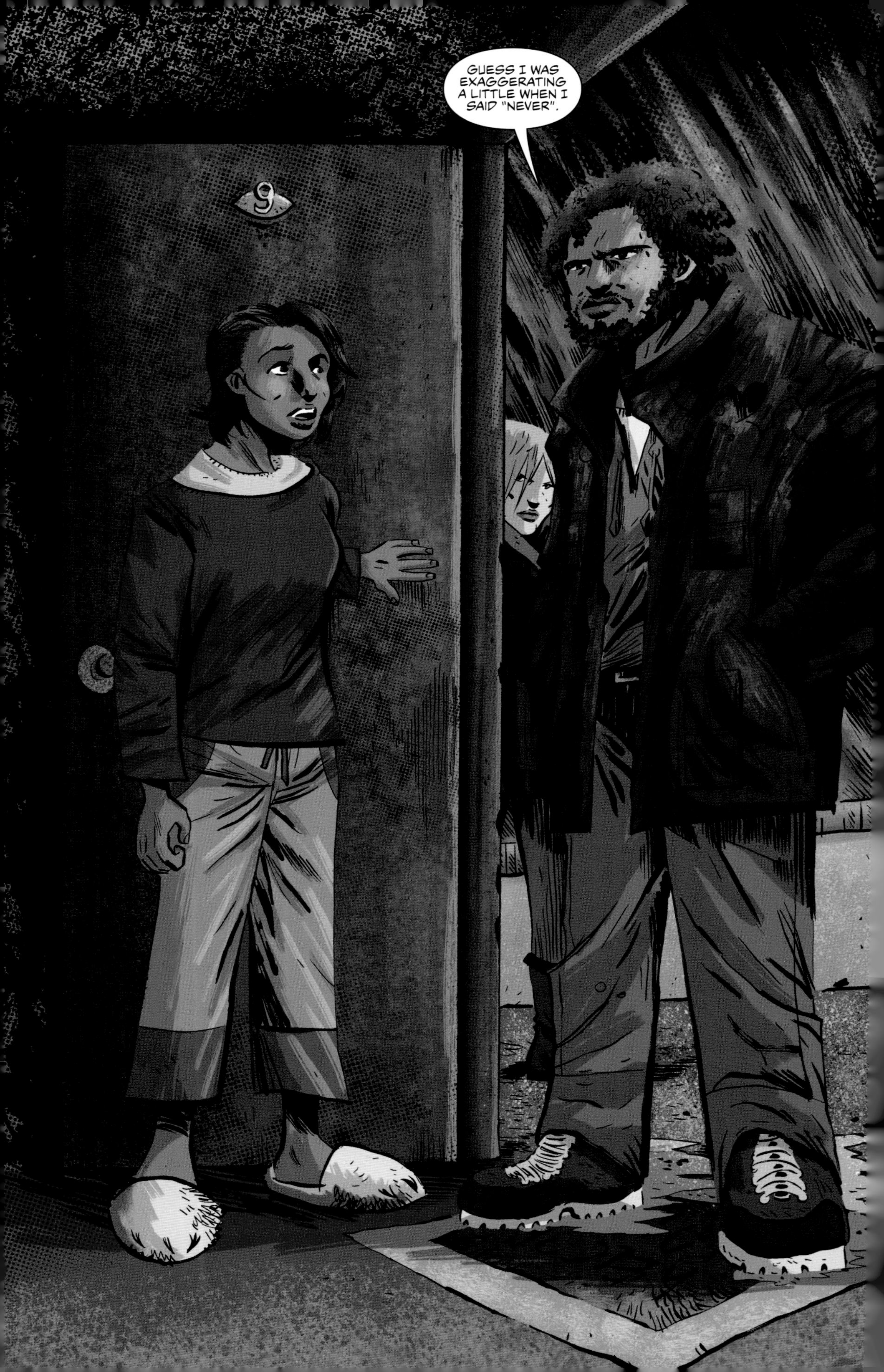
GUESS I WAS EXAGGERATING A LITTLE WHEN I SAID "NEVER".

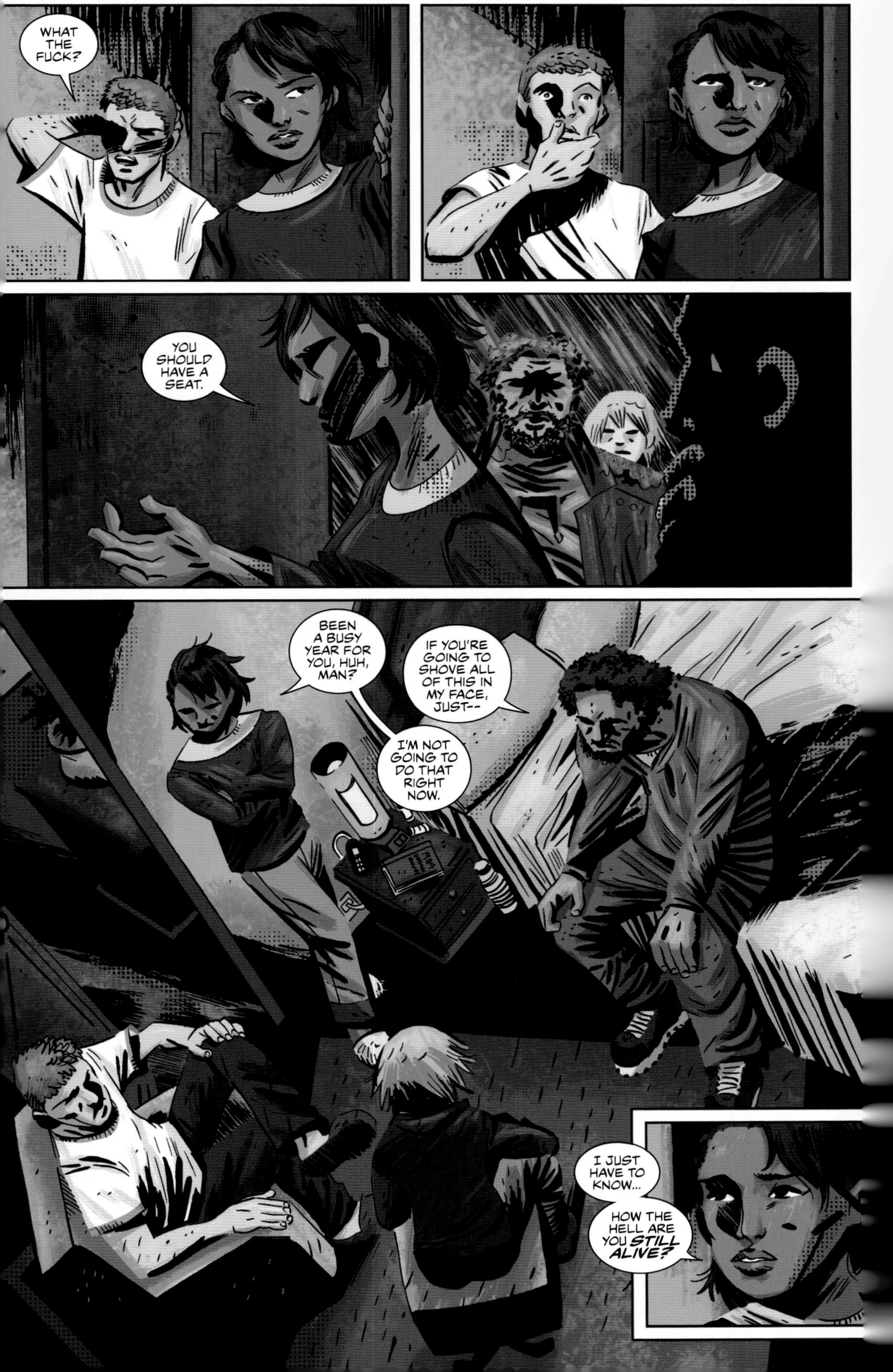
WHAT THE FUCK?
YOU SHOULD HAVE A SEAT.
BEEN A BUSY YEAR FOR YOU, HUH, MAN?
IF YOU'RE GOING TO SHOVE ALL OF THIS IN MY FACE, JUST--
I'M NOT GOING TO DO THAT RIGHT NOW.
I JUST HAVE TO KNOW...
HOW THE HELL ARE YOU STILL ALIVE?

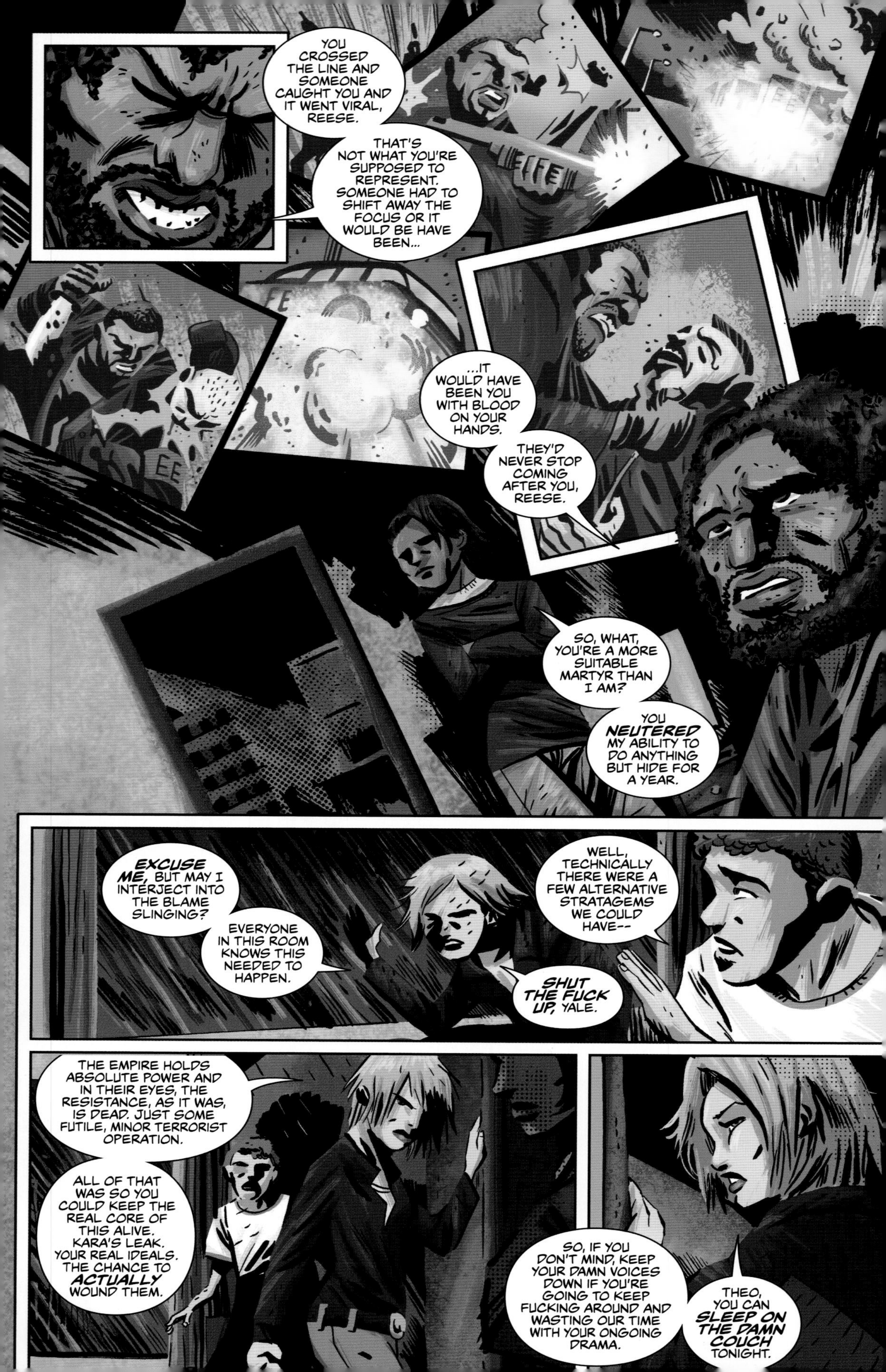
YOU CROSSED THE LINE AND SOMEONE CAUGHT YOU AND IT WENT VIRAL, REESE.
THAT'S NOT WHAT YOU'RE SUPPOSED TO REPRESENT. SOMEONE HAD TO SHIFT AWAY THE FOCUS OR IT WOULD BE HAVE BEEN...
...IT WOULD HAVE BEEN YOU WITH BLOOD ON YOUR HANDS.
THEY'D NEVER STOP COMING AFTER YOU, REESE.
SO, WHAT, YOU'RE A MORE SUITABLE MARTYR THAN I AM?
YOU NEUTERED MY ABILITY TO DO ANYTHING BUT HIDE FOR A YEAR.
EXCUSE ME, BUT MAY I INTERJECT INTO THE BLAME SLINGING?
EVERYONE IN THIS ROOM KNOWS THIS NEEDED TO HAPPEN.
WELL, TECHNICALLY THERE WERE A FEW ALTERNATIVE STRATAGEMS WE COULD HAVE--
SHUT THE FUCK UP, YALE.
THE EMPIRE HOLDS ABSOLUTE POWER AND IN THEIR EYES, THE RESISTANCE, AS IT WAS, IS DEAD. JUST SOME FUTILE, MINOR TERRORIST OPERATION.
ALL OF THAT WAS SO YOU COULD KEEP THE REAL CORE OF THIS ALIVE. KARA'S LEAK. YOUR REAL IDEALS. THE CHANCE TO ACTUALLY WOUND THEM.
SO, IF YOU DON'T MIND, KEEP YOUR DAMN VOICES DOWN IF YOU'RE GOING TO KEEP FUCKING AROUND AND WASTING OUR TIME WITH YOUR ONGOING DRAMA.
THEO, YOU CAN SLEEP ON THE DAMN COUCH TONIGHT.

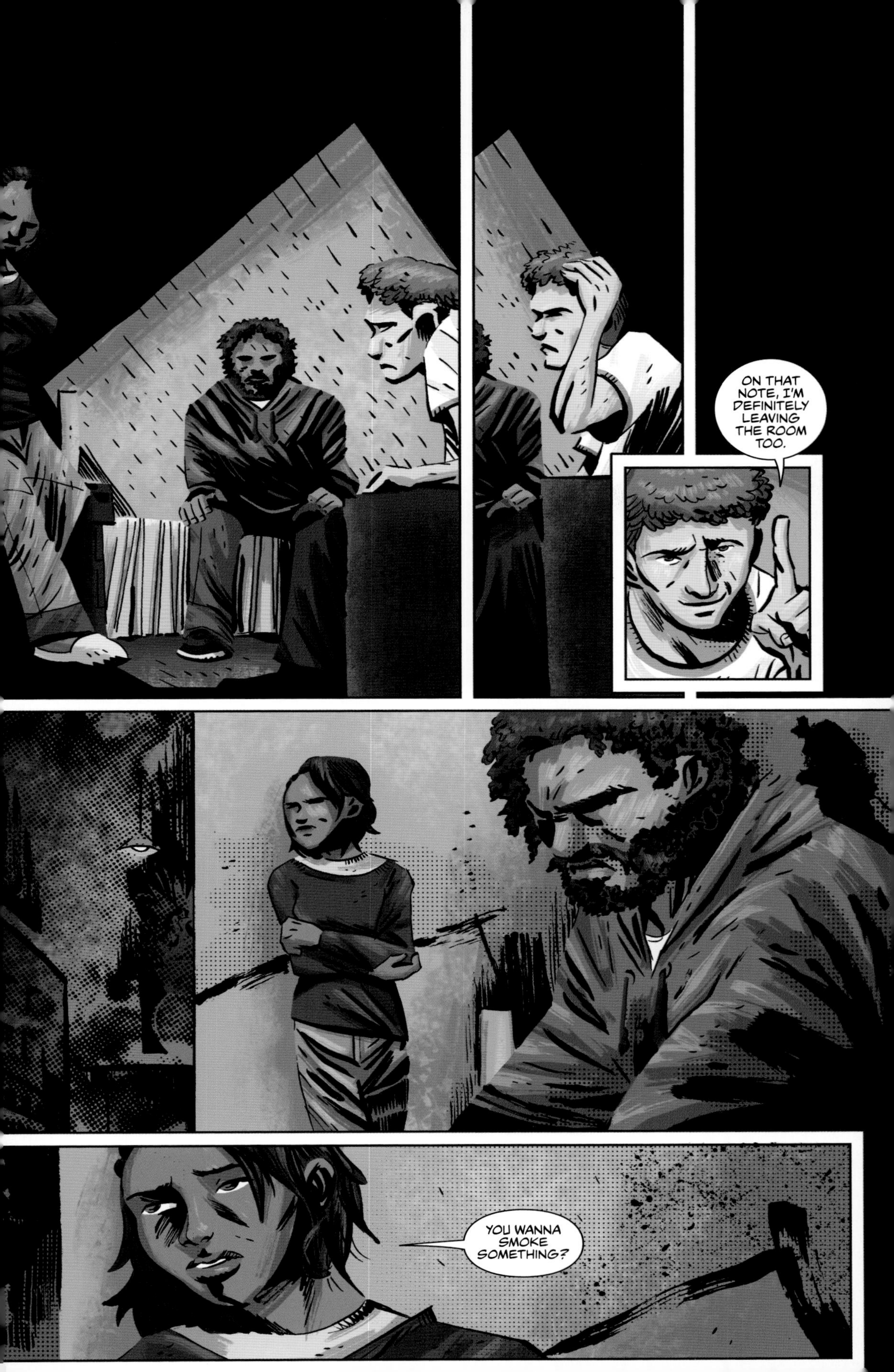
ON THAT NOTE, I'M DEFINITELY LEAVING THE ROOM TOO.
YOU WANNA SMOKE SOMETHING?

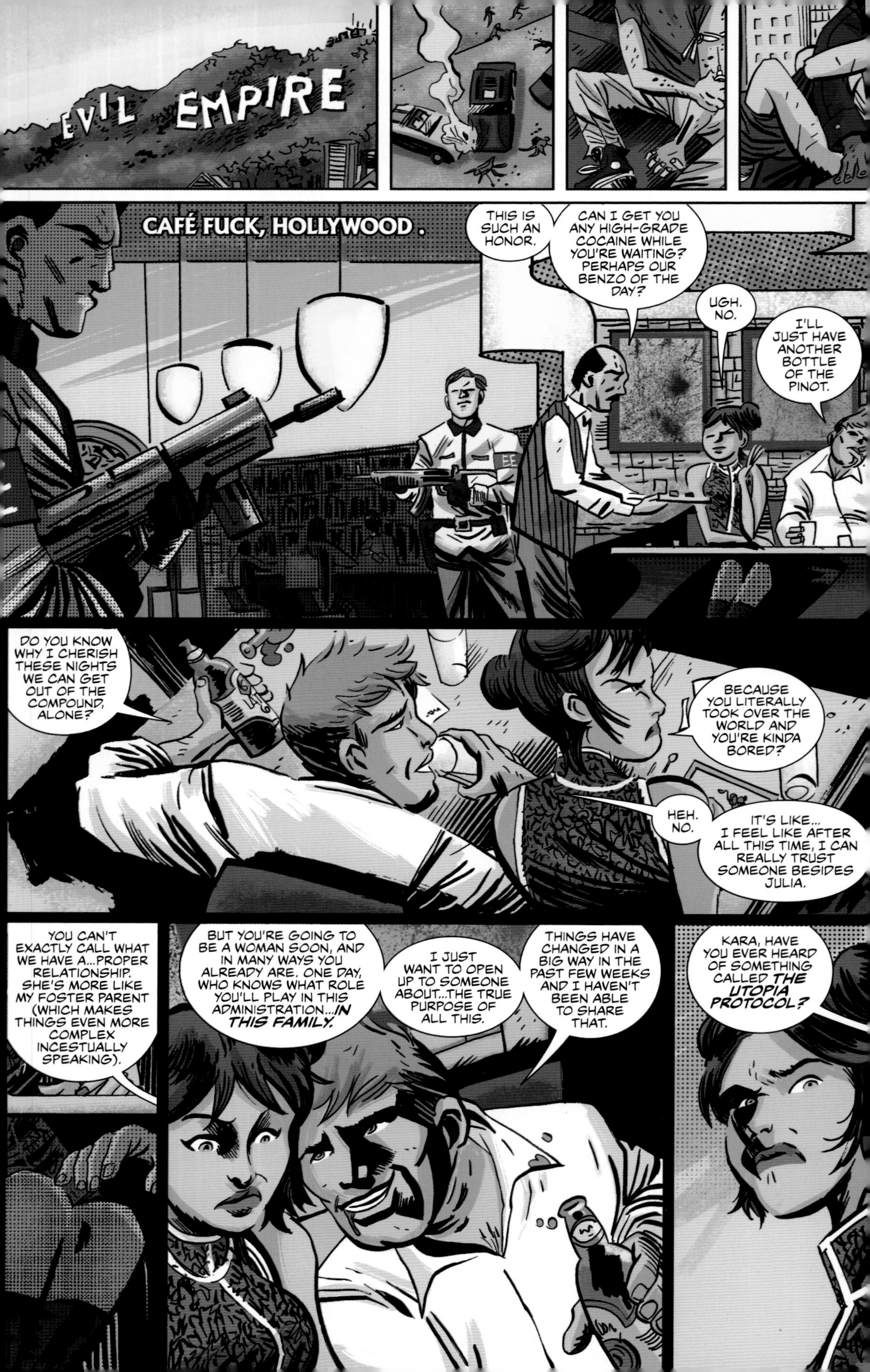
EVIL EMPIRE
CAFÉ FUCK, HOLLYWOOD.
THIS IS SUCH AN HONOR.
CAN I GET YOU ANY HIGH-GRADE COCAINE WHILE YOU'RE WAITING? PERHAPS OUR BENZO OF THE DAY?
UGH. NO.
I'LL JUST HAVE ANOTHER BOTTLE OF THE PINOT.
EE
DO YOU KNOW WHY I CHERISH THESE NIGHTS WE CAN GET OUT OF THE COMPOUND, ALONE?
BECAUSE YOU LITERALLY TOOK OVER THE WORLD AND YOU'RE KINDA BORED?
HEH. NO.
IT'S LIKE... I FEEL LIKE AFTER ALL THIS TIME, I CAN REALLY TRUST SOMEONE BESIDES JULIA.
YOU CAN'T EXACTLY CALL WHAT WE HAVE A...PROPER RELATIONSHIP. SHE'S MORE LIKE MY FOSTER PARENT (WHICH MAKES THINGS EVEN MORE COMPLEX INCESTUALLY SPEAKING).
BUT YOU'RE GOING TO BE A WOMAN SOON, AND IN MANY WAYS YOU ALREADY ARE. ONE DAY, WHO KNOWS WHAT ROLE YOU'LL PLAY IN THIS ADMINISTRATION...*IN THIS FAMILY.*
I JUST WANT TO OPEN UP TO SOMEONE ABOUT...THE TRUE PURPOSE OF ALL THIS.
THINGS HAVE CHANGED IN A BIG WAY IN THE PAST FEW WEEKS AND I HAVEN'T BEEN ABLE TO SHARE THAT.
KARA, HAVE YOU EVER HEARD OF SOMETHING CALLED *THE UTOPIA PROTOCOL?*

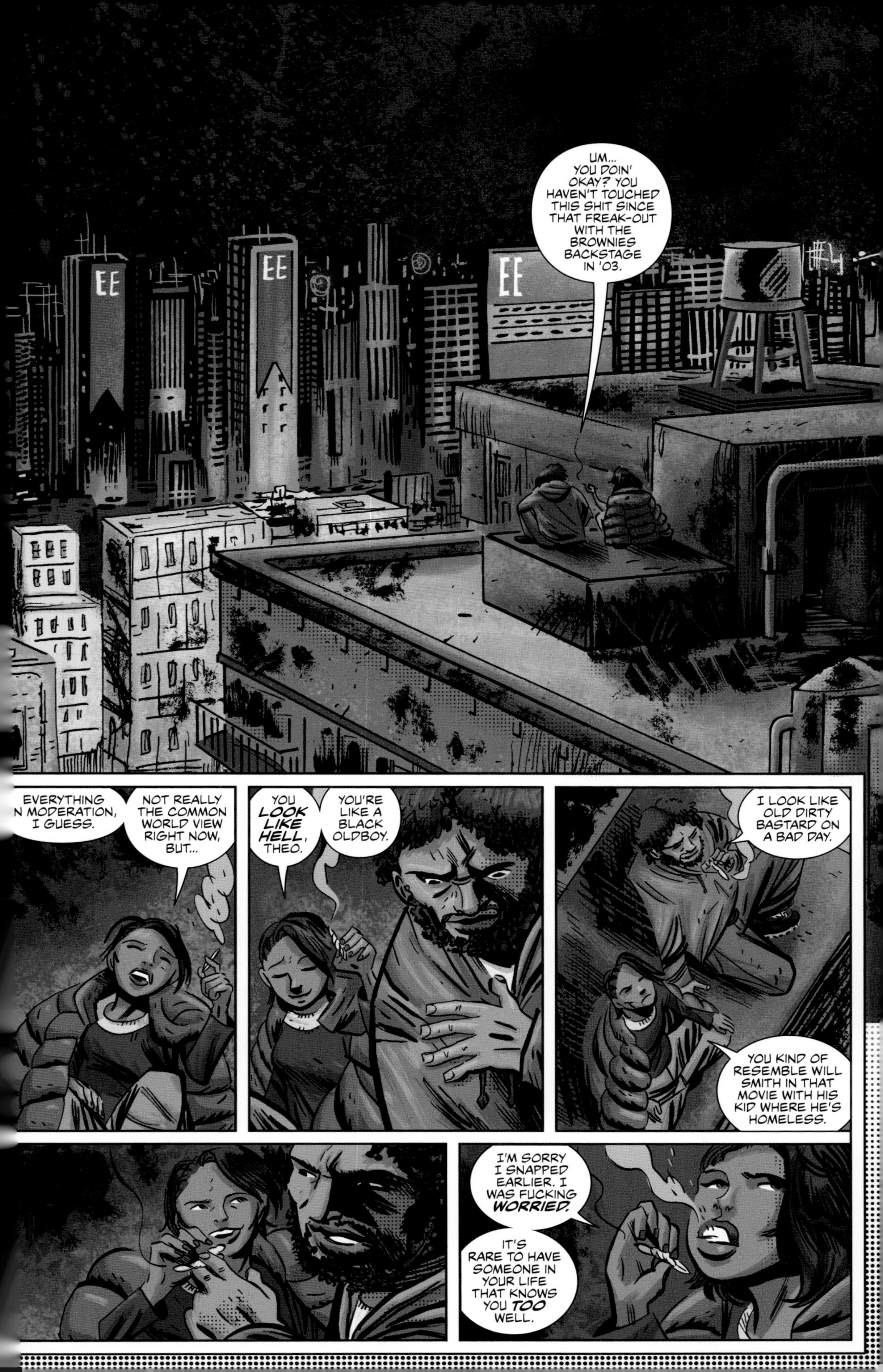
UM... YOU DOIN' OKAY? YOU HAVEN'T TOUCHED THIS SHIT SINCE THAT FREAK-OUT WITH THE BROWNIES BACKSTAGE IN '03.
EVERYTHING IN MODERATION, I GUESS.
NOT REALLY THE COMMON WORLD VIEW RIGHT NOW, BUT...
YOU LOOK LIKE HELL, THEO.
YOU'RE LIKE A BLACK OLDBOY.
I LOOK LIKE OLD DIRTY BASTARD ON A BAD DAY.
YOU KIND OF RESEMBLE WILL SMITH IN THAT MOVIE WITH HIS KID WHERE HE'S HOMELESS.
I'M SORRY I SNAPPED EARLIER. I WAS FUCKING WORRIED.
IT'S RARE TO HAVE SOMEONE IN YOUR LIFE THAT KNOWS YOU TOO WELL.

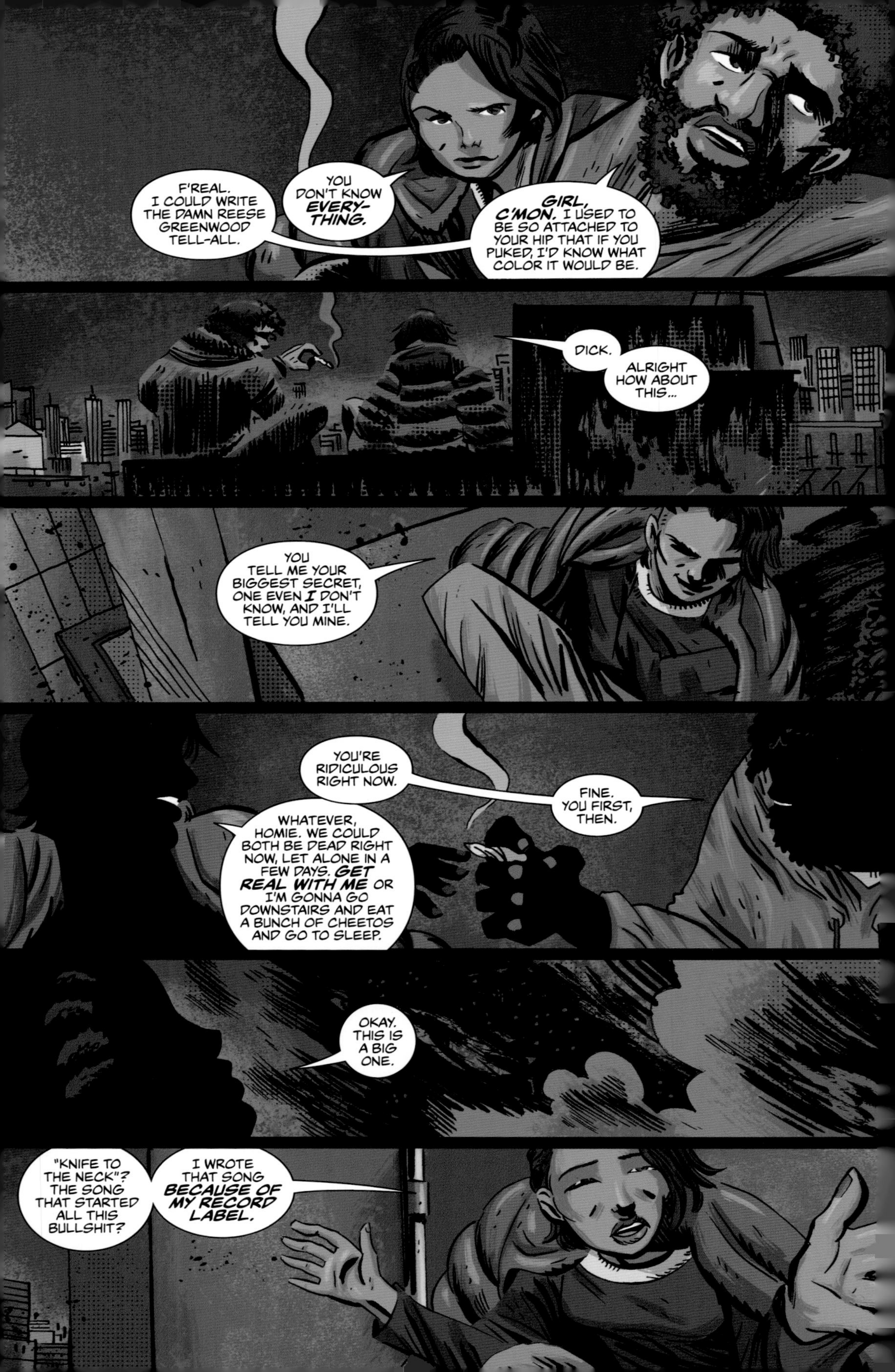
F'REAL. I COULD WRITE THE DAMN REESE GREENWOOD TELL-ALL.
YOU DON'T KNOW EVERY-THING.
GIRL, C'MON. I USED TO BE SO ATTACHED TO YOUR HIP THAT IF YOU PUKED, I'D KNOW WHAT COLOR IT WOULD BE.
DICK.
ALRIGHT HOW ABOUT THIS...
YOU TELL ME YOUR BIGGEST SECRET, ONE EVEN I DON'T KNOW, AND I'LL TELL YOU MINE.
YOU'RE RIDICULOUS RIGHT NOW.
FINE. YOU FIRST, THEN.
WHATEVER, HOMIE. WE COULD BOTH BE DEAD RIGHT NOW, LET ALONE IN A FEW DAYS. GET REAL WITH ME OR I'M GONNA GO DOWNSTAIRS AND EAT A BUNCH OF CHEETOS AND GO TO SLEEP.
OKAY. THIS IS A BIG ONE.
I WROTE THAT SONG BECAUSE OF MY RECORD LABEL.
"KNIFE TO THE NECK"? THE SONG THAT STARTED ALL THIS BULLSHIT?

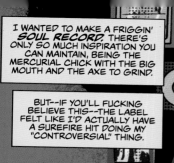

I WANTED TO MAKE A FRIGGIN' *SOUL RECORD.* THERE'S ONLY SO MUCH INSPIRATION YOU CAN MAINTAIN, BEING THE MERCURIAL CHICK WITH THE BIG MOUTH AND THE AXE TO GRIND.

BUT--IF YOU'LL FUCKING BELIEVE THIS--THE LABEL FELT LIKE I'D ACTUALLY HAVE A SUREFIRE HIT DOING MY "CONTROVERSIAL" THING.

BECAUSE THAT'S ALL I WAS GOOD FOR. WHAT I'M *STILL* GOOD FOR. THEY WANTED TO KEEP MARKETING *THAT.* SO THEY SENT ME BACK INTO THE STUDIO, AND THAT'S WHAT I SPAT OUT.

IT'S NOT THAT I DIDN'T BELIEVE IN THE WORDS I WROTE...BUT I'LL NEVER FORGIVE MYSELF. WRITING THAT PUNK SONG PURELY BECAUSE A BUNCH OF RICH, POWERFUL WHITE MEN BASICALLY DEMANDED IT OF ME.

SHIT, REESE.

I KNOW.

YOU REALIZE THAT MISTAKE WAS THE BEST THING THAT EVER HAPPENED TO US, RIGHT?

WELL... WHATEVER.

NOW YOU.

OKAY, WELL...

I ALSO LIKE *GUYS.*

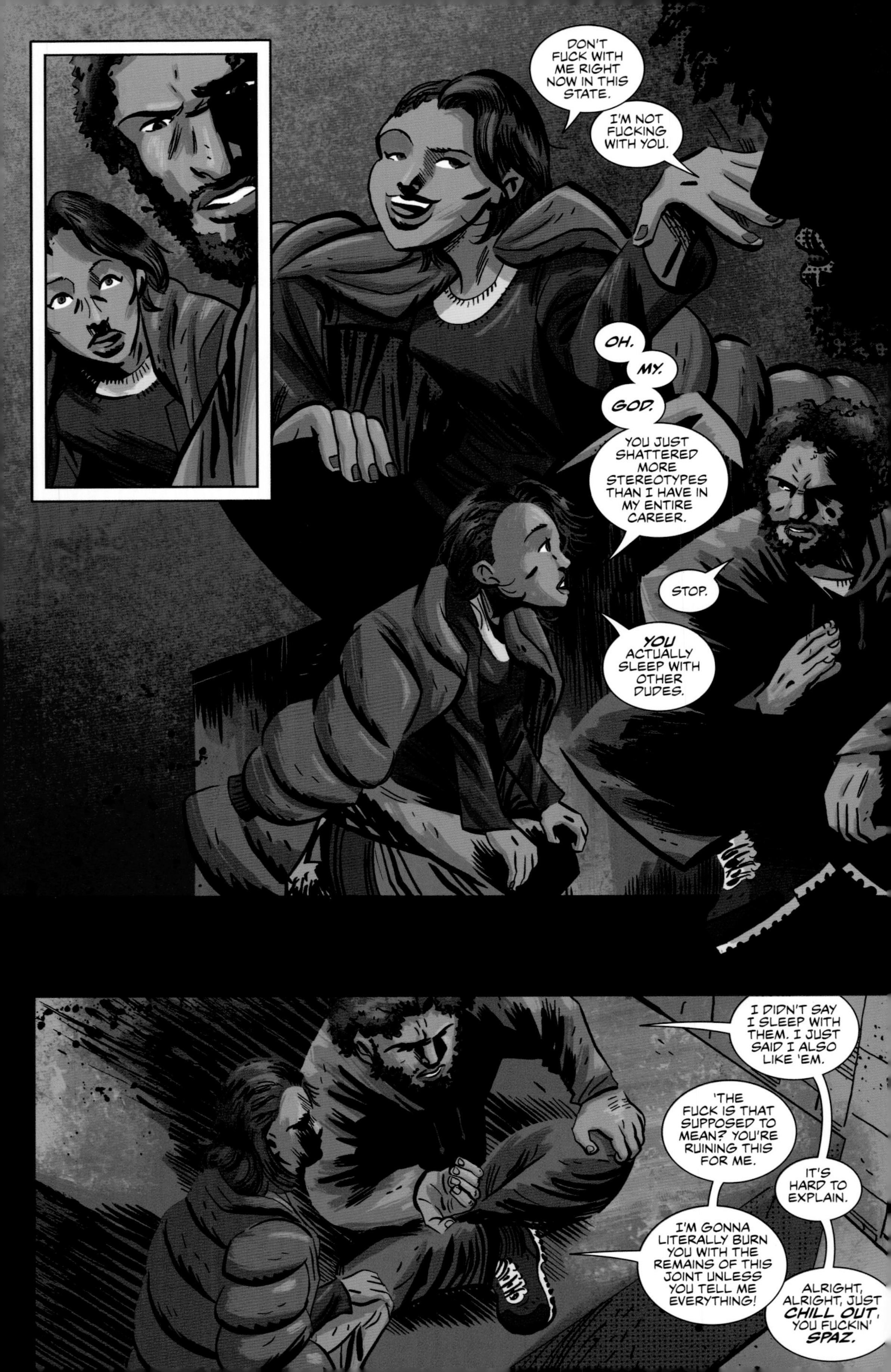
DON'T FUCK WITH ME RIGHT NOW IN THIS STATE.
I'M NOT FUCKING WITH YOU.
OH.
MY.
GOD.
YOU JUST SHATTERED MORE STEREOTYPES THAN I HAVE IN MY ENTIRE CAREER.
STOP.
YOU ACTUALLY SLEEP WITH OTHER DUDES.
I DIDN'T SAY I SLEEP WITH THEM. I JUST SAID I ALSO LIKE 'EM.
'THE FUCK IS THAT SUPPOSED TO MEAN? YOU'RE RUINING THIS FOR ME.
IT'S HARD TO EXPLAIN.
I'M GONNA LITERALLY BURN YOU WITH THE REMAINS OF THIS JOINT UNLESS YOU TELL ME EVERYTHING!
ALRIGHT, ALRIGHT, JUST CHILL OUT, YOU FUCKIN' SPAZ.

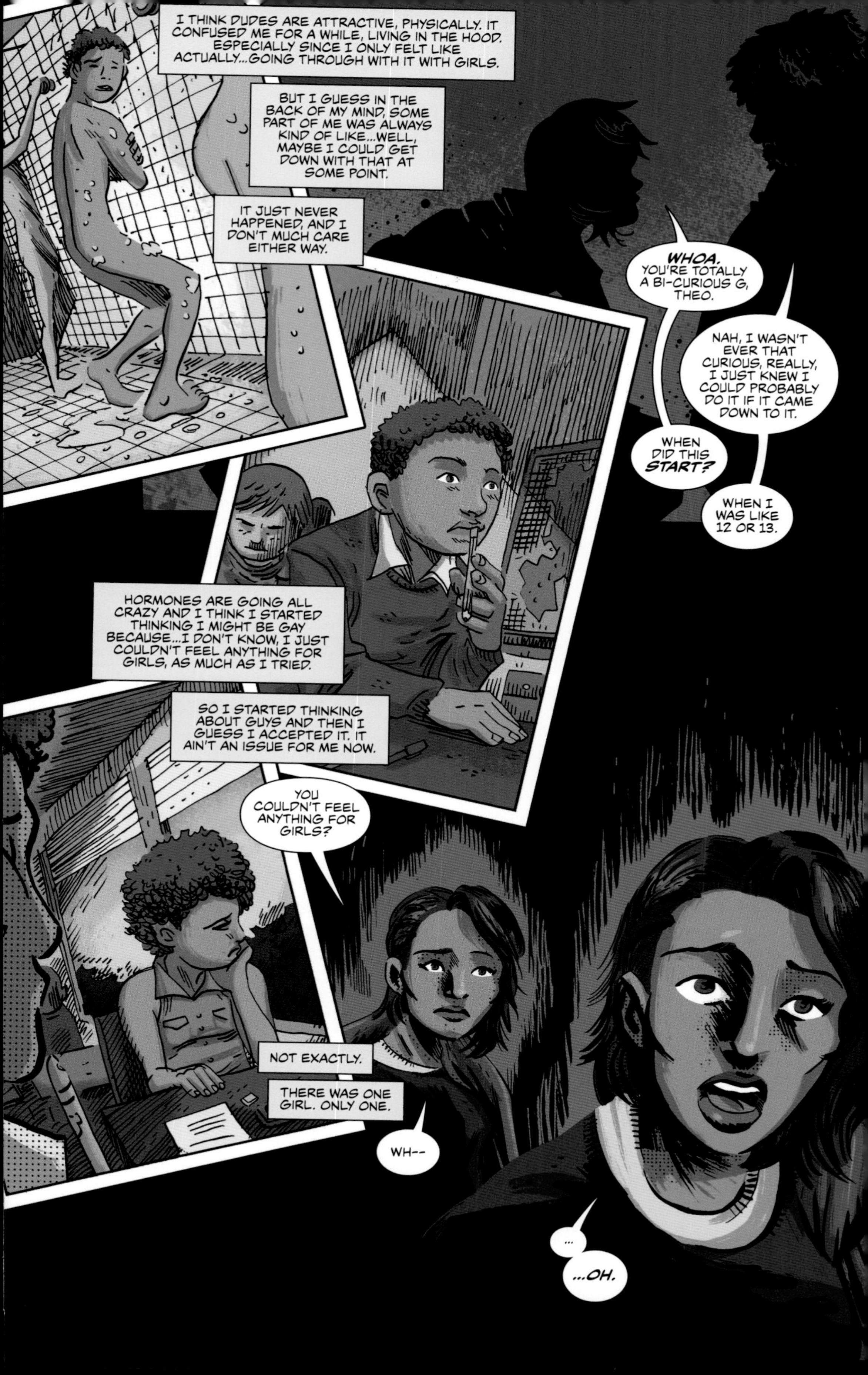
I THINK DUDES ARE ATTRACTIVE, PHYSICALLY. IT CONFUSED ME FOR A WHILE, LIVING IN THE HOOD. ESPECIALLY SINCE I ONLY FELT LIKE ACTUALLY...GOING THROUGH WITH IT WITH GIRLS.
BUT I GUESS IN THE BACK OF MY MIND, SOME PART OF ME WAS ALWAYS KIND OF LIKE...WELL, MAYBE I COULD GET DOWN WITH THAT AT SOME POINT.
IT JUST NEVER HAPPENED, AND I DON'T MUCH CARE EITHER WAY.
WHOA. YOU'RE TOTALLY A BI-CURIOUS G, THEO.
NAH, I WASN'T EVER THAT CURIOUS, REALLY, I JUST KNEW I COULD PROBABLY DO IT IF IT CAME DOWN TO IT.
WHEN DID THIS START?
WHEN I WAS LIKE 12 OR 13.
HORMONES ARE GOING ALL CRAZY AND I THINK I STARTED THINKING I MIGHT BE GAY BECAUSE...I DON'T KNOW, I JUST COULDN'T FEEL ANYTHING FOR GIRLS, AS MUCH AS I TRIED.
SO I STARTED THINKING ABOUT GUYS AND THEN I GUESS I ACCEPTED IT. IT AIN'T AN ISSUE FOR ME NOW.
YOU COULDN'T FEEL ANYTHING FOR GIRLS?
NOT EXACTLY.
THERE WAS ONE GIRL. ONLY ONE.
WH--
...
...OH.

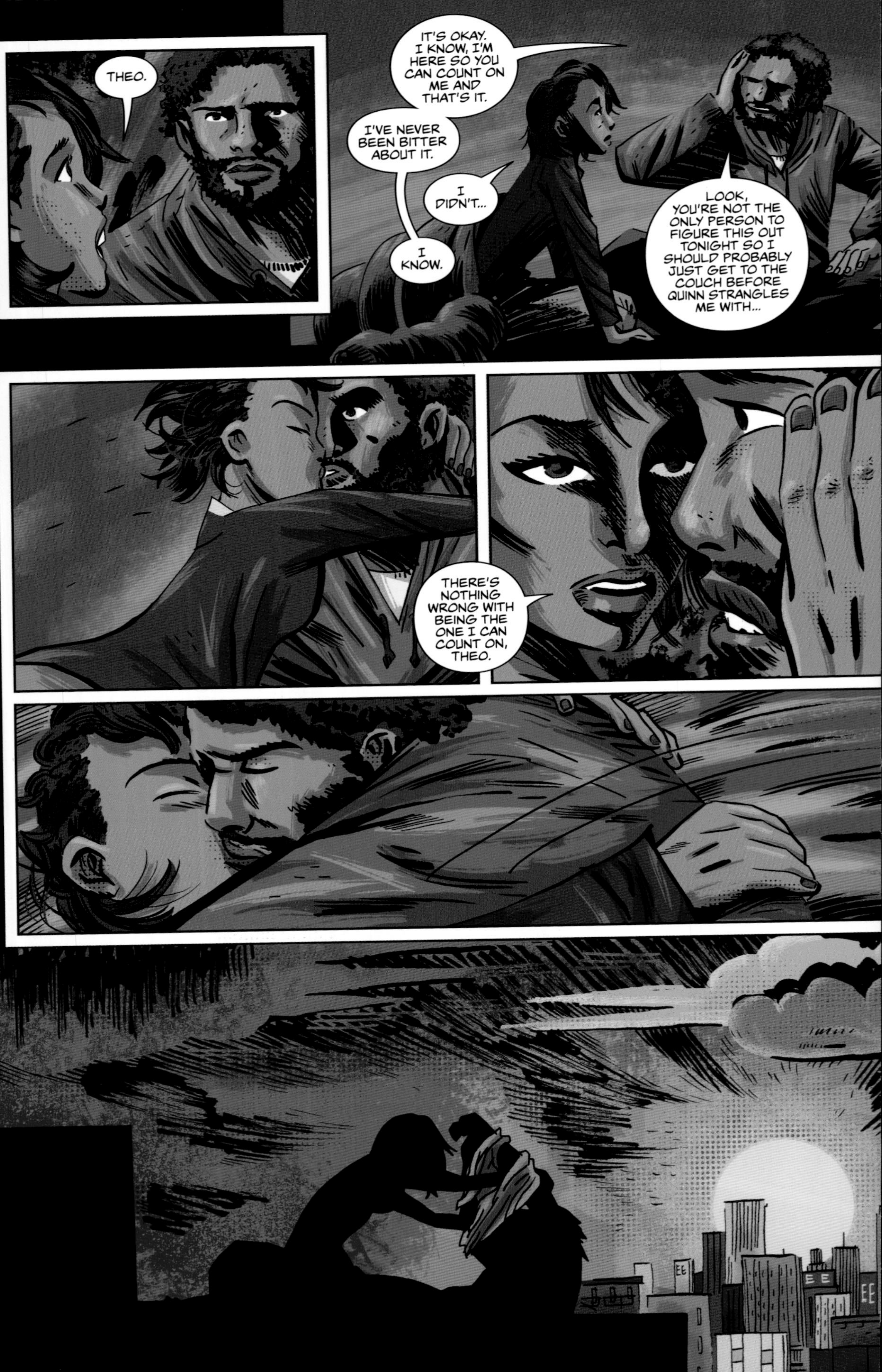
THEO.
IT'S OKAY. I KNOW, I'M HERE SO YOU CAN COUNT ON ME AND THAT'S IT.
I'VE NEVER BEEN BITTER ABOUT IT.
I DIDN'T...
I KNOW.
LOOK, YOU'RE NOT THE ONLY PERSON TO FIGURE THIS OUT TONIGHT SO I SHOULD PROBABLY JUST GET TO THE COUCH BEFORE QUINN STRANGLES ME WITH...
THERE'S NOTHING WRONG WITH BEING THE ONE I CAN COUNT ON, THEO.

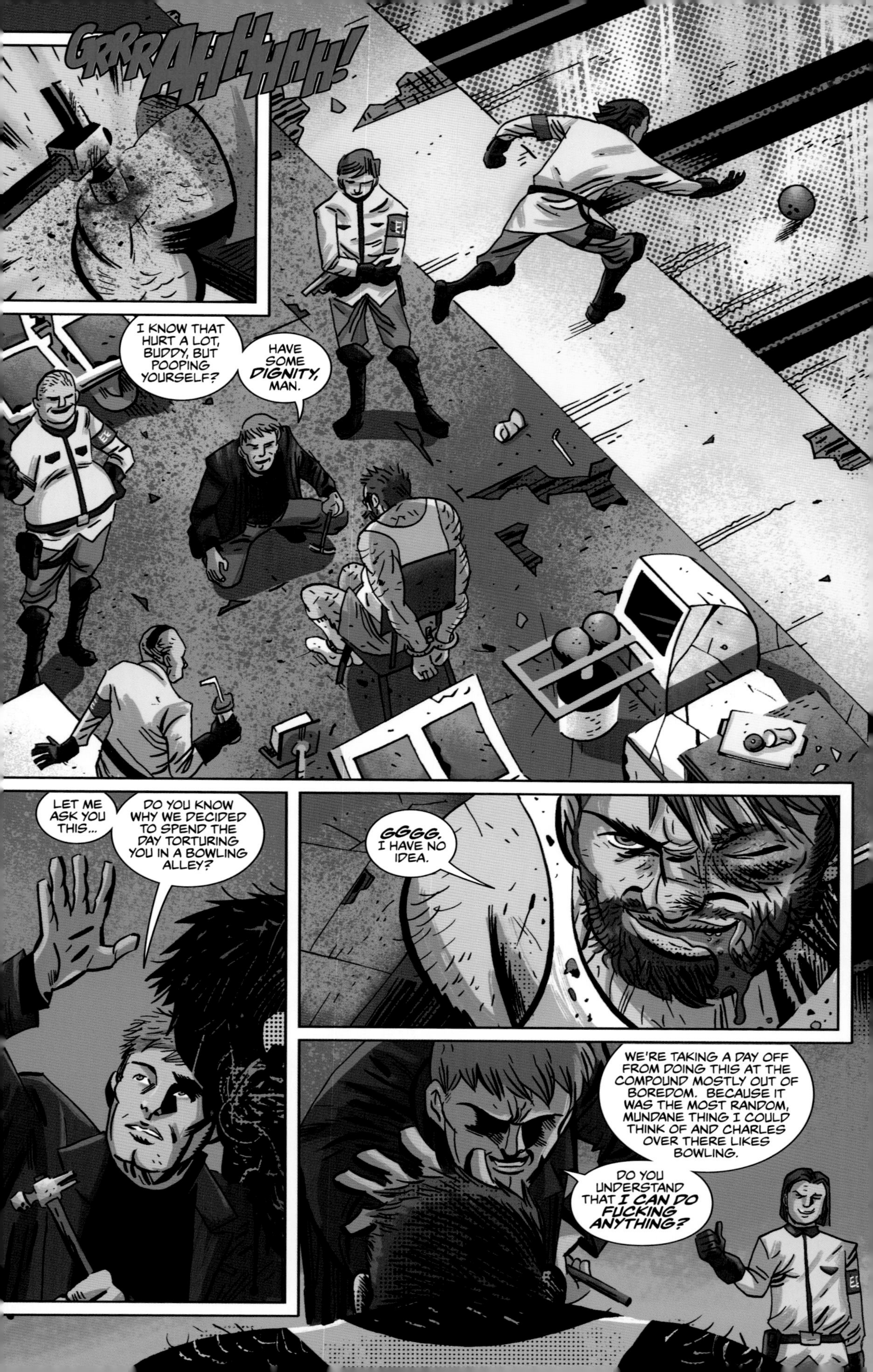
GRRRAHHHHHH!
I KNOW THAT HURT A LOT, BUDDY, BUT POOPING YOURSELF?
HAVE SOME DIGNITY, MAN.
LET ME ASK YOU THIS...
DO YOU KNOW WHY WE DECIDED TO SPEND THE DAY TORTURING YOU IN A BOWLING ALLEY?
GGGG. I HAVE NO IDEA.
WE'RE TAKING A DAY OFF FROM DOING THIS AT THE COMPOUND MOSTLY OUT OF BOREDOM. BECAUSE IT WAS THE MOST RANDOM, MUNDANE THING I COULD THINK OF AND CHARLES OVER THERE LIKES BOWLING.
DO YOU UNDERSTAND THAT I CAN DO FUCKING ANYTHING?

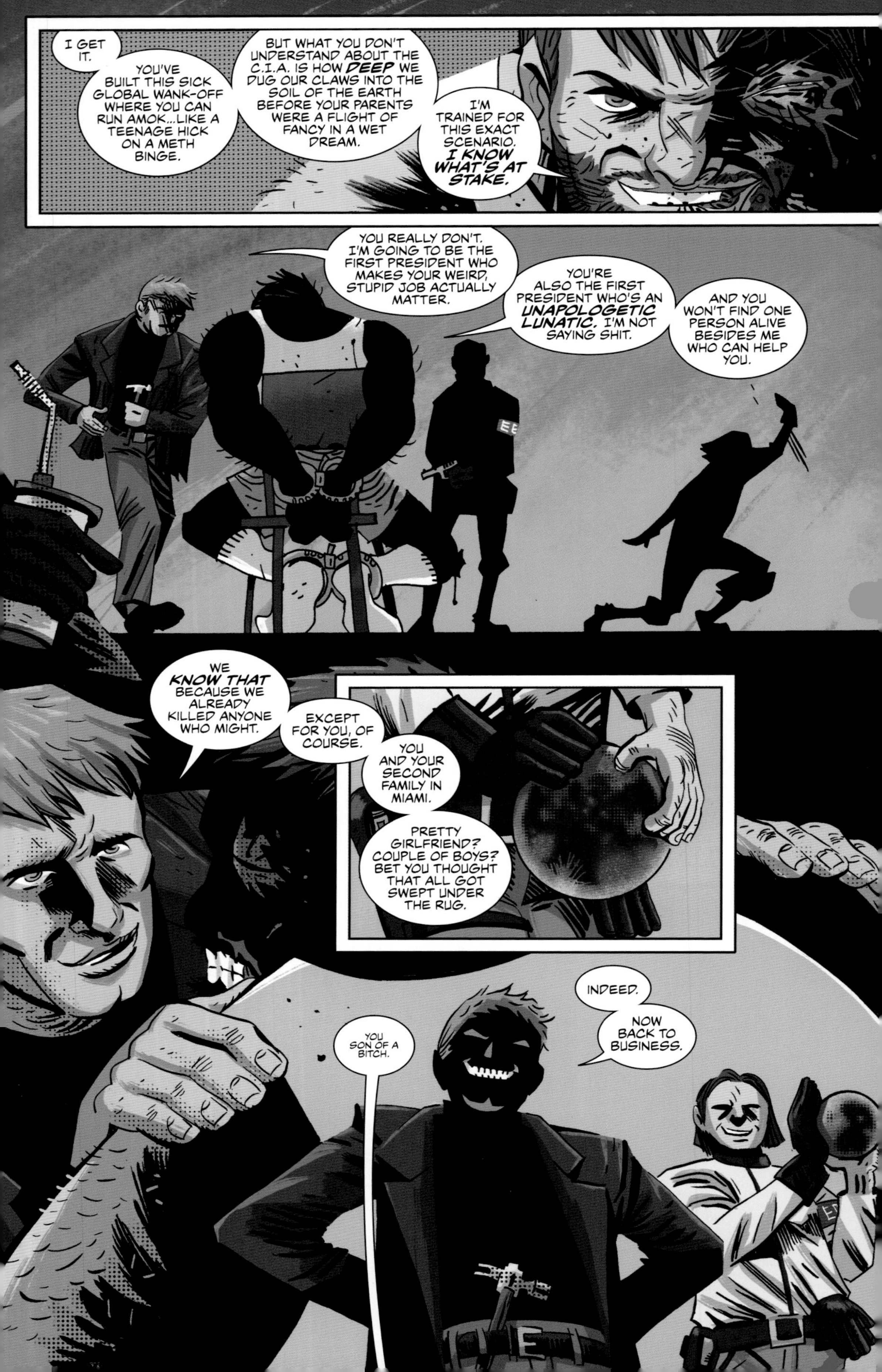
I GET IT.
YOU'VE BUILT THIS SICK GLOBAL WANK-OFF WHERE YOU CAN RUN AMOK...LIKE A TEENAGE HICK ON A METH BINGE.
BUT WHAT YOU DON'T UNDERSTAND ABOUT THE C.I.A. IS HOW *DEEP* WE DUG OUR CLAWS INTO THE SOIL OF THE EARTH BEFORE YOUR PARENTS WERE A FLIGHT OF FANCY IN A WET DREAM.
I'M TRAINED FOR THIS EXACT SCENARIO. **I KNOW WHAT'S AT STAKE.**
YOU REALLY DON'T. I'M GOING TO BE THE FIRST PRESIDENT WHO MAKES YOUR WEIRD, STUPID JOB ACTUALLY MATTER.
YOU'RE ALSO THE FIRST PRESIDENT WHO'S AN ***UNAPOLOGETIC LUNATIC.*** I'M NOT SAYING SHIT.
AND YOU WON'T FIND ONE PERSON ALIVE BESIDES ME WHO CAN HELP YOU.
WE ***KNOW THAT*** BECAUSE WE ALREADY KILLED ANYONE WHO MIGHT.
EXCEPT FOR YOU, OF COURSE.
YOU AND YOUR SECOND FAMILY IN MIAMI.
PRETTY GIRLFRIEND? COUPLE OF BOYS? BET YOU THOUGHT THAT ALL GOT SWEPT UNDER THE RUG.
YOU SON OF A BITCH.
INDEED.
NOW BACK TO BUSINESS.

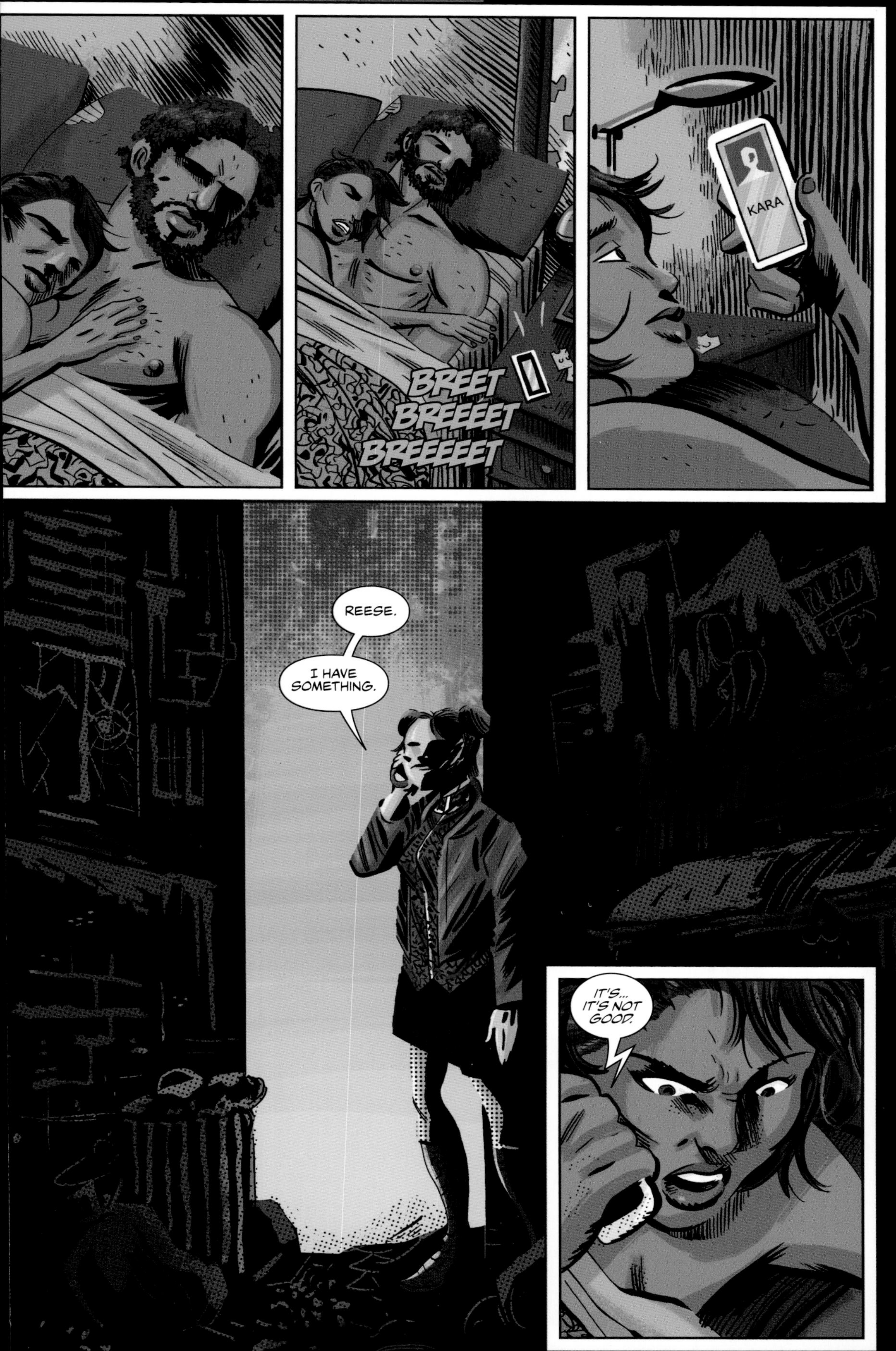
BREET
BREEEET
BREEEEET
KARA
REESE.
I HAVE SOMETHING.
IT'S... IT'S NOT GOOD.

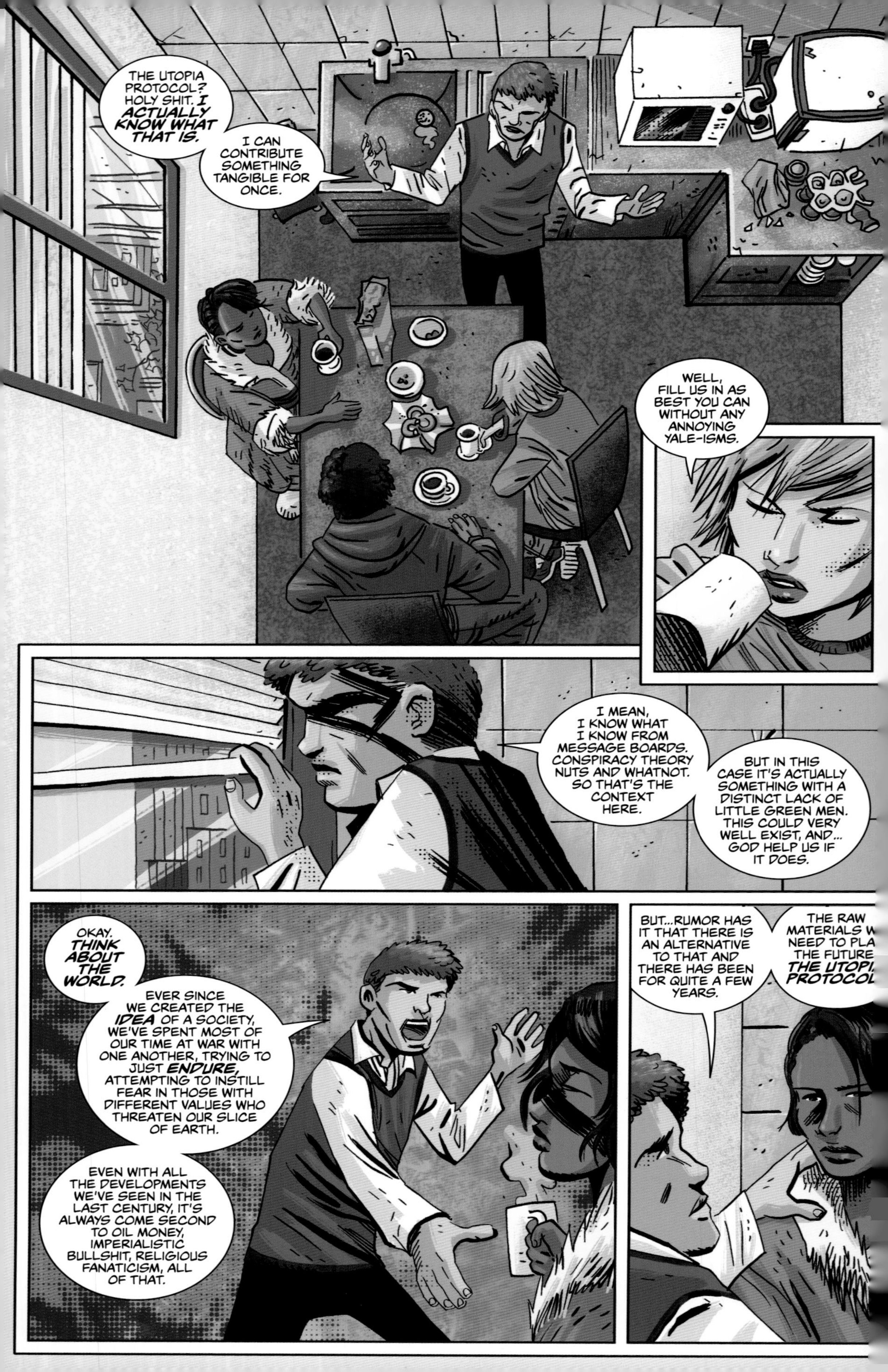

THE UTOPIA PROTOCOL? HOLY SHIT. ***I ACTUALLY KNOW WHAT THAT IS.***
I CAN CONTRIBUTE SOMETHING TANGIBLE FOR ONCE.
WELL, FILL US IN AS BEST YOU CAN WITHOUT ANY ANNOYING YALE-ISMS.
I MEAN, I KNOW WHAT I KNOW FROM MESSAGE BOARDS. CONSPIRACY THEORY NUTS AND WHATNOT. SO THAT'S THE CONTEXT HERE.
BUT IN THIS CASE IT'S ACTUALLY SOMETHING WITH A DISTINCT LACK OF LITTLE GREEN MEN. THIS COULD VERY WELL EXIST, AND... GOD HELP US IF IT DOES.
OKAY. ***THINK ABOUT THE WORLD.***
EVER SINCE WE CREATED THE ***IDEA*** OF A SOCIETY, WE'VE SPENT MOST OF OUR TIME AT WAR WITH ONE ANOTHER, TRYING TO JUST ***ENDURE,*** ATTEMPTING TO INSTILL FEAR IN THOSE WITH DIFFERENT VALUES WHO THREATEN OUR SLICE OF EARTH.
EVEN WITH ALL THE DEVELOPMENTS WE'VE SEEN IN THE LAST CENTURY, IT'S ALWAYS COME SECOND TO OIL MONEY, IMPERIALISTIC BULLSHIT, RELIGIOUS FANATICISM, ALL OF THAT.
BUT...RUMOR HAS IT THAT THERE IS AN ALTERNATIVE TO THAT AND THERE HAS BEEN FOR QUITE A FEW YEARS.
THE RAW MATERIALS W NEED TO PLA THE FUTURE ***THE UTOPI PROTOCOL***

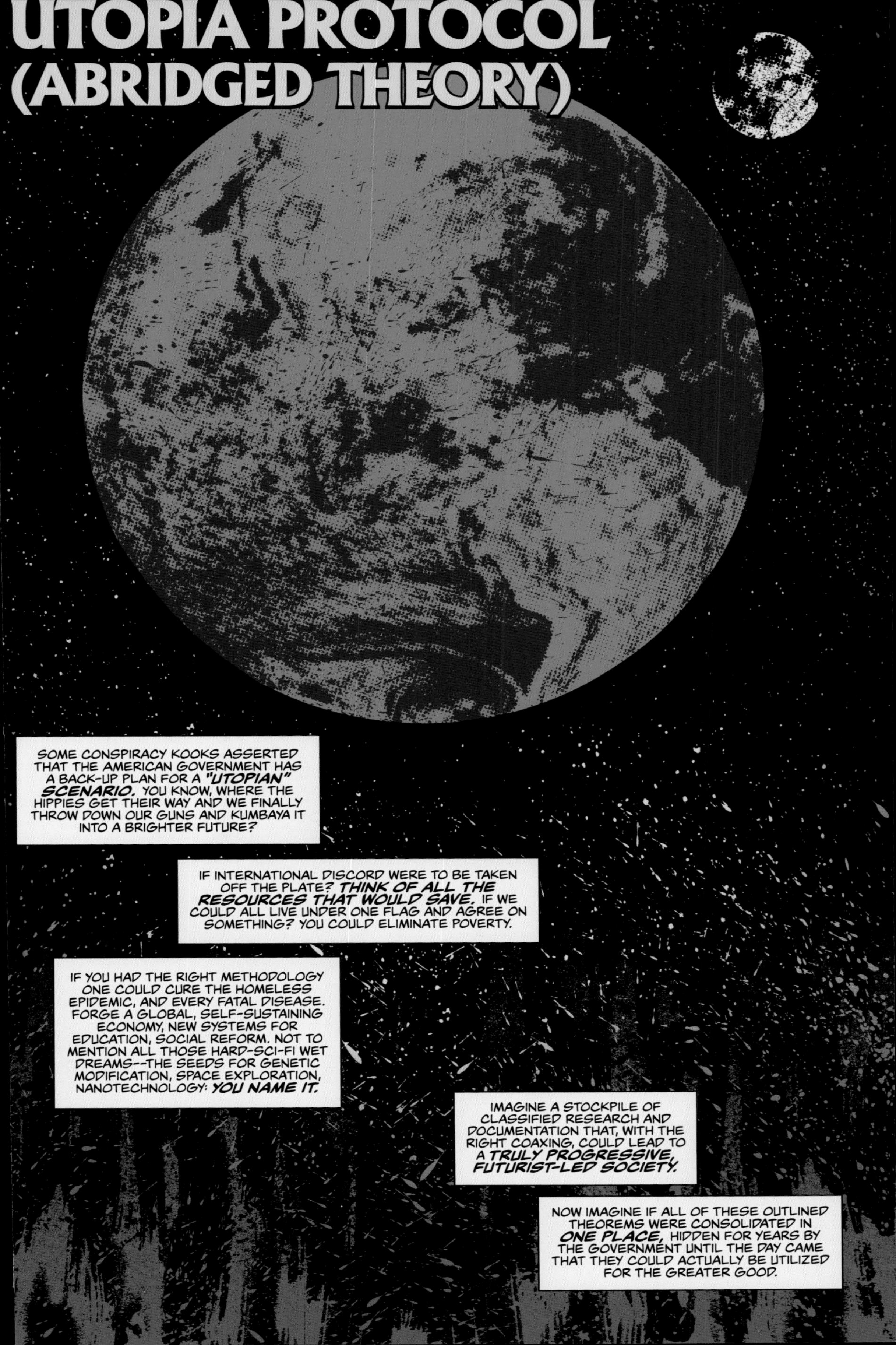
UTOPIA PROTOCOL (ABRIDGED THEORY)
SOME CONSPIRACY KOOKS ASSERTED THAT THE AMERICAN GOVERNMENT HAS A BACK-UP PLAN FOR A "UTOPIAN" SCENARIO. YOU KNOW, WHERE THE HIPPIES GET THEIR WAY AND WE FINALLY THROW DOWN OUR GUNS AND KUMBAYA IT INTO A BRIGHTER FUTURE?
IF INTERNATIONAL DISCORD WERE TO BE TAKEN OFF THE PLATE? THINK OF ALL THE RESOURCES THAT WOULD SAVE. IF WE COULD ALL LIVE UNDER ONE FLAG AND AGREE ON SOMETHING? YOU COULD ELIMINATE POVERTY.
IF YOU HAD THE RIGHT METHODOLOGY ONE COULD CURE THE HOMELESS EPIDEMIC, AND EVERY FATAL DISEASE. FORGE A GLOBAL, SELF-SUSTAINING ECONOMY, NEW SYSTEMS FOR EDUCATION, SOCIAL REFORM. NOT TO MENTION ALL THOSE HARD-SCI-FI WET DREAMS--THE SEEDS FOR GENETIC MODIFICATION, SPACE EXPLORATION, NANOTECHNOLOGY: YOU NAME IT.
IMAGINE A STOCKPILE OF CLASSIFIED RESEARCH AND DOCUMENTATION THAT, WITH THE RIGHT COAXING, COULD LEAD TO A TRULY PROGRESSIVE, FUTURIST-LED SOCIETY.
NOW IMAGINE IF ALL OF THESE OUTLINED THEOREMS WERE CONSOLIDATED IN ONE PLACE, HIDDEN FOR YEARS BY THE GOVERNMENT UNTIL THE DAY CAME THAT THEY COULD ACTUALLY BE UTILIZED FOR THE GREATER GOOD.

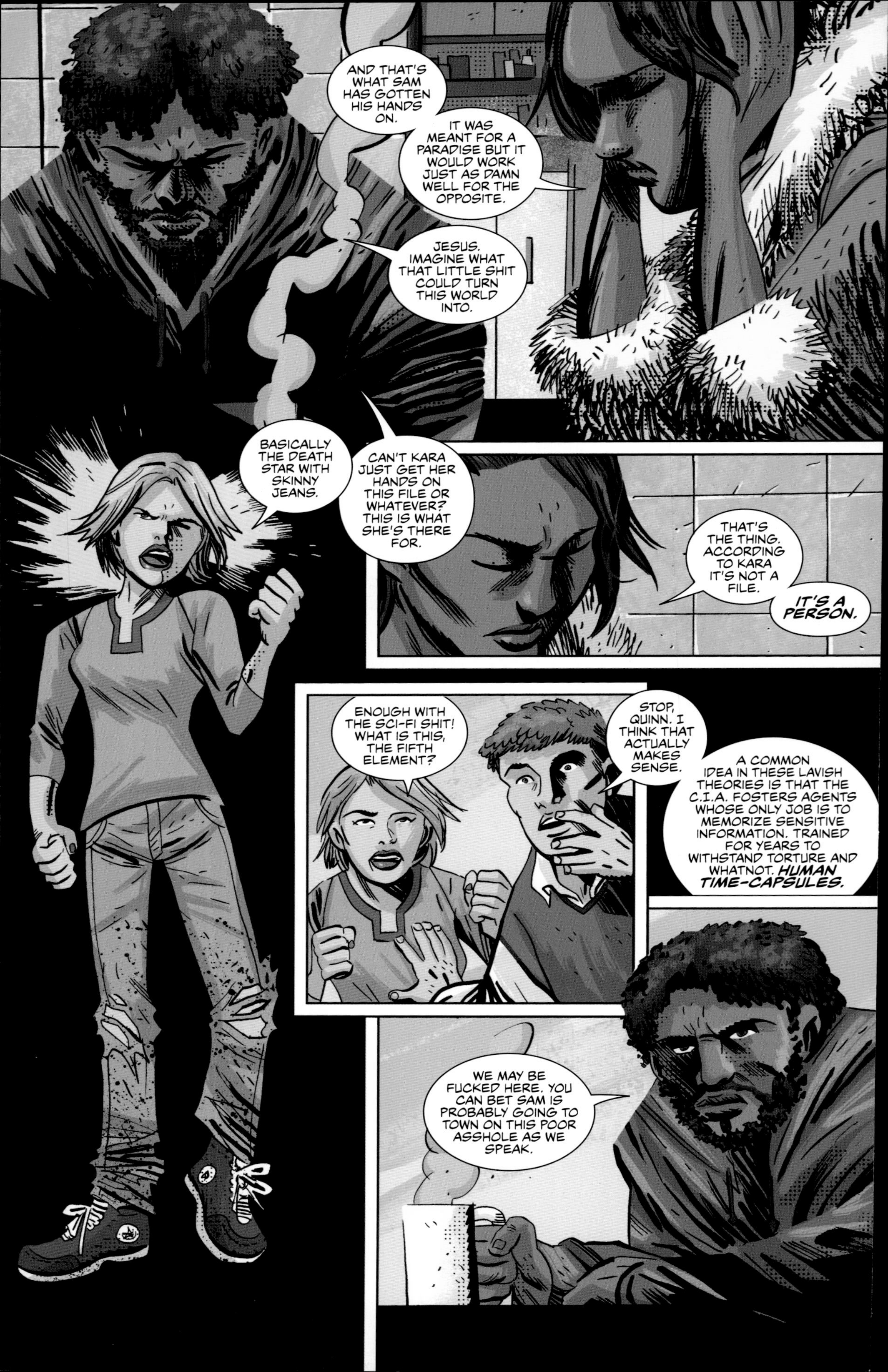
AND THAT'S WHAT SAM HAS GOTTEN HIS HANDS ON.
IT WAS MEANT FOR A PARADISE BUT IT WOULD WORK JUST AS DAMN WELL FOR THE OPPOSITE.
JESUS. IMAGINE WHAT THAT LITTLE SHIT COULD TURN THIS WORLD INTO.
BASICALLY THE DEATH STAR WITH SKINNY JEANS.
CAN'T KARA JUST GET HER HANDS ON THIS FILE OR WHATEVER? THIS IS WHAT SHE'S THERE FOR.
THAT'S THE THING. ACCORDING TO KARA IT'S NOT A FILE.
IT'S A PERSON.
ENOUGH WITH THE SCI-FI SHIT! WHAT IS THIS, THE FIFTH ELEMENT?
STOP, QUINN. I THINK THAT ACTUALLY MAKES SENSE.
A COMMON IDEA IN THESE LAVISH THEORIES IS THAT THE C.I.A. FOSTERS AGENTS WHOSE ONLY JOB IS TO MEMORIZE SENSITIVE INFORMATION. TRAINED FOR YEARS TO WITHSTAND TORTURE AND WHATNOT. HUMAN TIME-CAPSULES.
WE MAY BE FUCKED HERE. YOU CAN BET SAM IS PROBABLY GOING TO TOWN ON THIS POOR ASSHOLE AS WE SPEAK.

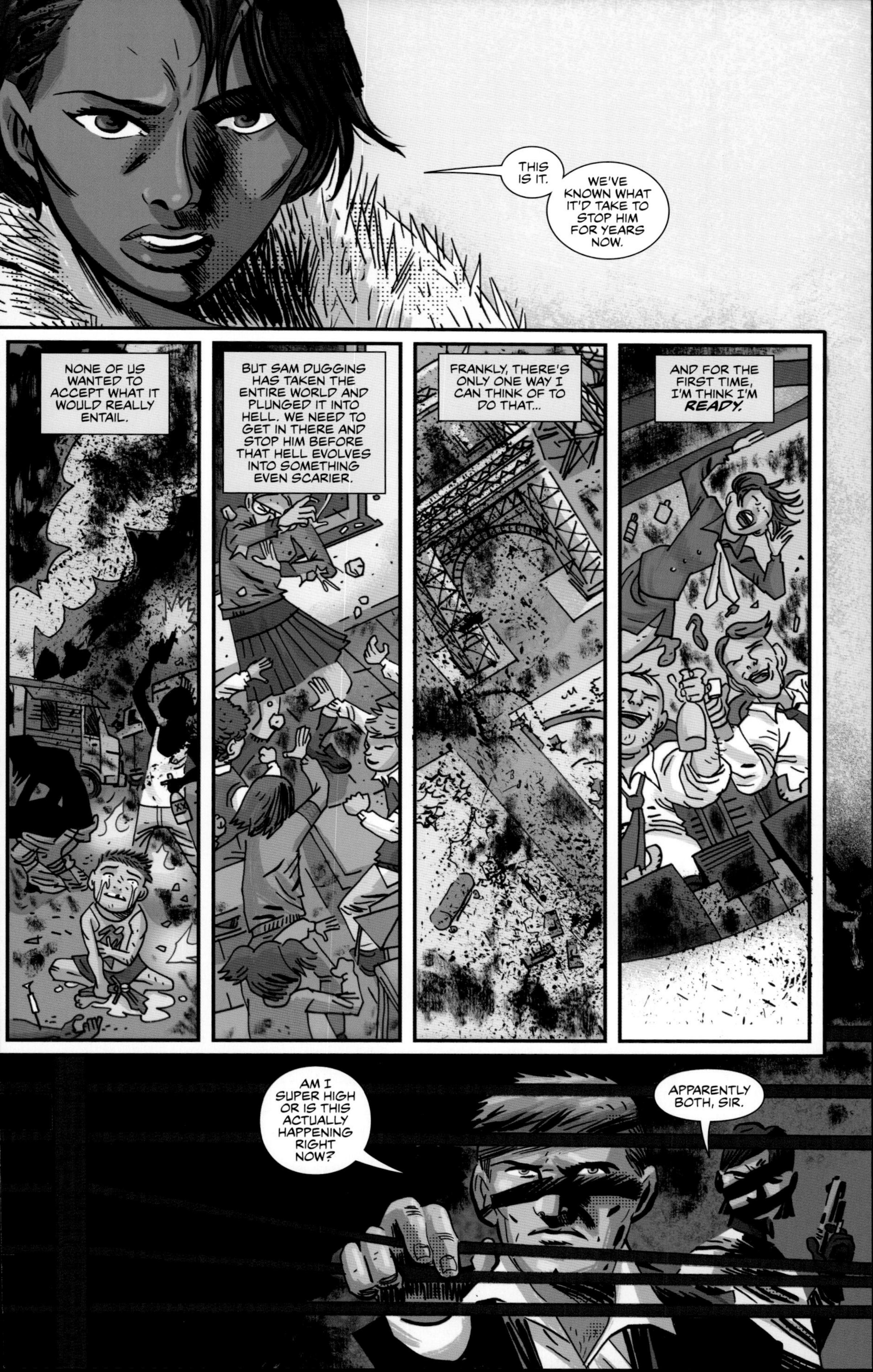
THIS IS IT.
WE'VE KNOWN WHAT IT'D TAKE TO STOP HIM FOR YEARS NOW.
NONE OF US WANTED TO ACCEPT WHAT IT WOULD REALLY ENTAIL.
BUT SAM DUGGINS HAS TAKEN THE ENTIRE WORLD AND PLUNGED IT INTO HELL. WE NEED TO GET IN THERE AND STOP HIM BEFORE THAT HELL EVOLVES INTO SOMETHING EVEN SCARIER.
FRANKLY, THERE'S ONLY ONE WAY I CAN THINK OF TO DO THAT...
AND FOR THE FIRST TIME, I'M THINK I'M READY.
AM I SUPER HIGH OR IS THIS ACTUALLY HAPPENING RIGHT NOW?
APPARENTLY BOTH, SIR.

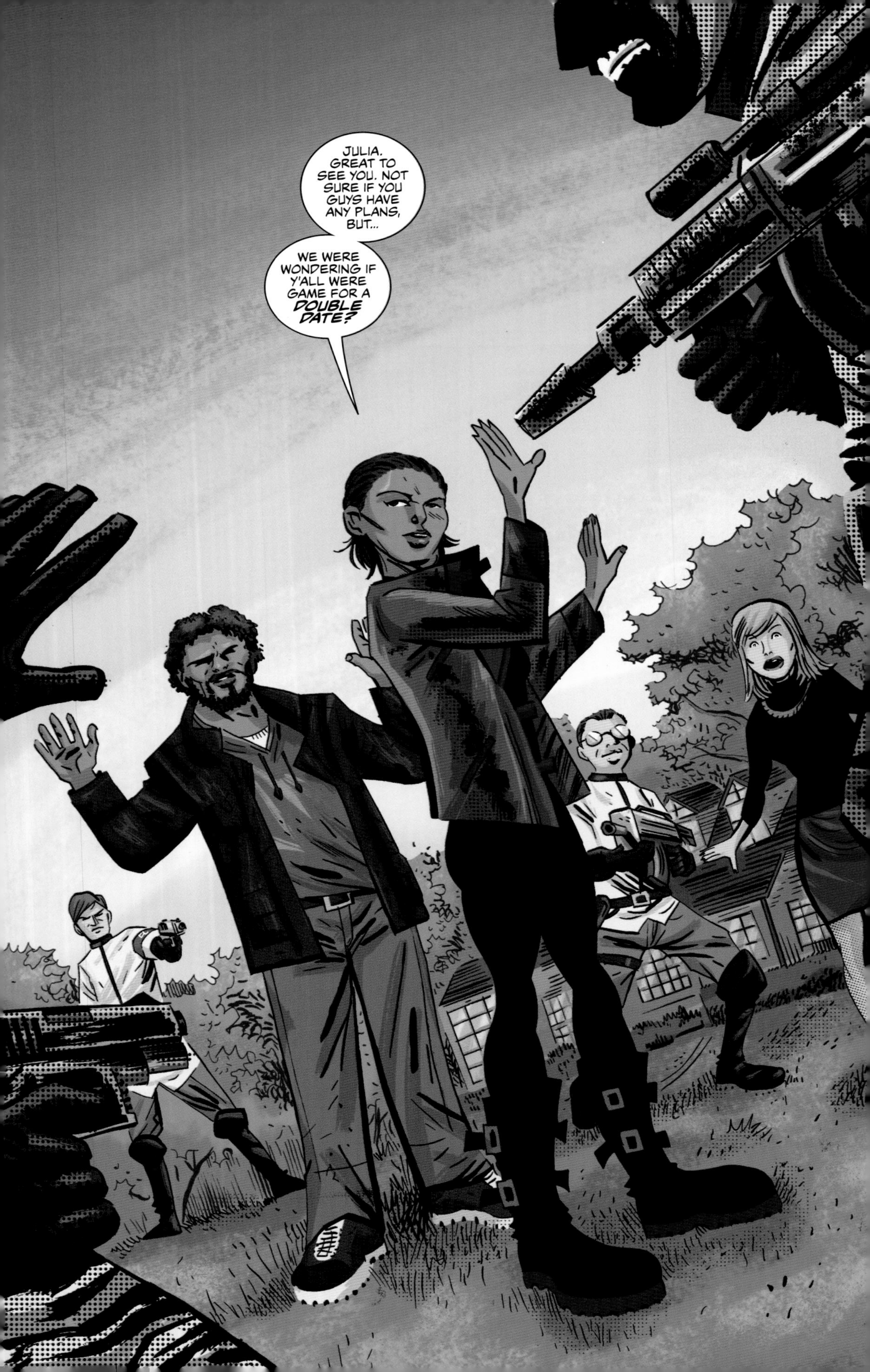
JULIA. GREAT TO SEE YOU. NOT SURE IF YOU GUYS HAVE ANY PLANS, BUT...
WE WERE WONDERING IF Y'ALL WERE GAME FOR A ***DOUBLE DATE?***

Maybe we're not supposed to dwell too long on the
nightmarish appeal of these visions.
exc. 4.0

CHAPTER
TWELVE
fig. 4

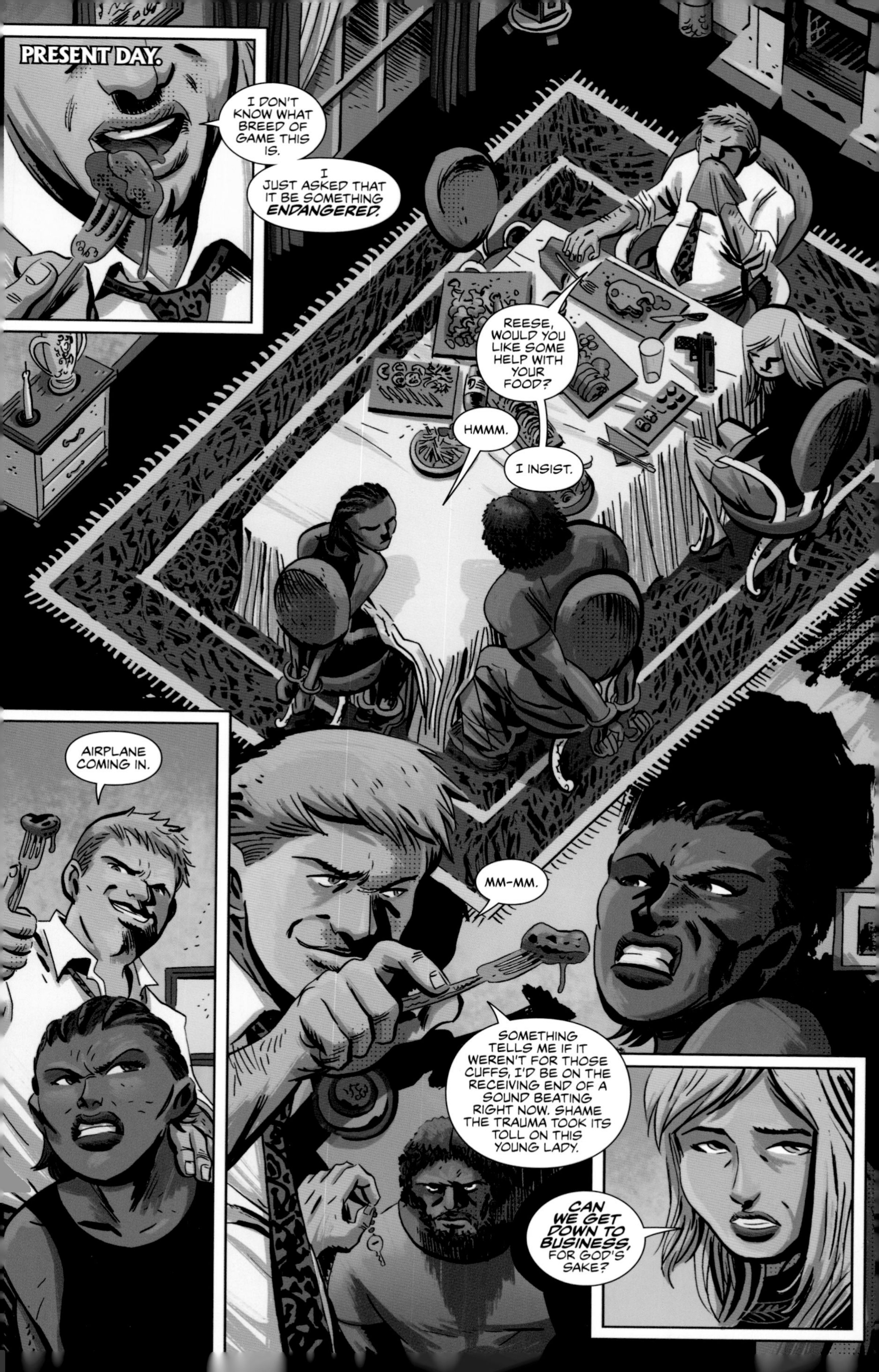
PRESENT DAY.
I DON'T KNOW WHAT BREED OF GAME THIS IS.
I JUST ASKED THAT IT BE SOMETHING ENDANGERED.
REESE, WOULD YOU LIKE SOME HELP WITH YOUR FOOD?
HMMM.
I INSIST.
AIRPLANE COMING IN.
MM-MM.
SOMETHING TELLS ME IF IT WEREN'T FOR THOSE CUFFS, I'D BE ON THE RECEIVING END OF A SOUND BEATING RIGHT NOW. SHAME THE TRAUMA TOOK ITS TOLL ON THIS YOUNG LADY.
CAN WE GET DOWN TO BUSINESS, FOR GOD'S SAKE?

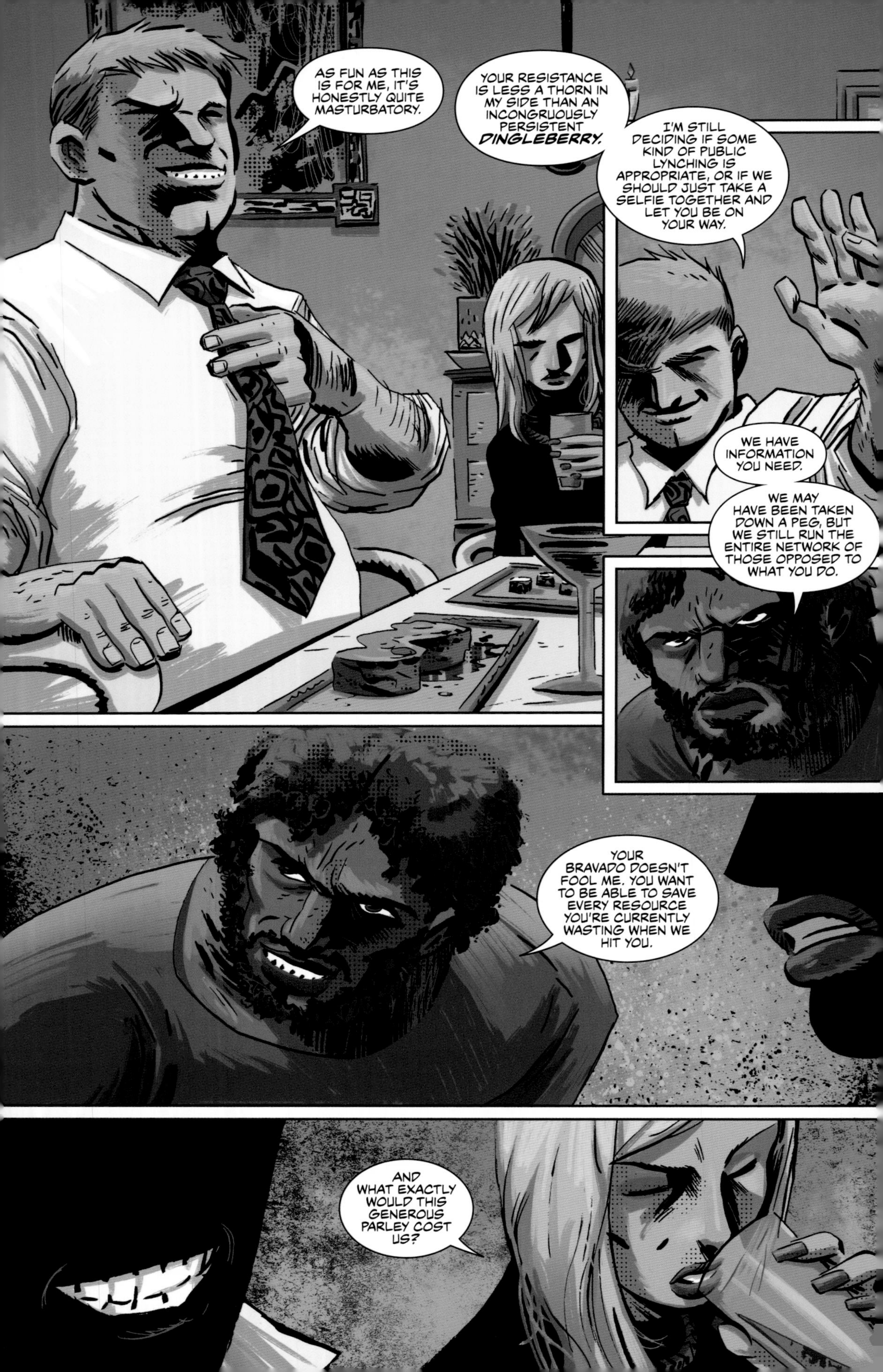
AS FUN AS THIS IS FOR ME, IT'S HONESTLY QUITE MASTURBATORY.
YOUR RESISTANCE IS LESS A THORN IN MY SIDE THAN AN INCONGRUOUSLY PERSISTENT DINGLEBERRY.
I'M STILL DECIDING IF SOME KIND OF PUBLIC LYNCHING IS APPROPRIATE, OR IF WE SHOULD JUST TAKE A SELFIE TOGETHER AND LET YOU BE ON YOUR WAY.
WE HAVE INFORMATION YOU NEED.
WE MAY HAVE BEEN TAKEN DOWN A PEG, BUT WE STILL RUN THE ENTIRE NETWORK OF THOSE OPPOSED TO WHAT YOU DO.
YOUR BRAVADO DOESN'T FOOL ME. YOU WANT TO BE ABLE TO SAVE EVERY RESOURCE YOU'RE CURRENTLY WASTING WHEN WE HIT YOU.
AND WHAT EXACTLY WOULD THIS GENEROUS PARLEY COST US?

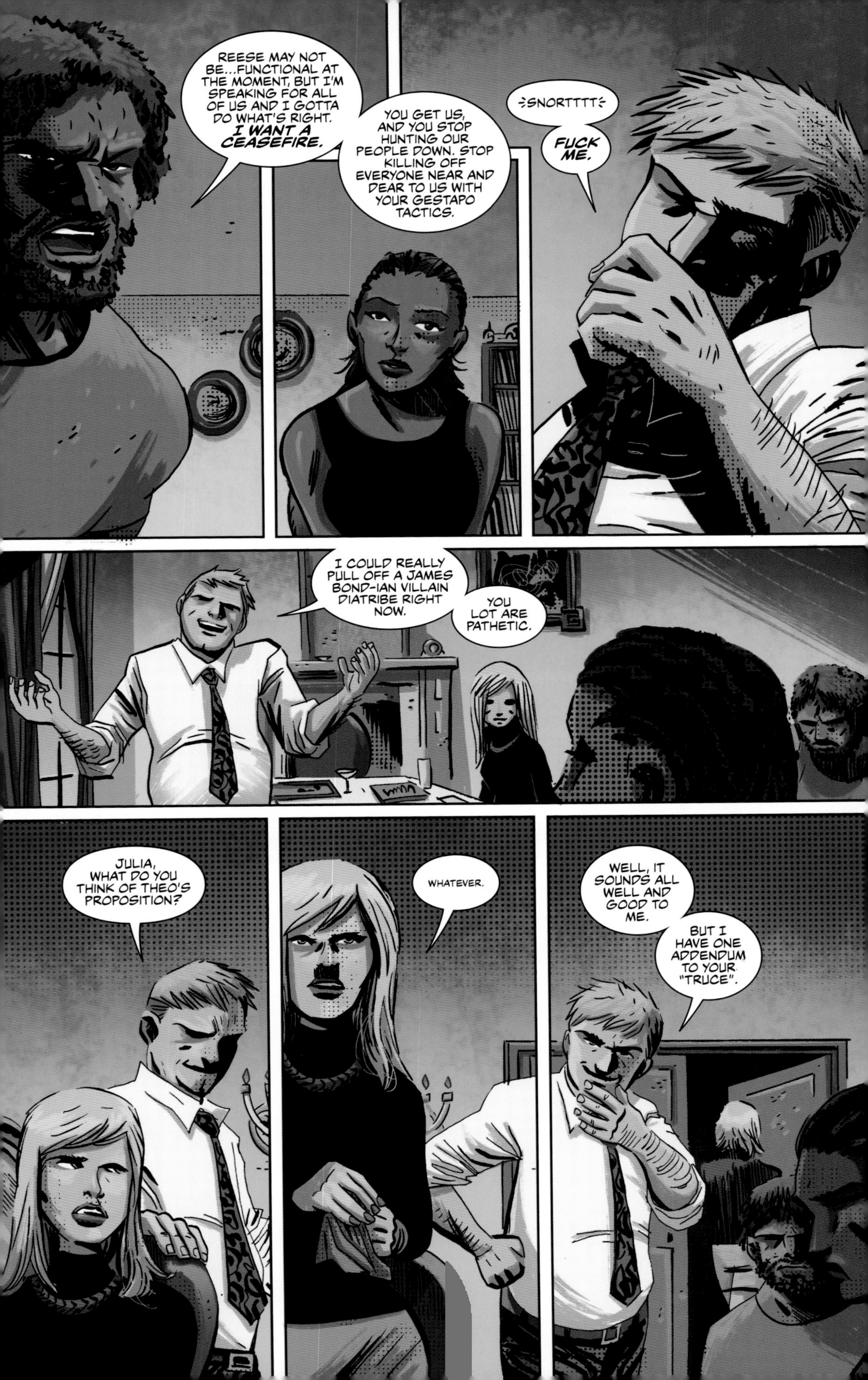
REESE MAY NOT BE...FUNCTIONAL AT THE MOMENT, BUT I'M SPEAKING FOR ALL OF US AND I GOTTA DO WHAT'S RIGHT. I WANT A CEASEFIRE.
YOU GET US, AND YOU STOP HUNTING OUR PEOPLE DOWN. STOP KILLING OFF EVERYONE NEAR AND DEAR TO US WITH YOUR GESTAPO TACTICS.
SNORTTTT
FUCK ME.
I COULD REALLY PULL OFF A JAMES BOND-IAN VILLAIN DIATRIBE RIGHT NOW.
YOU LOT ARE PATHETIC.
JULIA, WHAT DO YOU THINK OF THEO'S PROPOSITION?
WHATEVER.
WELL, IT SOUNDS ALL WELL AND GOOD TO ME.
BUT I HAVE ONE ADDENDUM TO YOUR "TRUCE".

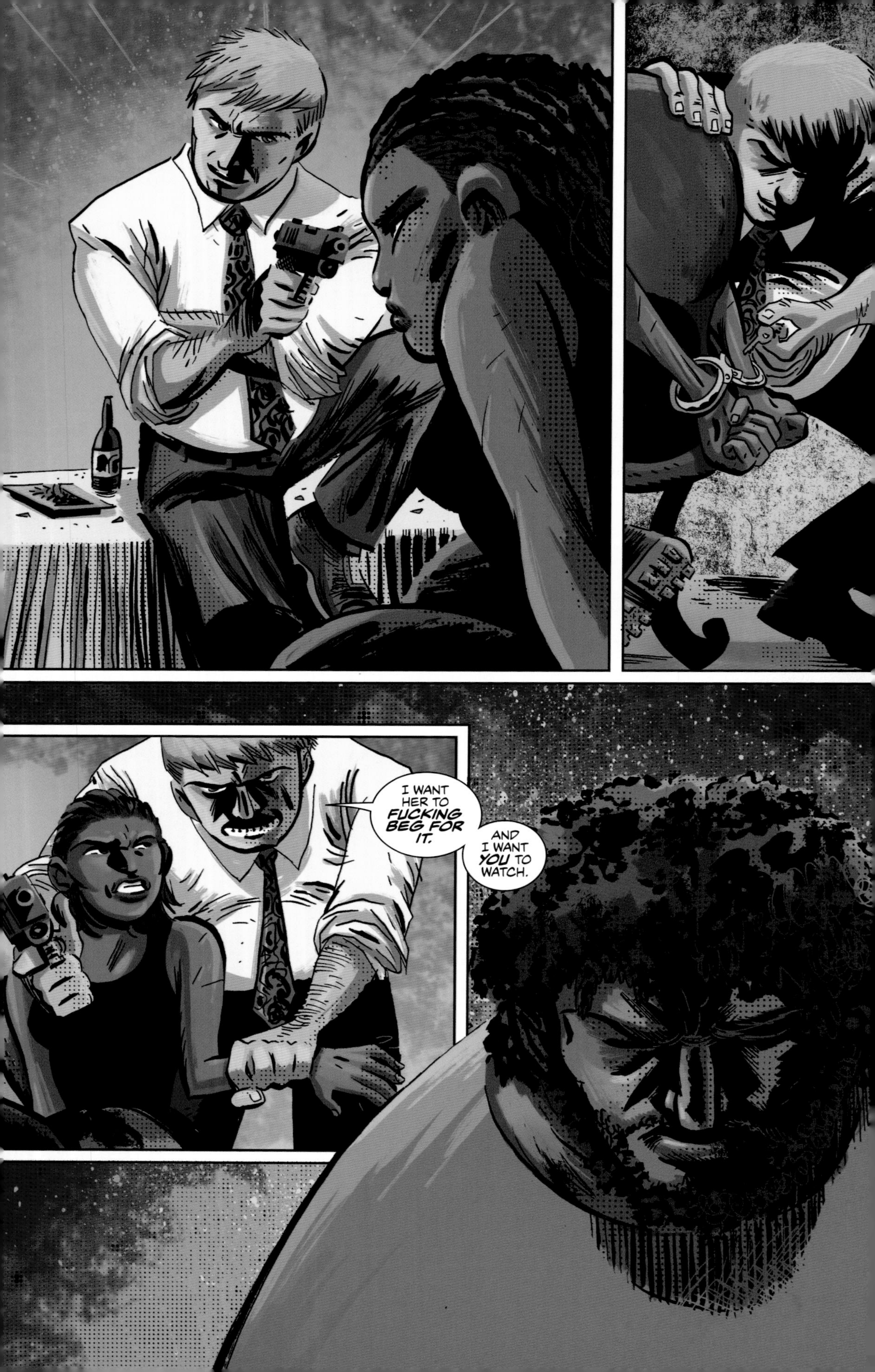

I WANT HER TO FUCKING BEG FOR IT.
AND I WANT YOU TO WATCH.

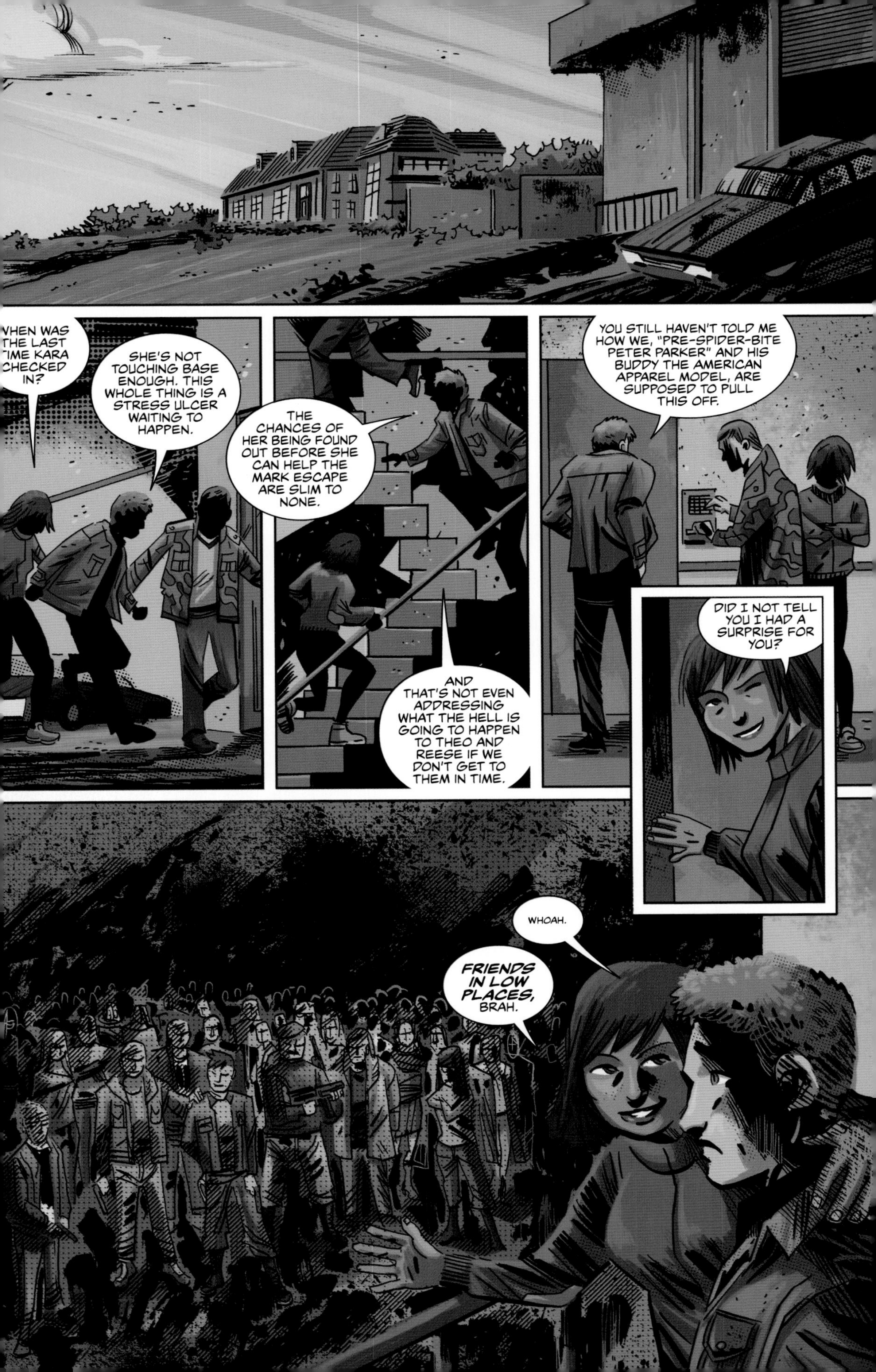
WHEN WAS THE LAST TIME KARA CHECKED IN?
SHE'S NOT TOUCHING BASE ENOUGH. THIS WHOLE THING IS A STRESS ULCER WAITING TO HAPPEN.
THE CHANCES OF HER BEING FOUND OUT BEFORE SHE CAN HELP THE MARK ESCAPE ARE SLIM TO NONE.
AND THAT'S NOT EVEN ADDRESSING WHAT THE HELL IS GOING TO HAPPEN TO THEO AND REESE IF WE DON'T GET TO THEM IN TIME.
YOU STILL HAVEN'T TOLD ME HOW WE, "PRE-SPIDER-BITE PETER PARKER" AND HIS BUDDY THE AMERICAN APPAREL MODEL, ARE SUPPOSED TO PULL THIS OFF.
DID I NOT TELL YOU I HAD A SURPRISE FOR YOU?
WHOAH.
FRIENDS IN LOW PLACES, BRAH.

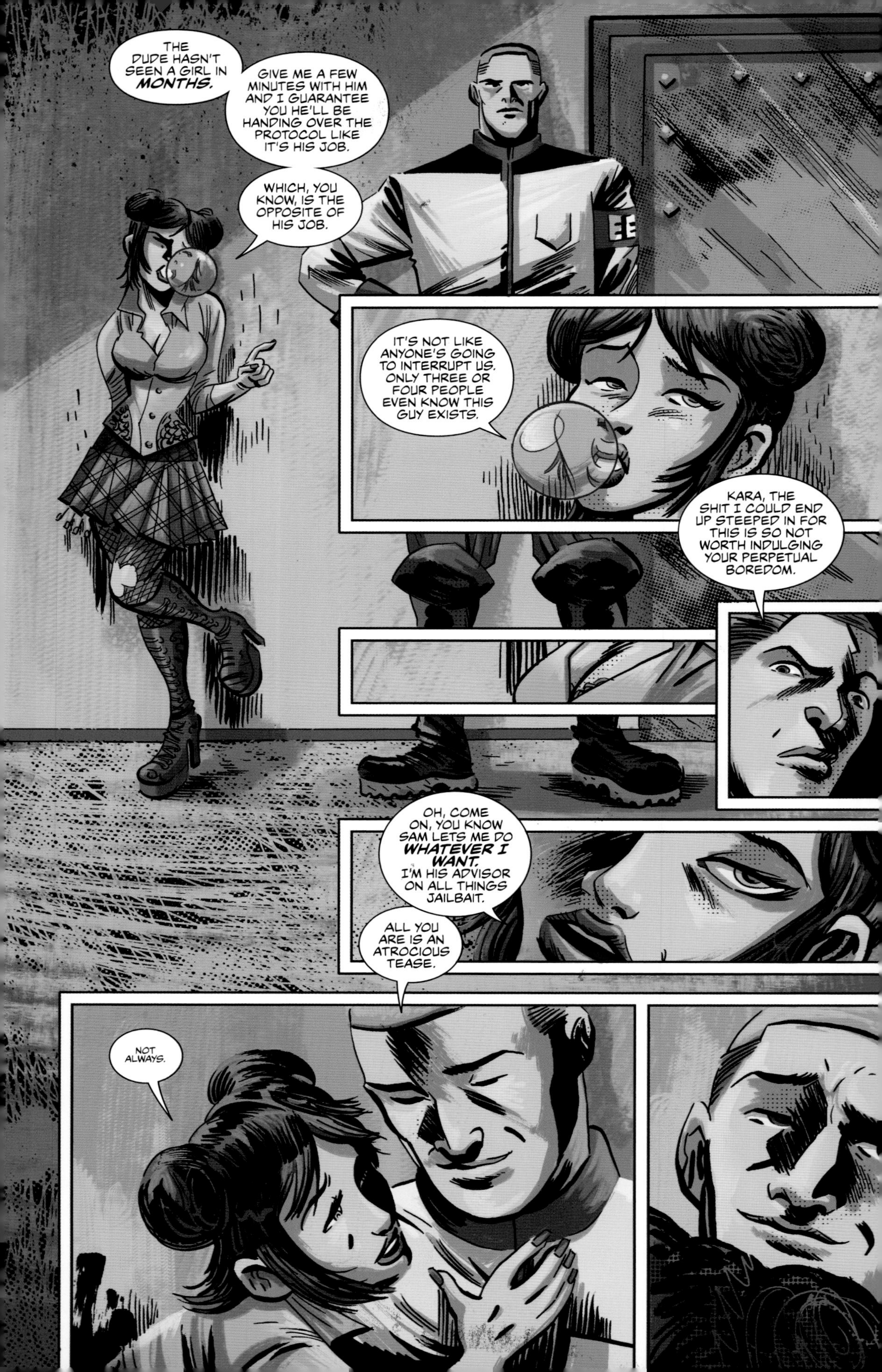
THE DUDE HASN'T SEEN A GIRL IN *MONTHS.*
GIVE ME A FEW MINUTES WITH HIM AND I GUARANTEE YOU HE'LL BE HANDING OVER THE PROTOCOL LIKE IT'S HIS JOB.
WHICH, YOU KNOW, IS THE OPPOSITE OF HIS JOB.
IT'S NOT LIKE ANYONE'S GOING TO INTERRUPT US. ONLY THREE OR FOUR PEOPLE EVEN KNOW THIS GUY EXISTS.
KARA, THE SHIT I COULD END UP STEEPED IN FOR THIS IS SO NOT WORTH INDULGING YOUR PERPETUAL BOREDOM.
OH, COME ON, YOU KNOW SAM LETS ME DO ***WHATEVER I WANT.*** I'M HIS ADVISOR ON ALL THINGS JAILBAIT.
ALL YOU ARE IS AN ATROCIOUS TEASE.
NOT ALWAYS.

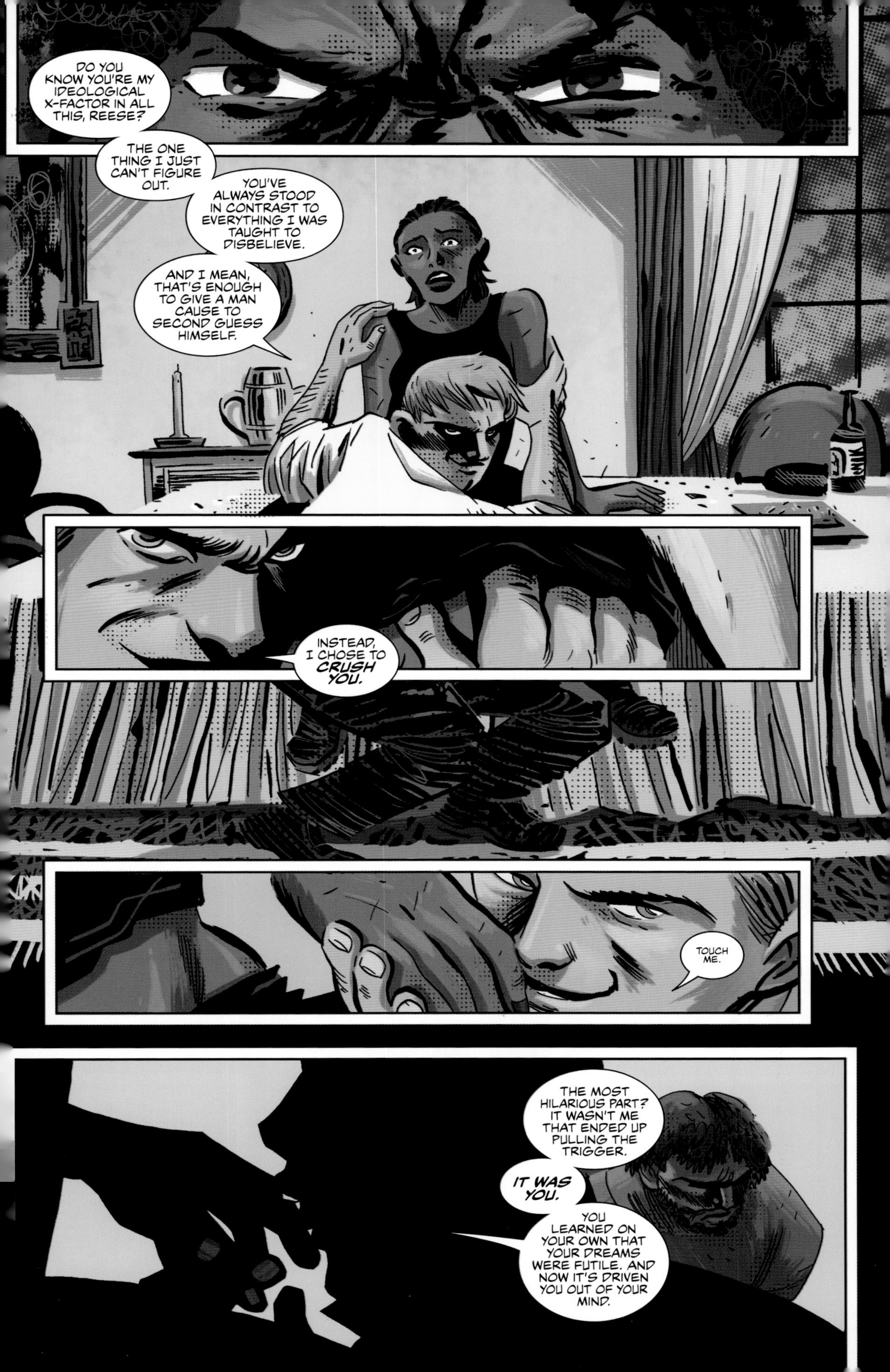
DO YOU KNOW YOU'RE MY IDEOLOGICAL X-FACTOR IN ALL THIS, REESE?
THE ONE THING I JUST CAN'T FIGURE OUT.
YOU'VE ALWAYS STOOD IN CONTRAST TO EVERYTHING I WAS TAUGHT TO DISBELIEVE.
AND I MEAN, THAT'S ENOUGH TO GIVE A MAN CAUSE TO SECOND GUESS HIMSELF.
INSTEAD, I CHOSE TO *CRUSH YOU.*
TOUCH ME.
THE MOST HILARIOUS PART? IT WASN'T ME THAT ENDED UP PULLING THE TRIGGER.
IT WAS YOU.
YOU LEARNED ON YOUR OWN THAT YOUR DREAMS WERE FUTILE. AND NOW IT'S DRIVEN YOU OUT OF YOUR MIND.

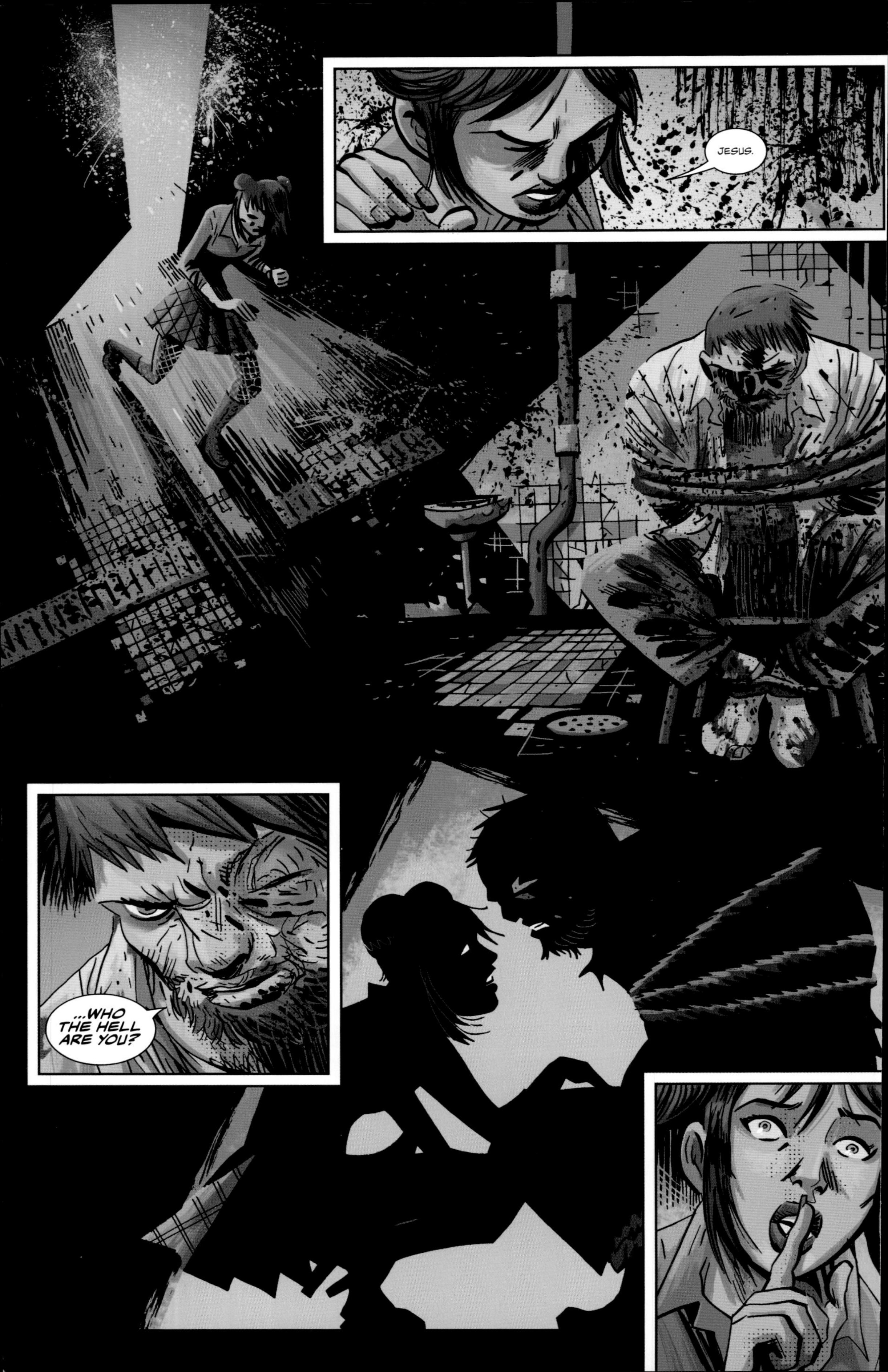
JESUS.
...WHO THE HELL ARE YOU?

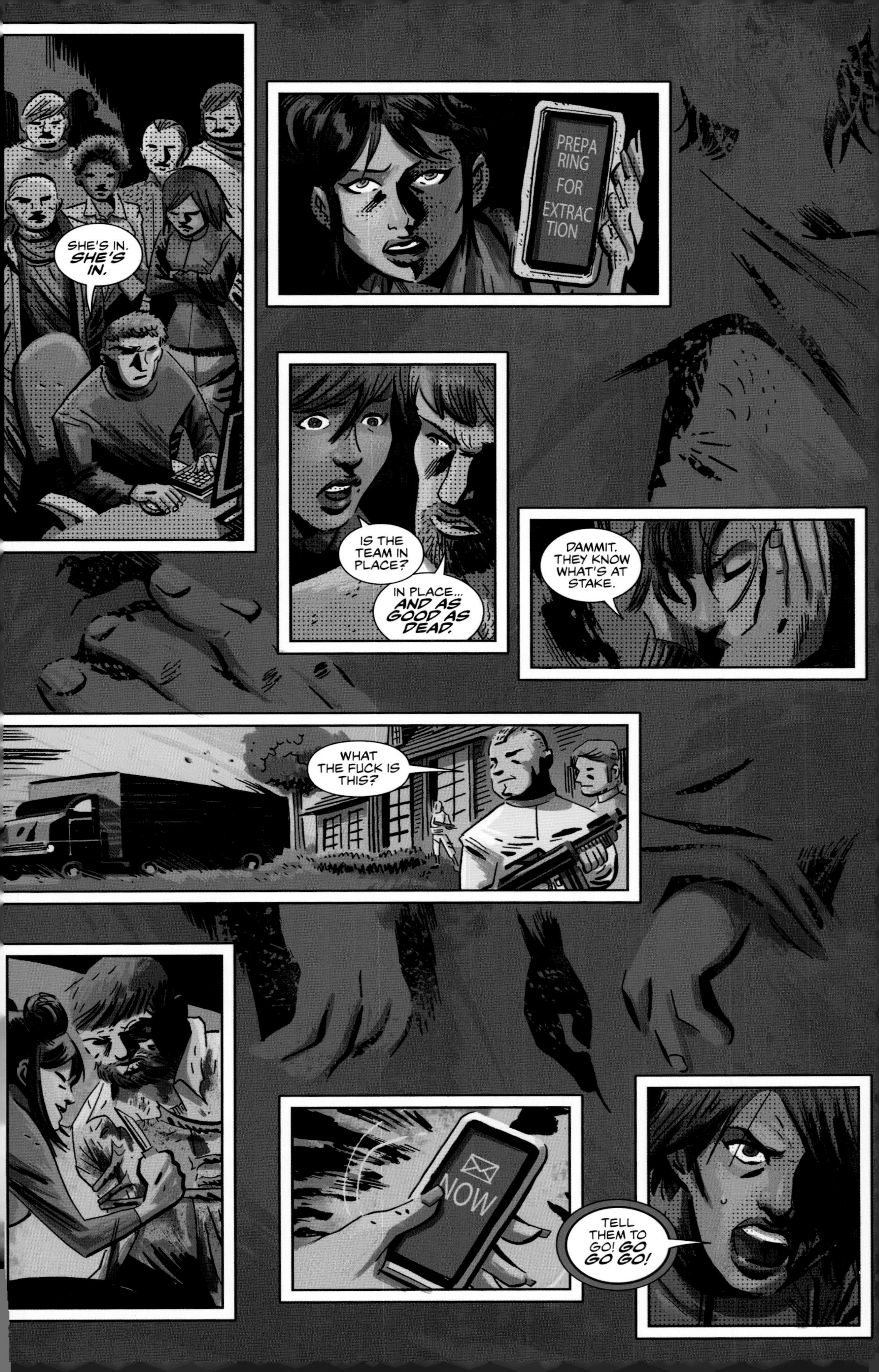
SHE'S IN. SHE'S IN.
PREPA RING FOR EXTRAC TION
IS THE TEAM IN PLACE?
IN PLACE... AND AS GOOD AS DEAD.
DAMMIT. THEY KNOW WHAT'S AT STAKE.
WHAT THE FUCK IS THIS?
NOW
TELL THEM TO GO! GO GO GO!

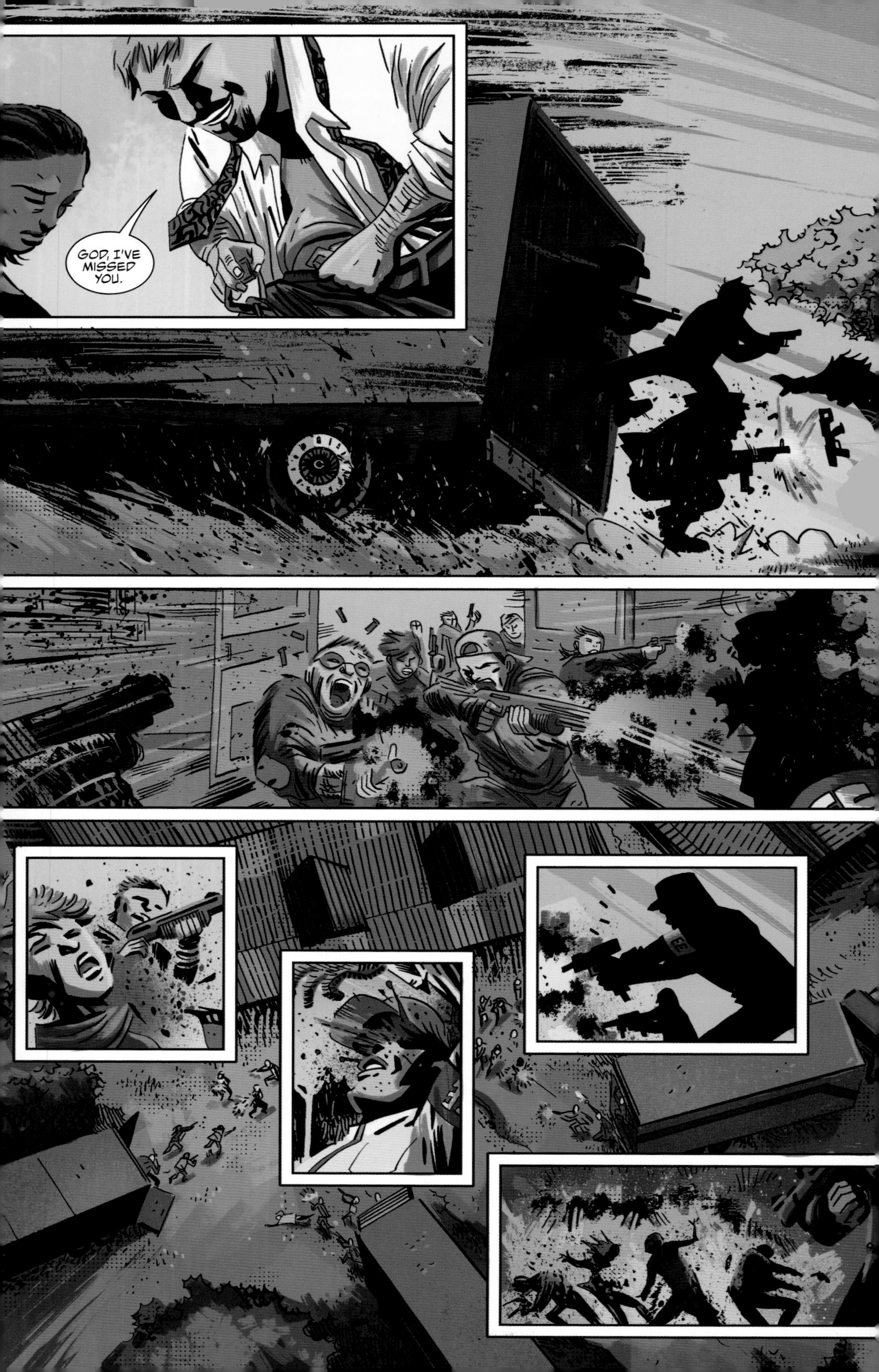
GOD, I'VE MISSED YOU.

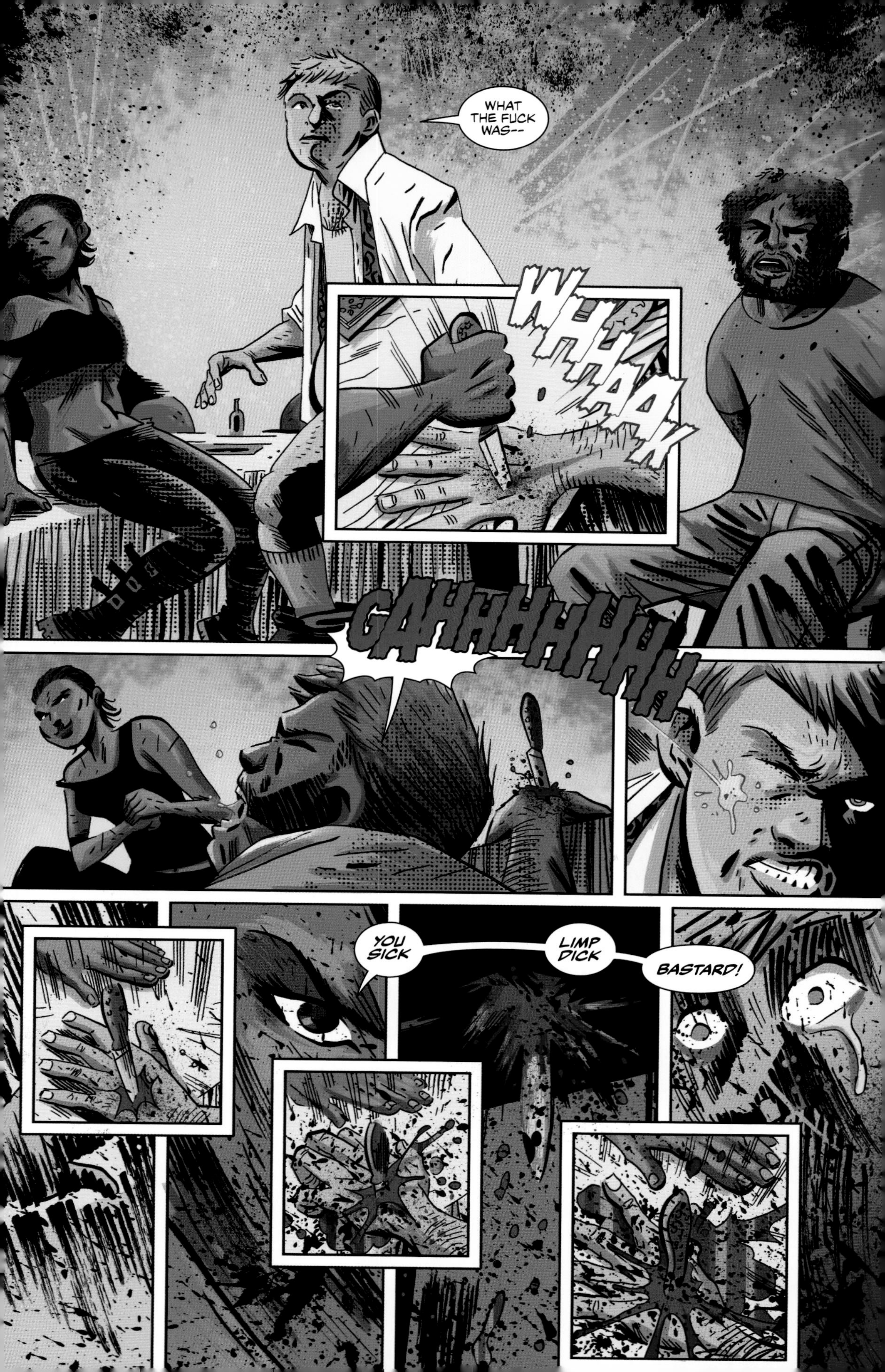
WHAT THE FUCK WAS--
WHHAAK
GAHHHHHHHH
YOU SICK
LIMP DICK
BASTARD!

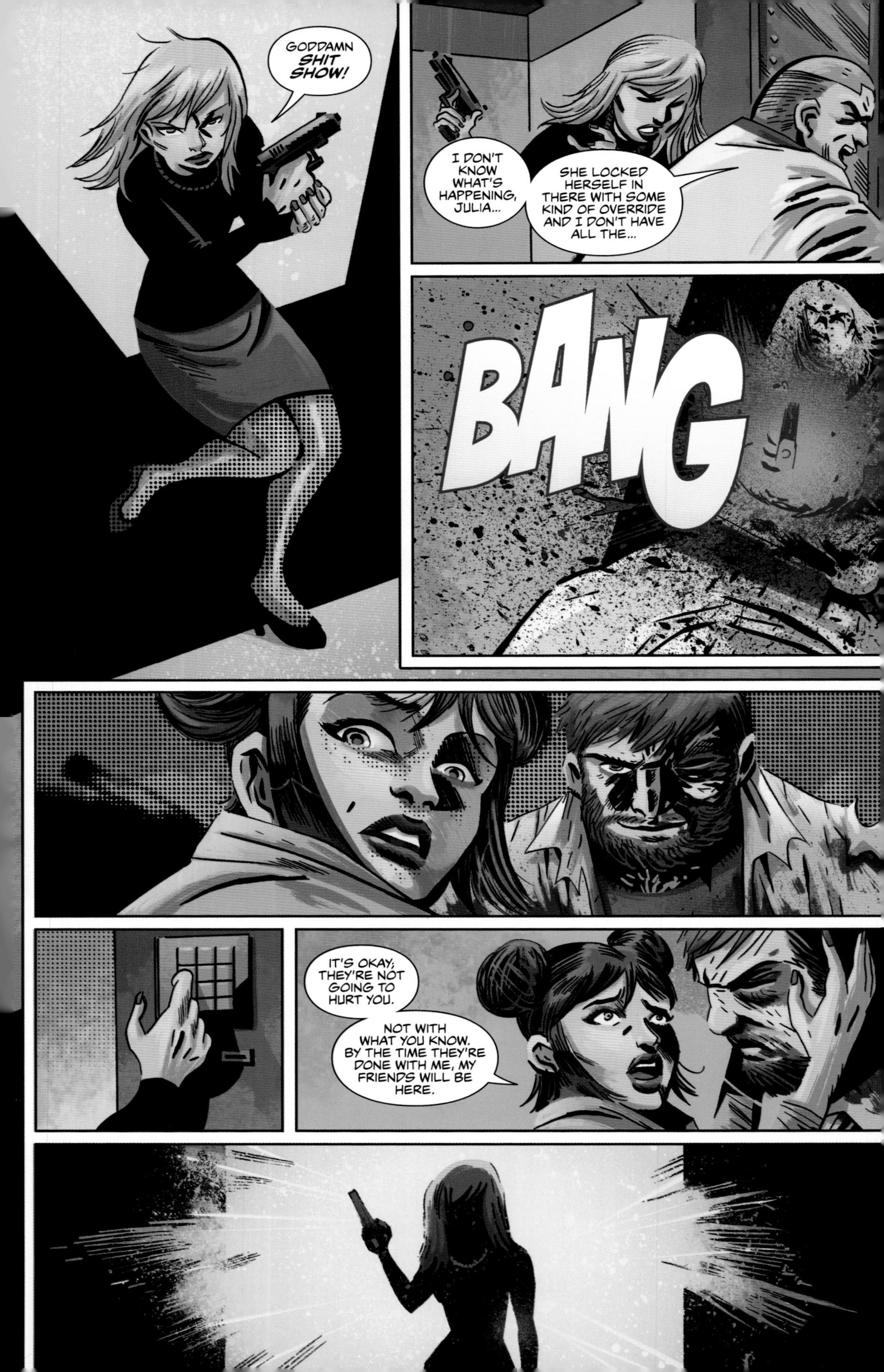
GODDAMN SHIT SHOW!
I DON'T KNOW WHAT'S HAPPENING, JULIA...
SHE LOCKED HERSELF IN THERE WITH SOME KIND OF OVERRIDE AND I DON'T HAVE ALL THE...
BANG
IT'S OKAY; THEY'RE NOT GOING TO HURT YOU.
NOT WITH WHAT YOU KNOW. BY THE TIME THEY'RE DONE WITH ME, MY FRIENDS WILL BE HERE.

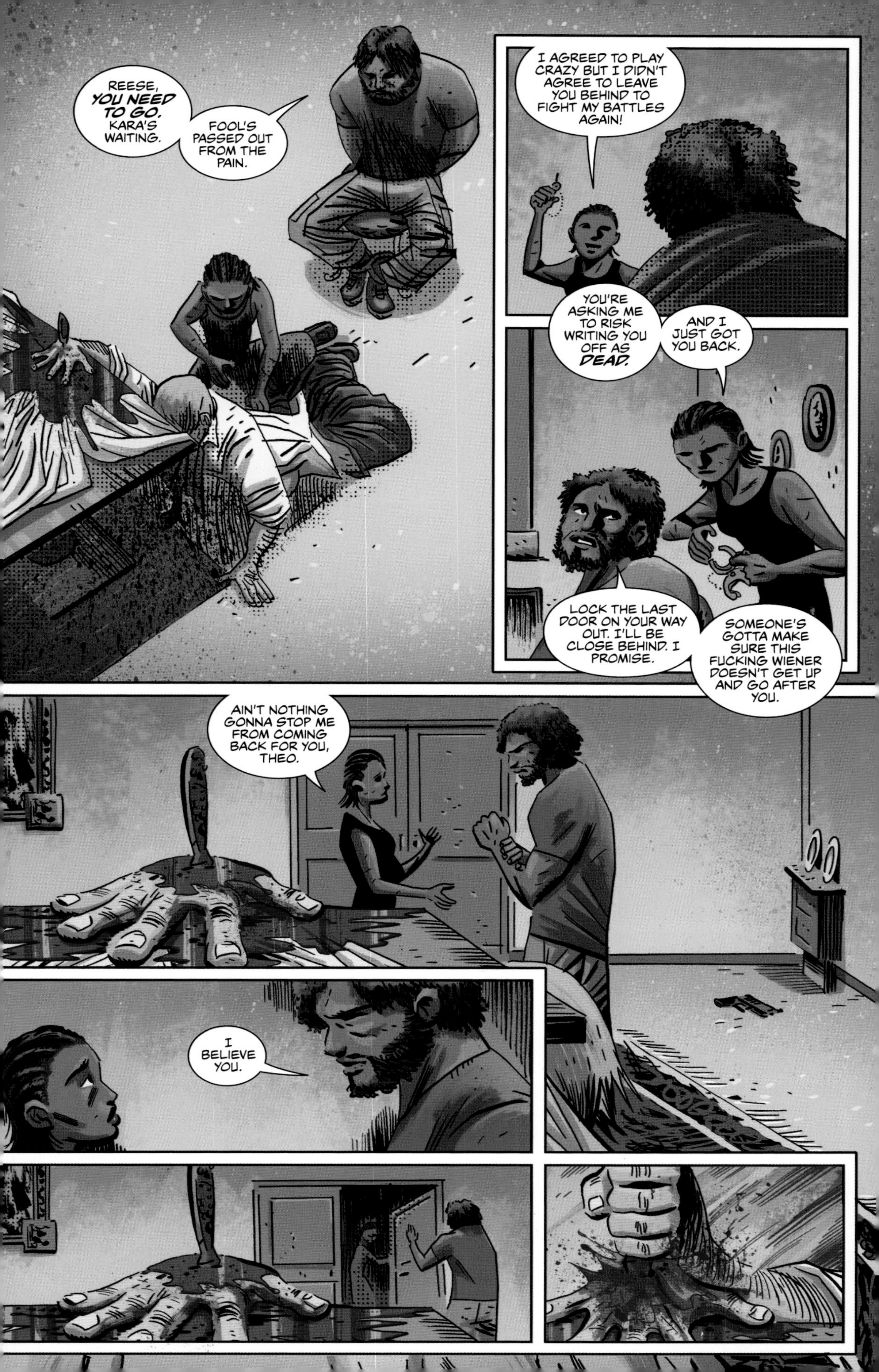
REESE, YOU NEED TO GO. KARA'S WAITING.
FOOL'S PASSED OUT FROM THE PAIN.
I AGREED TO PLAY CRAZY BUT I DIDN'T AGREE TO LEAVE YOU BEHIND TO FIGHT MY BATTLES AGAIN!
YOU'RE ASKING ME TO RISK WRITING YOU OFF AS DEAD.
AND I JUST GOT YOU BACK.
LOCK THE LAST DOOR ON YOUR WAY OUT. I'LL BE CLOSE BEHIND. I PROMISE.
SOMEONE'S GOTTA MAKE SURE THIS FUCKING WIENER DOESN'T GET UP AND GO AFTER YOU.
AIN'T NOTHING GONNA STOP ME FROM COMING BACK FOR YOU, THEO.
I BELIEVE YOU.

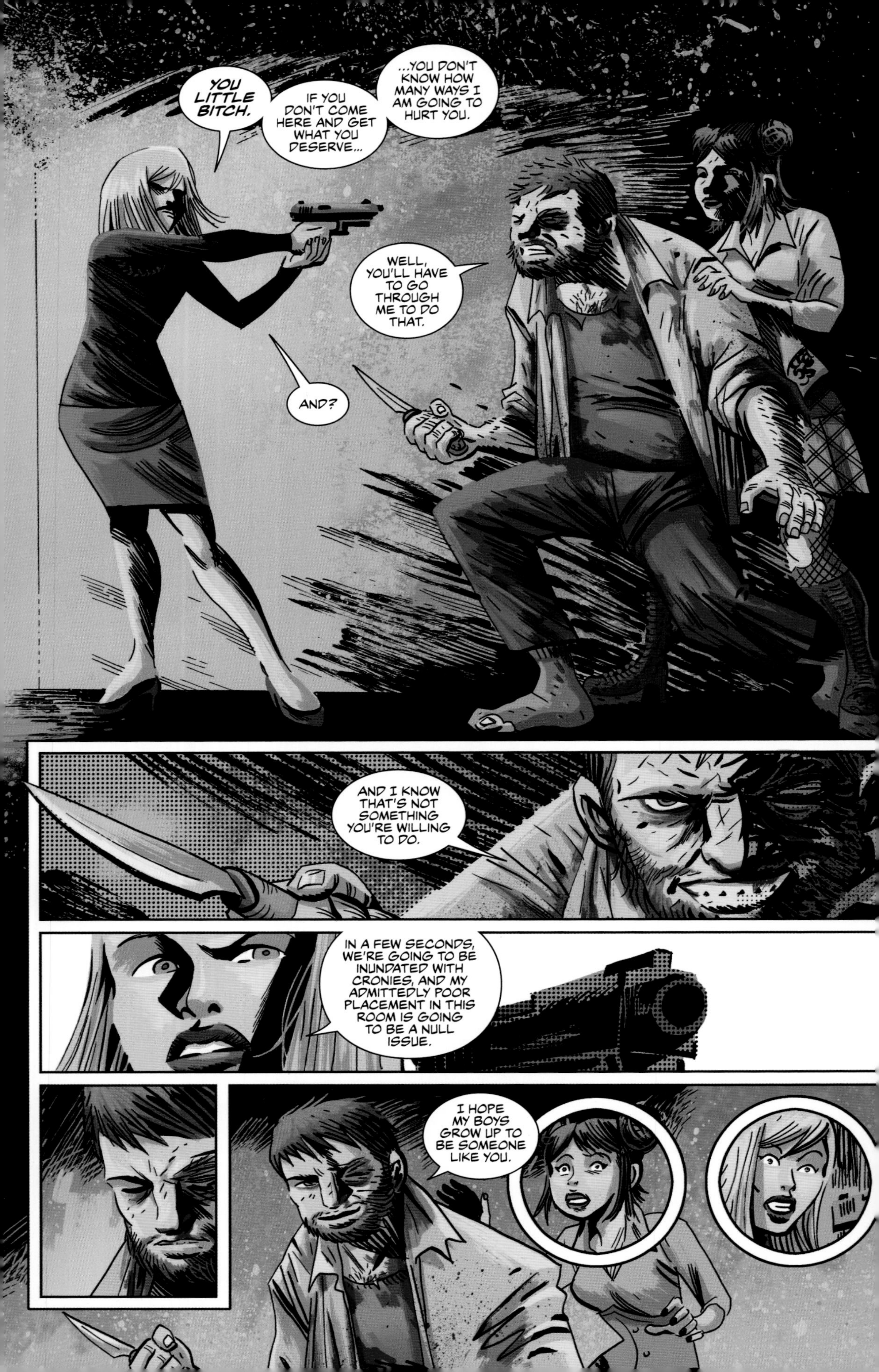
YOU LITTLE BITCH.
IF YOU DON'T COME HERE AND GET WHAT YOU DESERVE...
...YOU DON'T KNOW HOW MANY WAYS I AM GOING TO HURT YOU.
WELL, YOU'LL HAVE TO GO THROUGH ME TO DO THAT.
AND?
AND I KNOW THAT'S NOT SOMETHING YOU'RE WILLING TO DO.
IN A FEW SECONDS, WE'RE GOING TO BE INUNDATED WITH CRONIES, AND MY ADMITTEDLY POOR PLACEMENT IN THIS ROOM IS GOING TO BE A NULL ISSUE.
I HOPE MY BOYS GROW UP TO BE SOMEONE LIKE YOU.

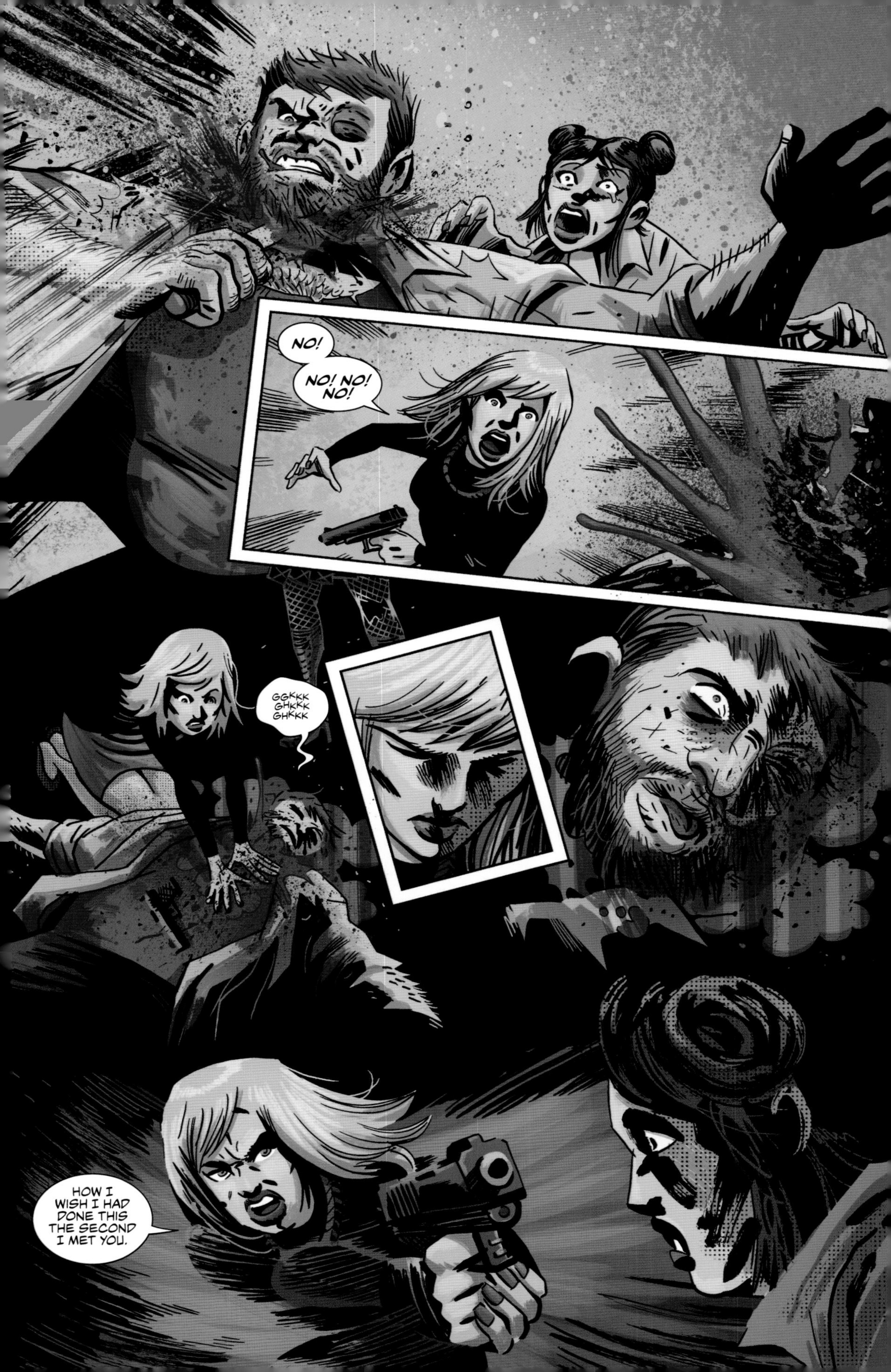
NO!
NO! NO! NO!
GGKKK GHKKK GHKKK
HOW I WISH I HAD DONE THIS THE SECOND I MET YOU.

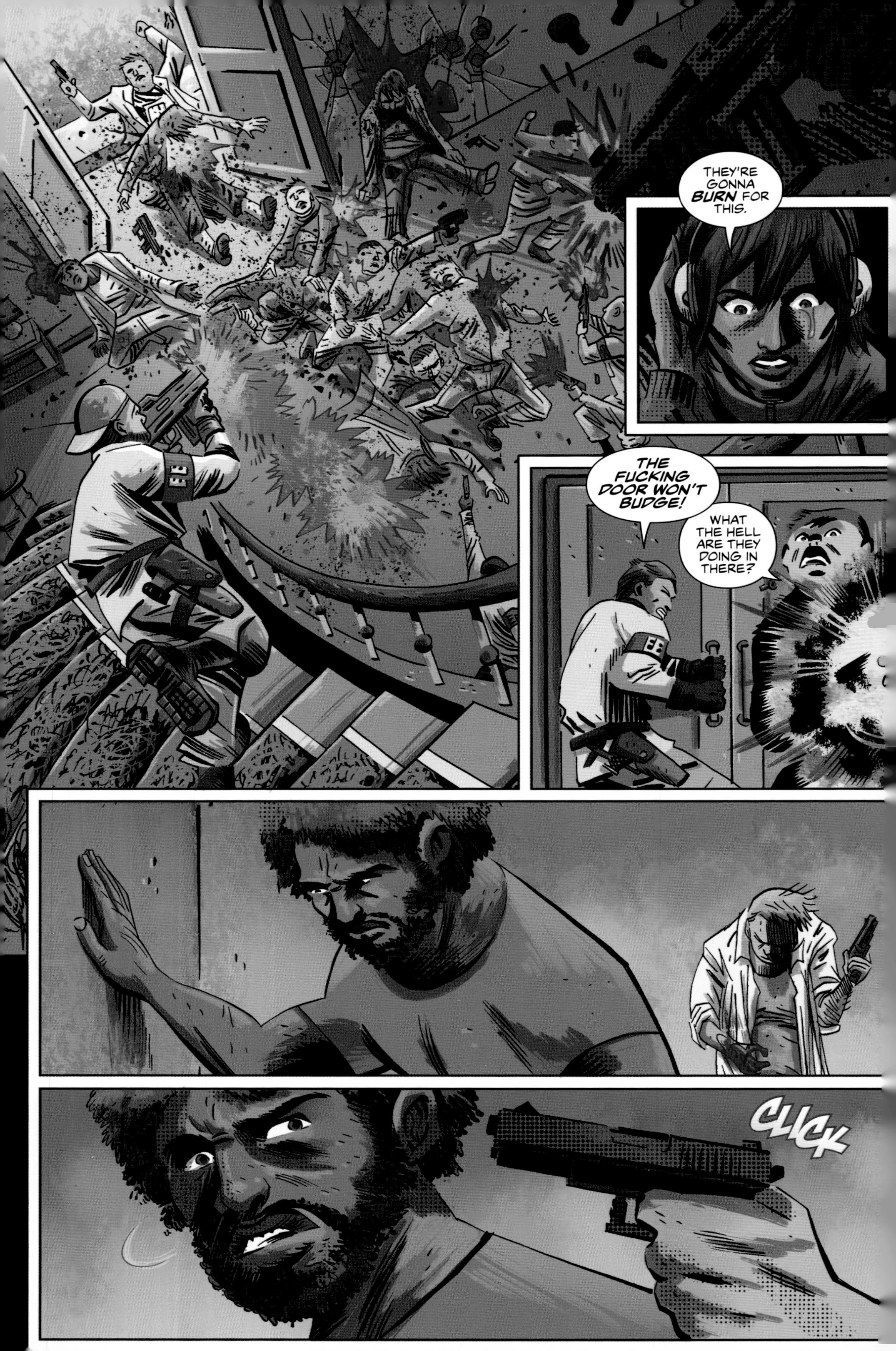
THEY'RE GONNA BURN FOR THIS.
THE FUCKING DOOR WON'T BUDGE!
WHAT THE HELL ARE THEY DOING IN THERE?
CLICK

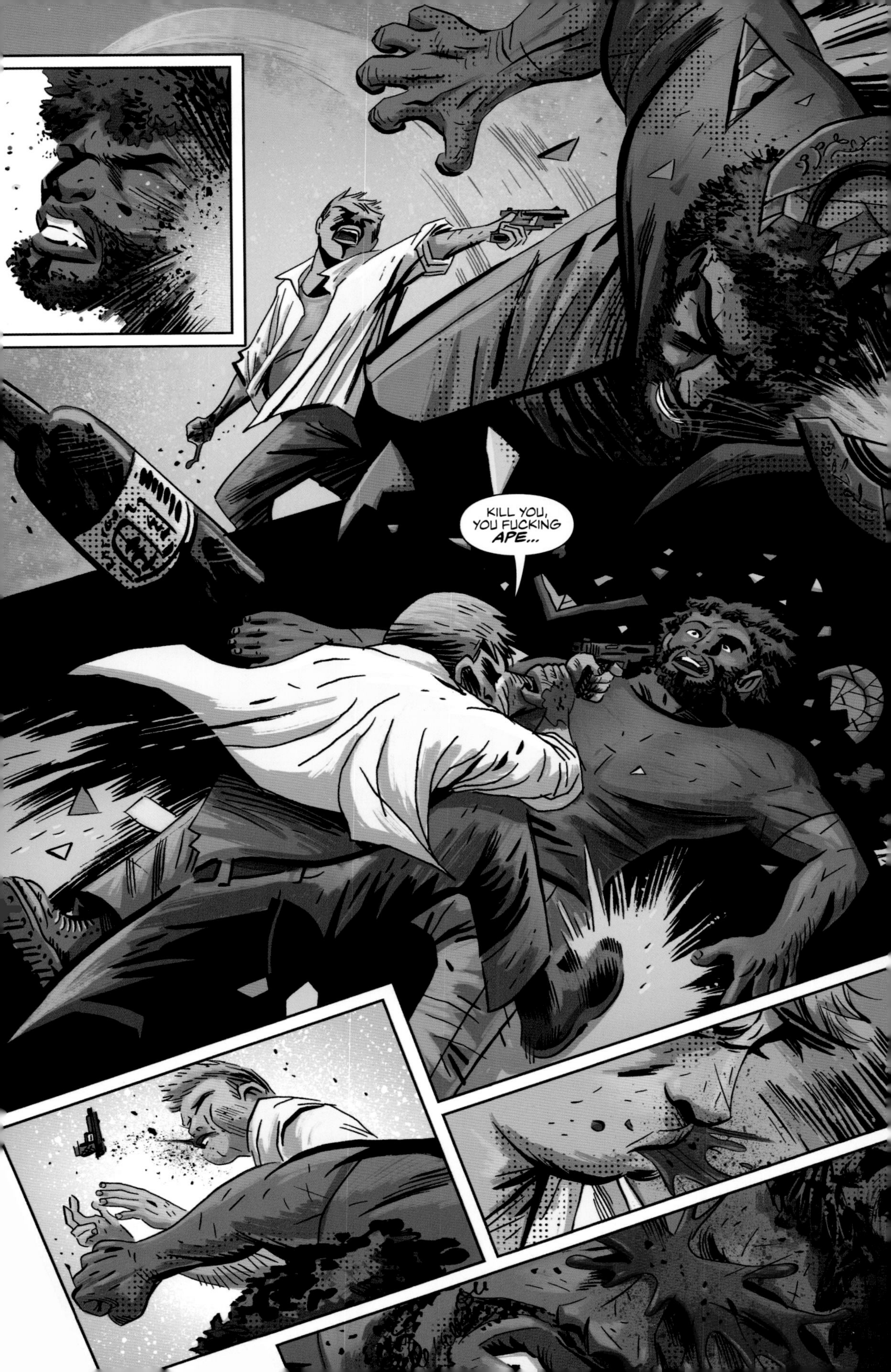
KILL YOU, YOU FUCKING *APE*...

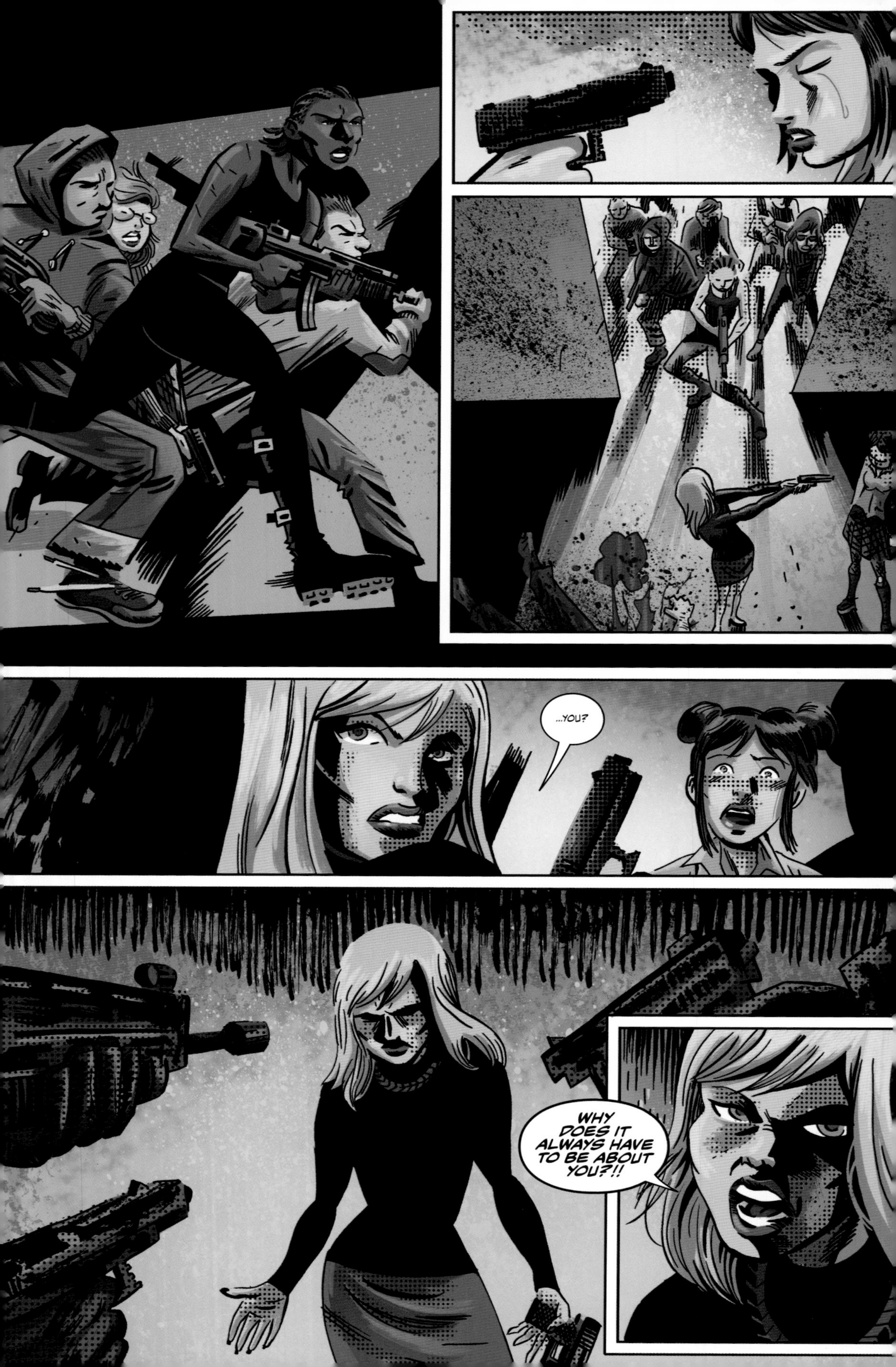
...YOU?
WHY DOES IT ALWAYS HAVE TO BE ABOUT YOU?!!

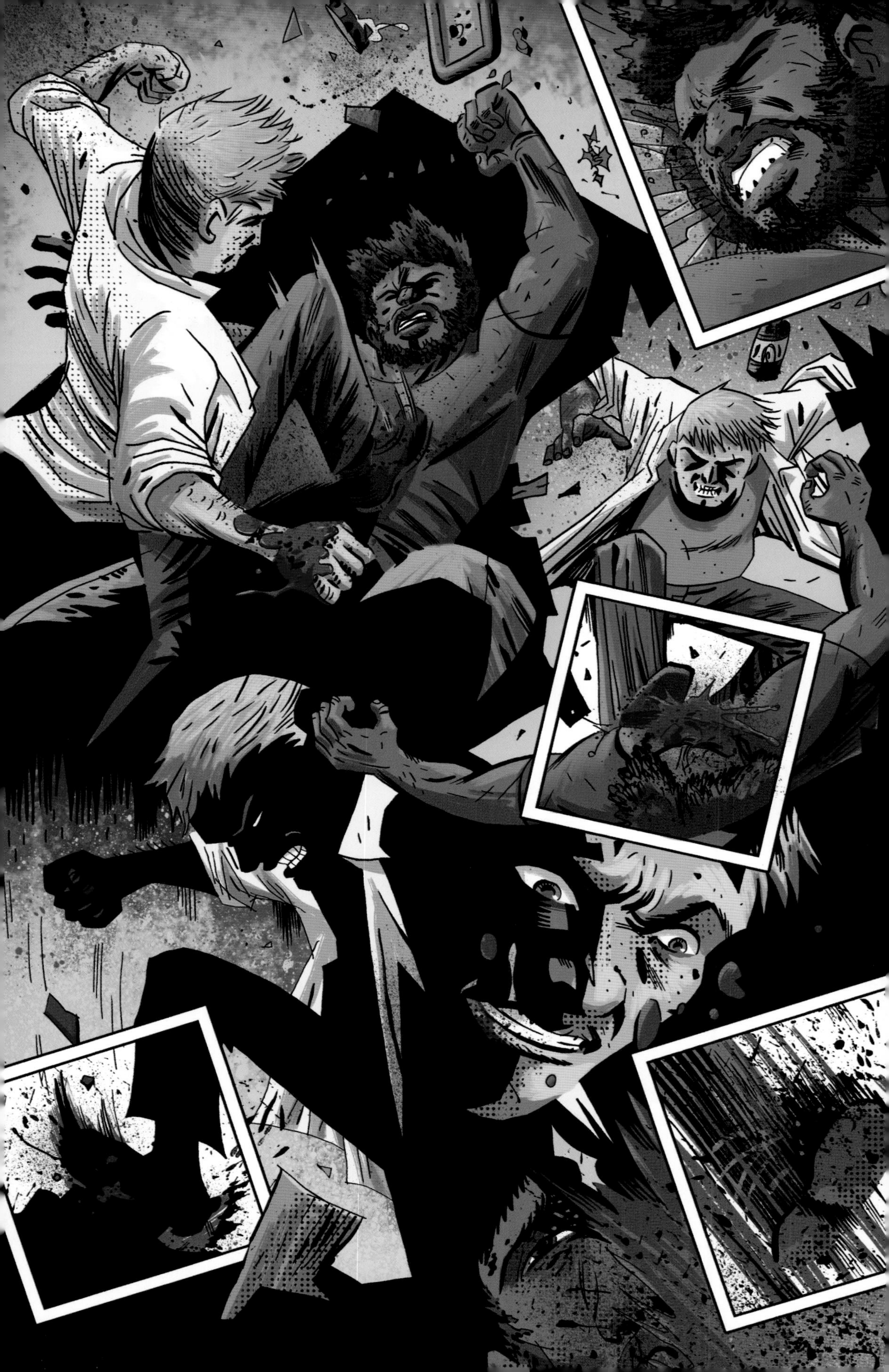

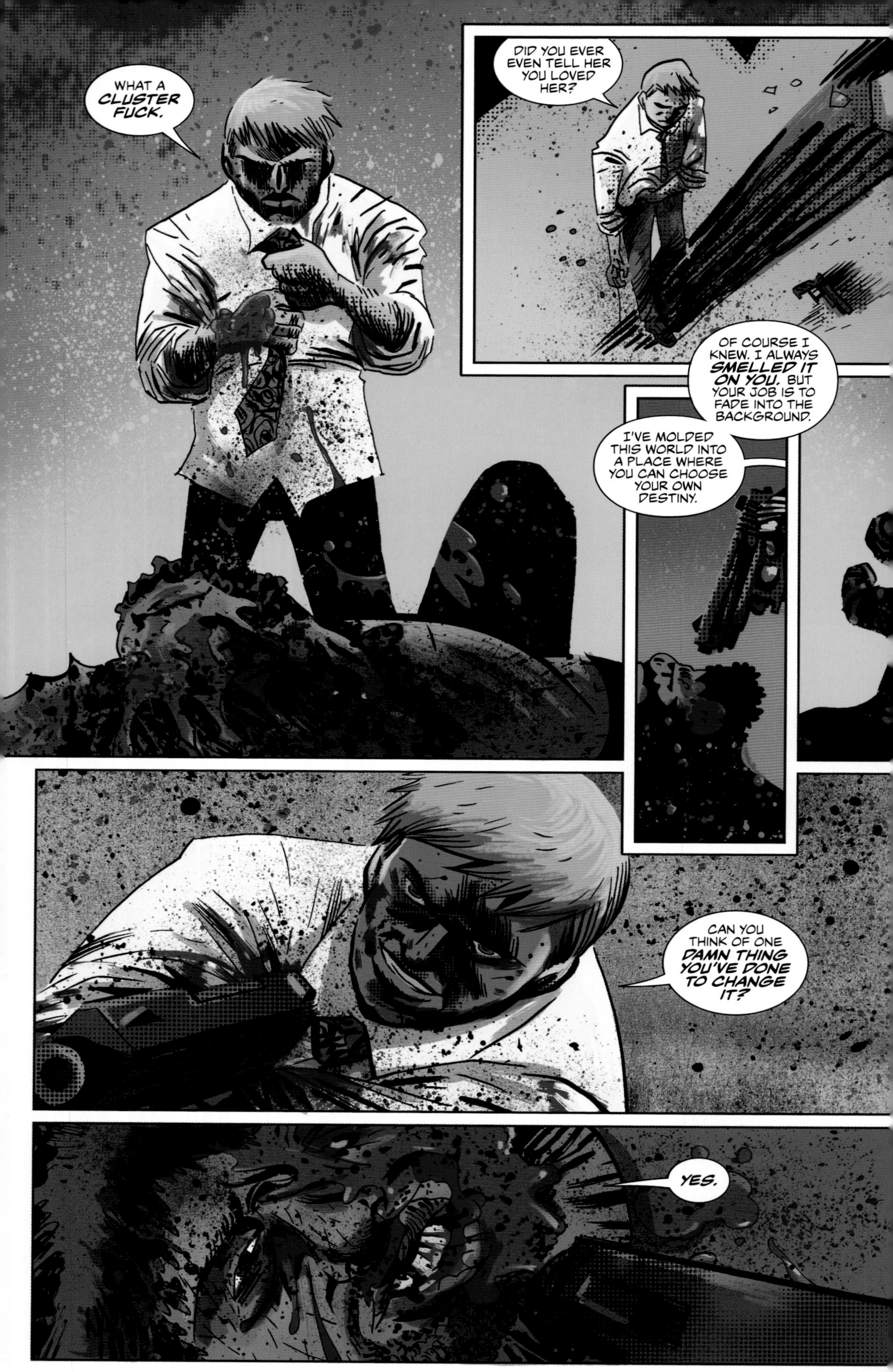
WHAT A CLUSTER FUCK.
DID YOU EVER EVEN TELL HER YOU LOVED HER?
OF COURSE I KNEW. I ALWAYS SMELLED IT ON YOU. BUT YOUR JOB IS TO FADE INTO THE BACKGROUND.
I'VE MOLDED THIS WORLD INTO A PLACE WHERE YOU CAN CHOOSE YOUR OWN DESTINY.
CAN YOU THINK OF ONE DAMN THING YOU'VE DONE TO CHANGE IT?
YES.

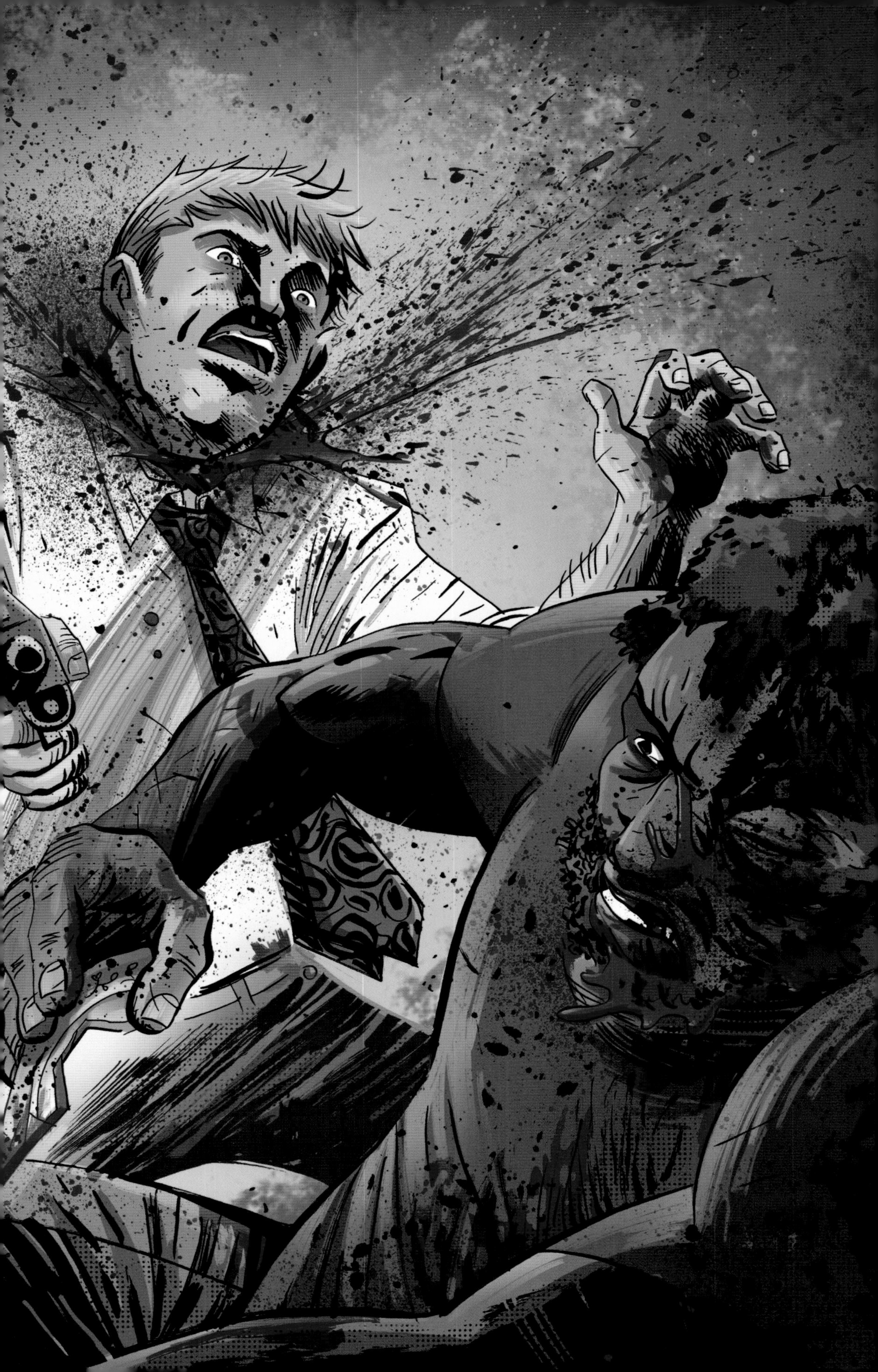

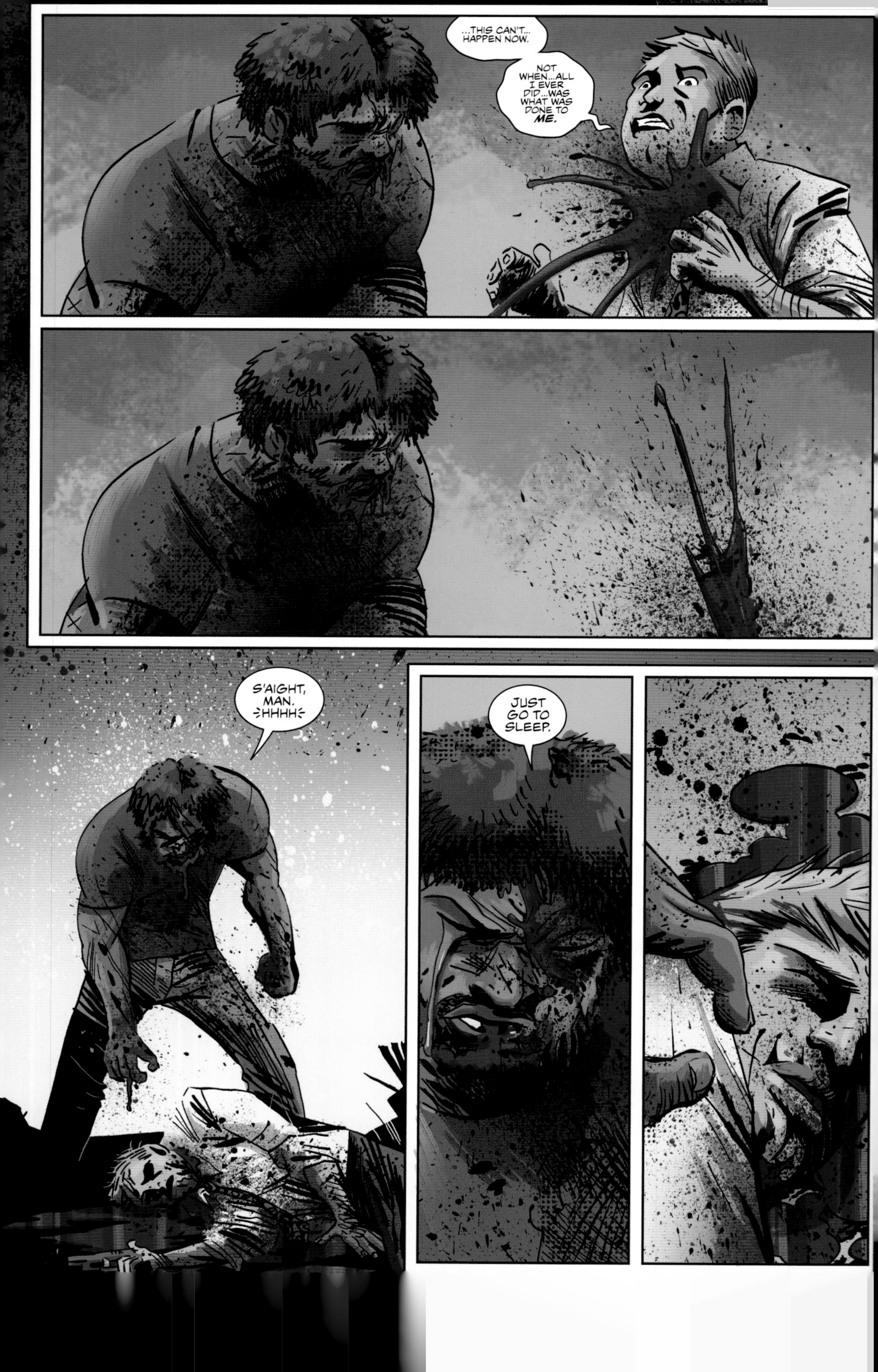
...THIS CAN'T... HAPPEN NOW.
NOT WHEN...ALL I EVER DID...WAS WHAT WAS DONE TO ME.
S'AIGHT, MAN. -HHHH-
JUST GO TO SLEEP.

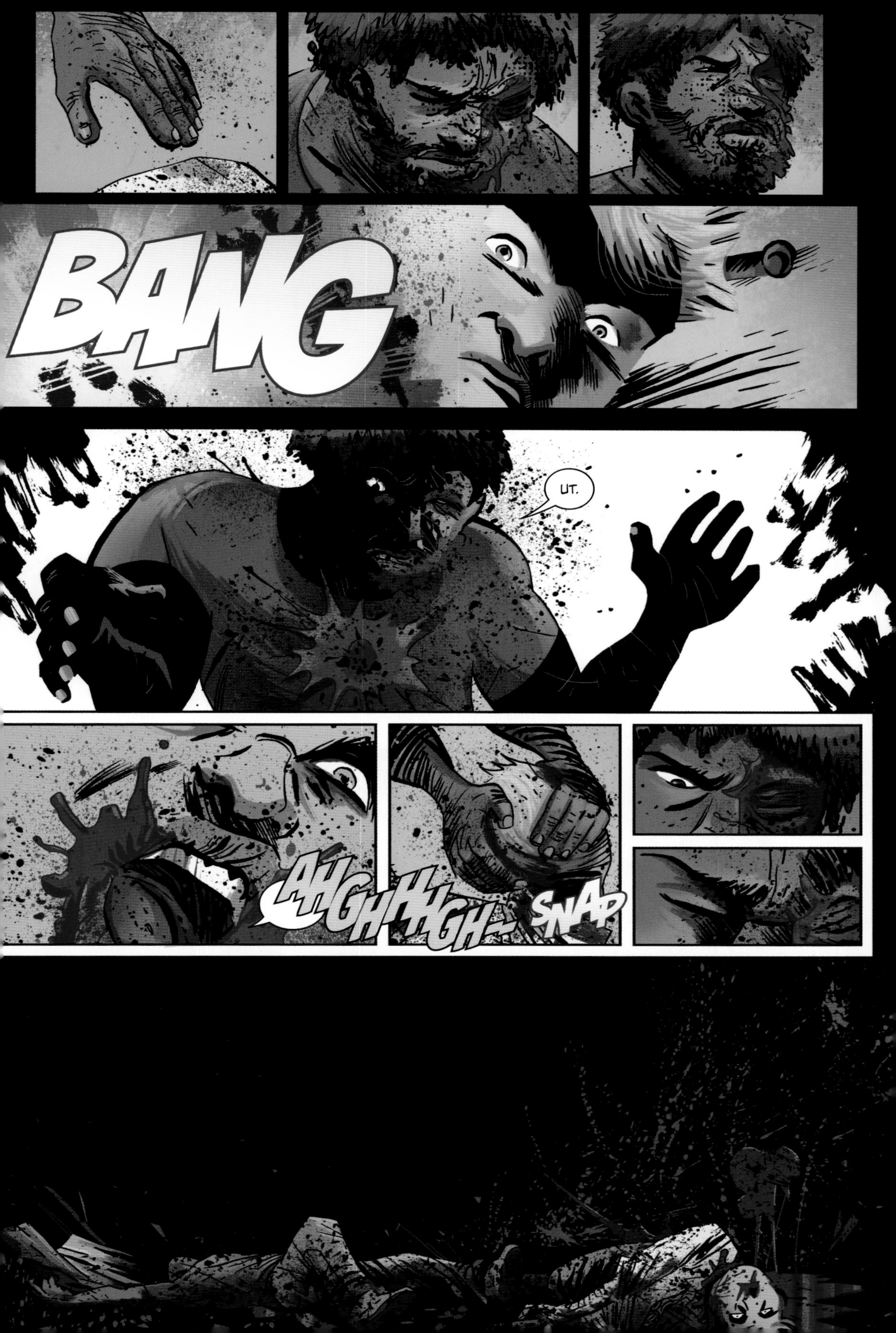

BANG
UT.
AHGHHGH--
SNAP

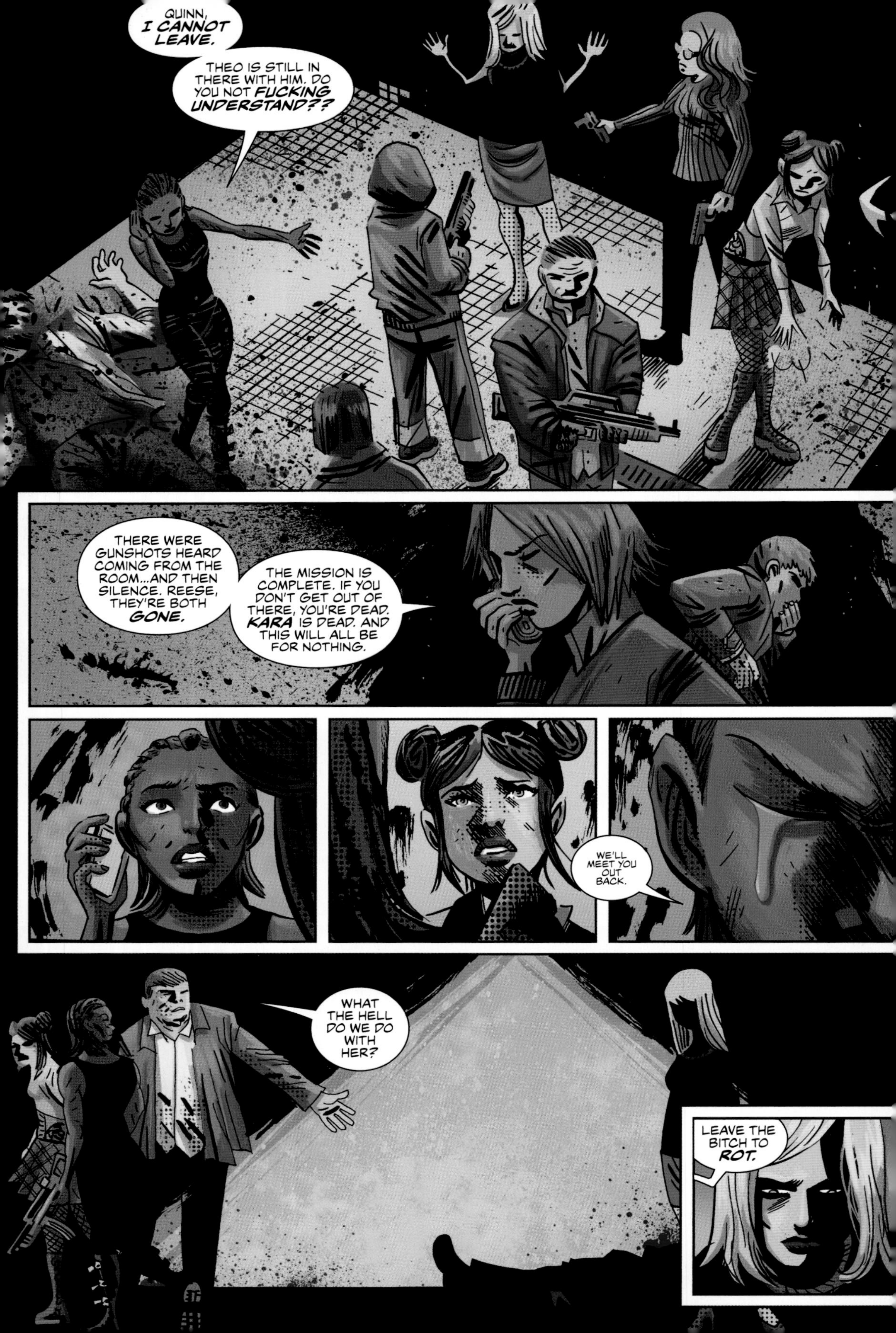
QUINN, I CANNOT LEAVE.
THEO IS STILL IN THERE WITH HIM. DO YOU NOT FUCKING UNDERSTAND??
THERE WERE GUNSHOTS HEARD COMING FROM THE ROOM...AND THEN SILENCE. REESE, THEY'RE BOTH GONE.
THE MISSION IS COMPLETE. IF YOU DON'T GET OUT OF THERE, YOU'RE DEAD. KARA IS DEAD. AND THIS WILL ALL BE FOR NOTHING.
WE'LL MEET YOU OUT BACK.
WHAT THE HELL DO WE DO WITH HER?
LEAVE THE BITCH TO ROT.

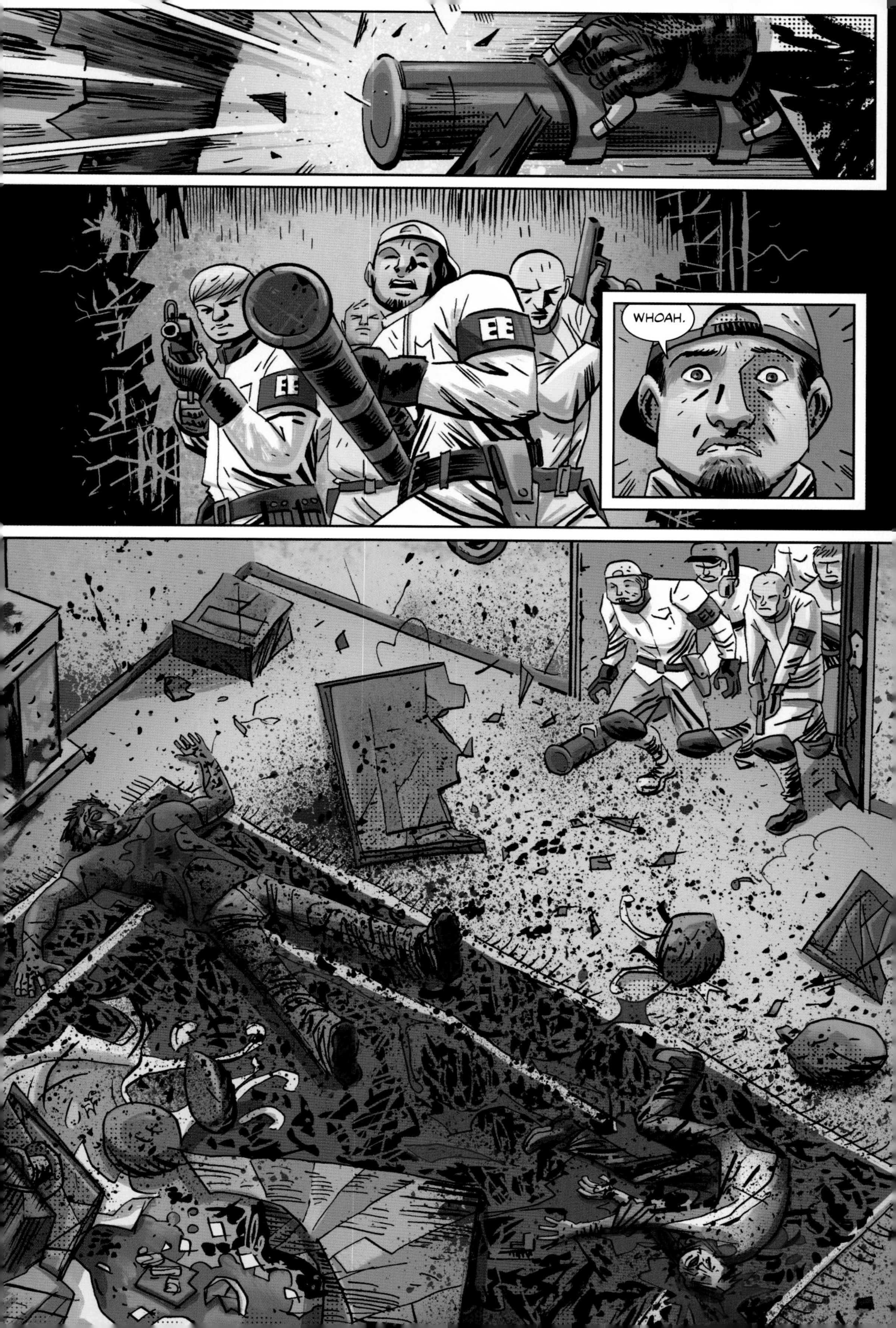

EE
WHOAH.

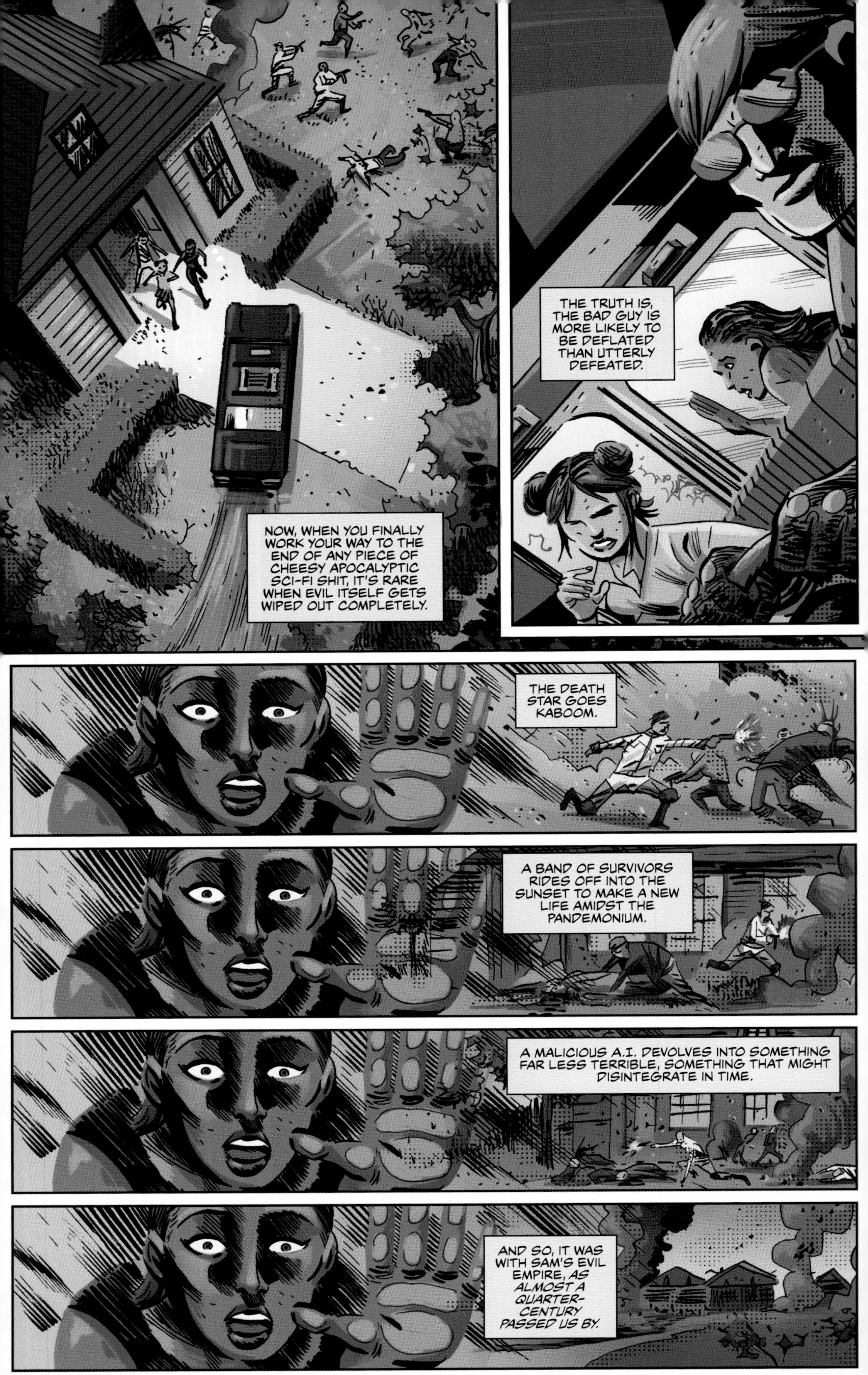
NOW, WHEN YOU FINALLY WORK YOUR WAY TO THE END OF ANY PIECE OF CHEESY APOCALYPTIC SCI-FI SHIT, IT'S RARE WHEN EVIL ITSELF GETS WIPED OUT COMPLETELY.
THE TRUTH IS, THE BAD GUY IS MORE LIKELY TO BE DEFLATED THAN UTTERLY DEFEATED.
THE DEATH STAR GOES KABOOM.
A BAND OF SURVIVORS RIDES OFF INTO THE SUNSET TO MAKE A NEW LIFE AMIDST THE PANDEMONIUM.
A MALICIOUS A.I. DEVOLVES INTO SOMETHING FAR LESS TERRIBLE, SOMETHING THAT MIGHT DISINTEGRATE IN TIME.
AND SO, IT WAS WITH SAM'S EVIL EMPIRE, AS *ALMOST A QUARTER-CENTURY PASSED US BY.*

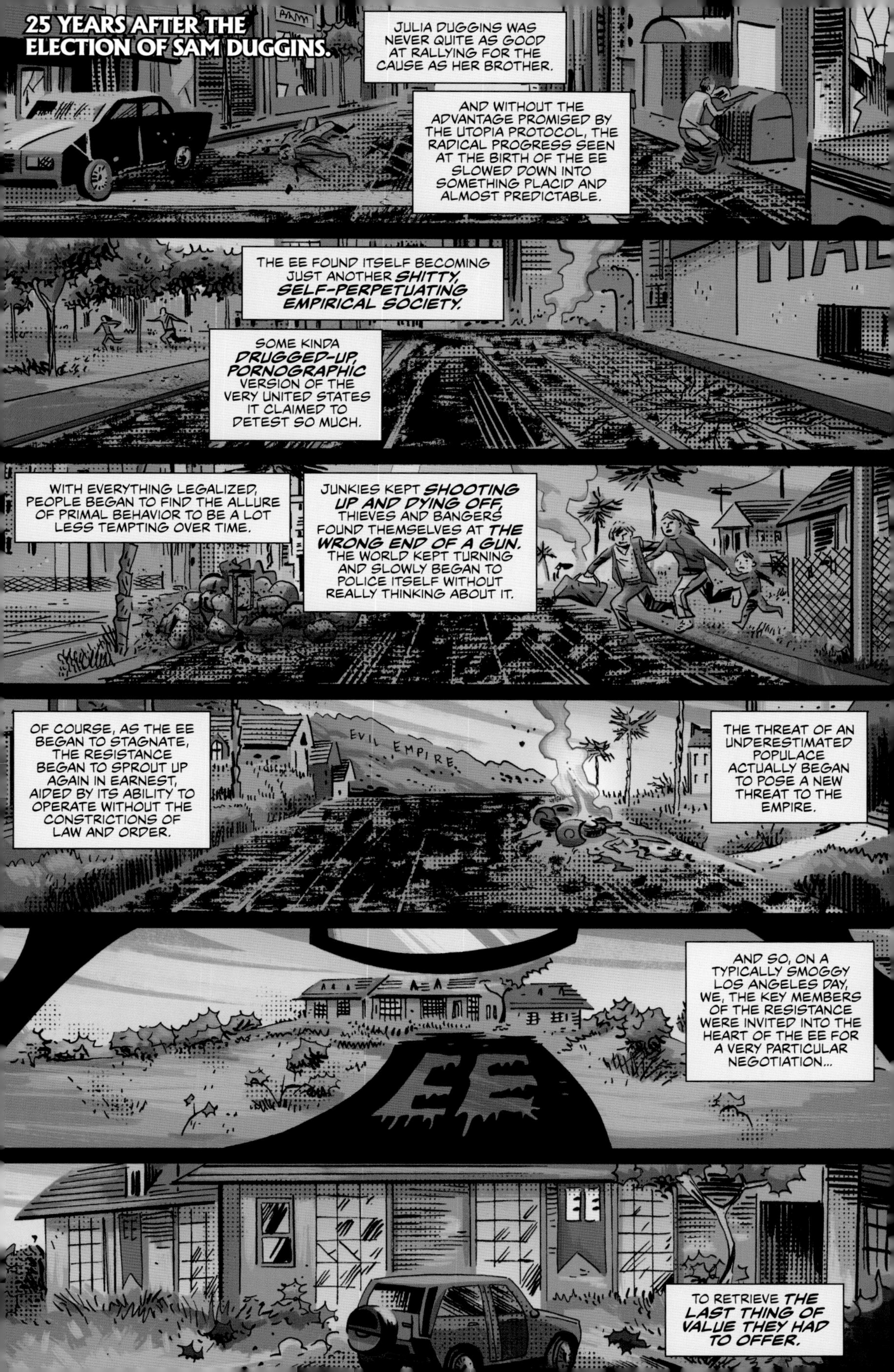
25 YEARS AFTER THE ELECTION OF SAM DUGGINS.
JULIA DUGGINS WAS NEVER QUITE AS GOOD AT RALLYING FOR THE CAUSE AS HER BROTHER.
AND WITHOUT THE ADVANTAGE PROMISED BY THE UTOPIA PROTOCOL, THE RADICAL PROGRESS SEEN AT THE BIRTH OF THE EE SLOWED DOWN INTO SOMETHING PLACID AND ALMOST PREDICTABLE.
THE EE FOUND ITSELF BECOMING JUST ANOTHER SHITTY, SELF-PERPETUATING EMPIRICAL SOCIETY.
SOME KINDA DRUGGED-UP, PORNOGRAPHIC VERSION OF THE VERY UNITED STATES IT CLAIMED TO DETEST SO MUCH.
WITH EVERYTHING LEGALIZED, PEOPLE BEGAN TO FIND THE ALLURE OF PRIMAL BEHAVIOR TO BE A LOT LESS TEMPTING OVER TIME.
JUNKIES KEPT SHOOTING UP AND DYING OFF, THIEVES AND BANGERS FOUND THEMSELVES AT THE WRONG END OF A GUN. THE WORLD KEPT TURNING AND SLOWLY BEGAN TO POLICE ITSELF WITHOUT REALLY THINKING ABOUT IT.
OF COURSE, AS THE EE BEGAN TO STAGNATE, THE RESISTANCE BEGAN TO SPROUT UP AGAIN IN EARNEST, AIDED BY ITS ABILITY TO OPERATE WITHOUT THE CONSTRICTIONS OF LAW AND ORDER.
EVIL EMPIRE
THE THREAT OF AN UNDERESTIMATED POPULACE ACTUALLY BEGAN TO POSE A NEW THREAT TO THE EMPIRE.
AND SO, ON A TYPICALLY SMOGGY LOS ANGELES DAY, WE, THE KEY MEMBERS OF THE RESISTANCE WERE INVITED INTO THE HEART OF THE EE FOR A VERY PARTICULAR NEGOTIATION...
TO RETRIEVE THE LAST THING OF VALUE THEY HAD TO OFFER.

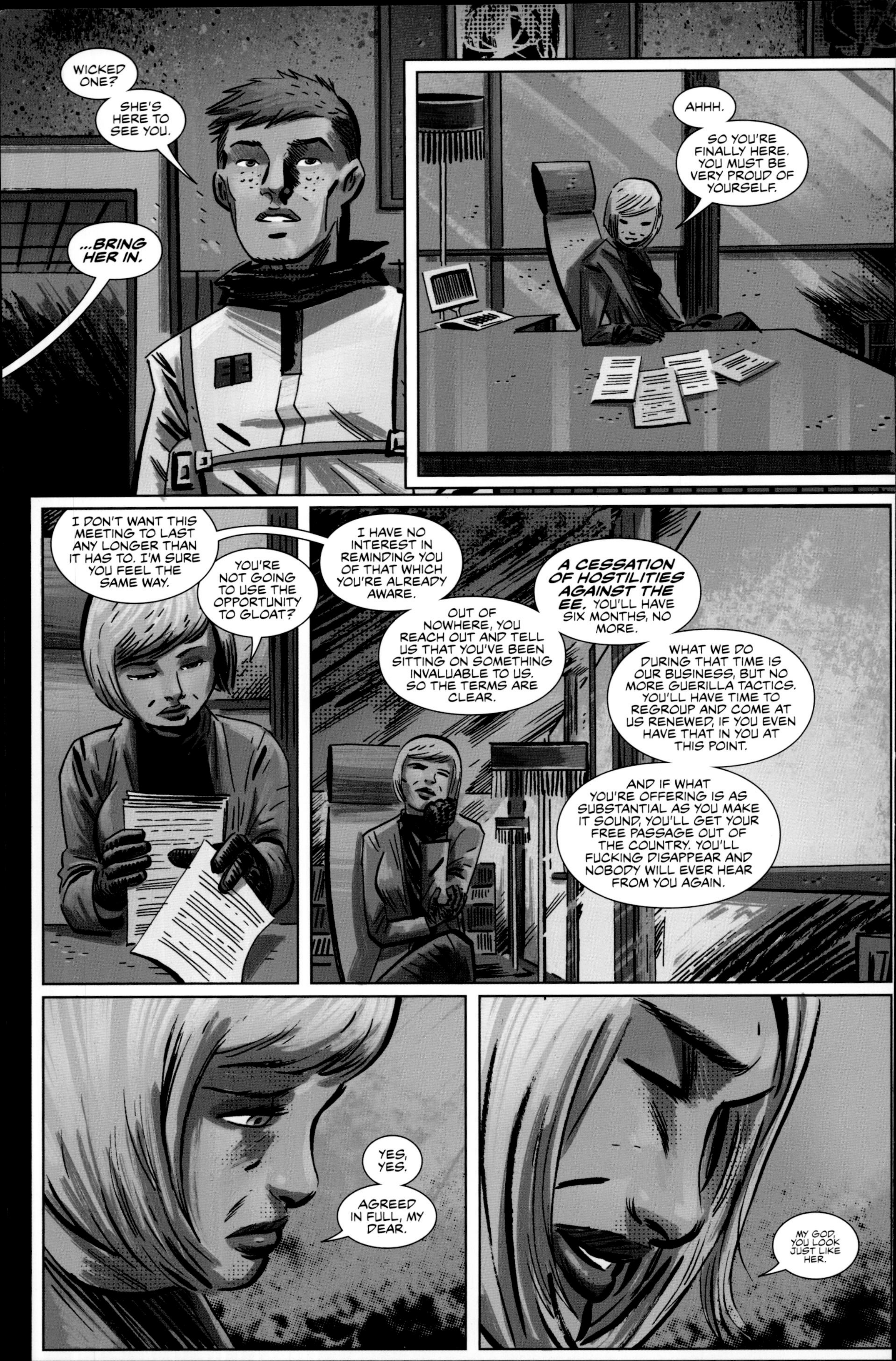
WICKED ONE?
SHE'S HERE TO SEE YOU.
...BRING HER IN.
AHHH.
SO YOU'RE FINALLY HERE. YOU MUST BE VERY PROUD OF YOURSELF.
I DON'T WANT THIS MEETING TO LAST ANY LONGER THAN IT HAS TO. I'M SURE YOU FEEL THE SAME WAY.
YOU'RE NOT GOING TO USE THE OPPORTUNITY TO GLOAT?
I HAVE NO INTEREST IN REMINDING YOU OF THAT WHICH YOU'RE ALREADY AWARE.
OUT OF NOWHERE, YOU REACH OUT AND TELL US THAT YOU'VE BEEN SITTING ON SOMETHING INVALUABLE TO US. SO THE TERMS ARE CLEAR.
A CESSATION OF HOSTILITIES AGAINST THE EE. YOU'LL HAVE SIX MONTHS, NO MORE.
WHAT WE DO DURING THAT TIME IS OUR BUSINESS, BUT NO MORE GUERILLA TACTICS. YOU'LL HAVE TIME TO REGROUP AND COME AT US RENEWED, IF YOU EVEN HAVE THAT IN YOU AT THIS POINT.
AND IF WHAT YOU'RE OFFERING IS AS SUBSTANTIAL AS YOU MAKE IT SOUND, YOU'LL GET YOUR FREE PASSAGE OUT OF THE COUNTRY. YOU'LL FUCKING DISAPPEAR AND NOBODY WILL EVER HEAR FROM YOU AGAIN.
YES, YES.
AGREED IN FULL, MY DEAR.
MY GOD, YOU LOOK JUST LIKE HER.

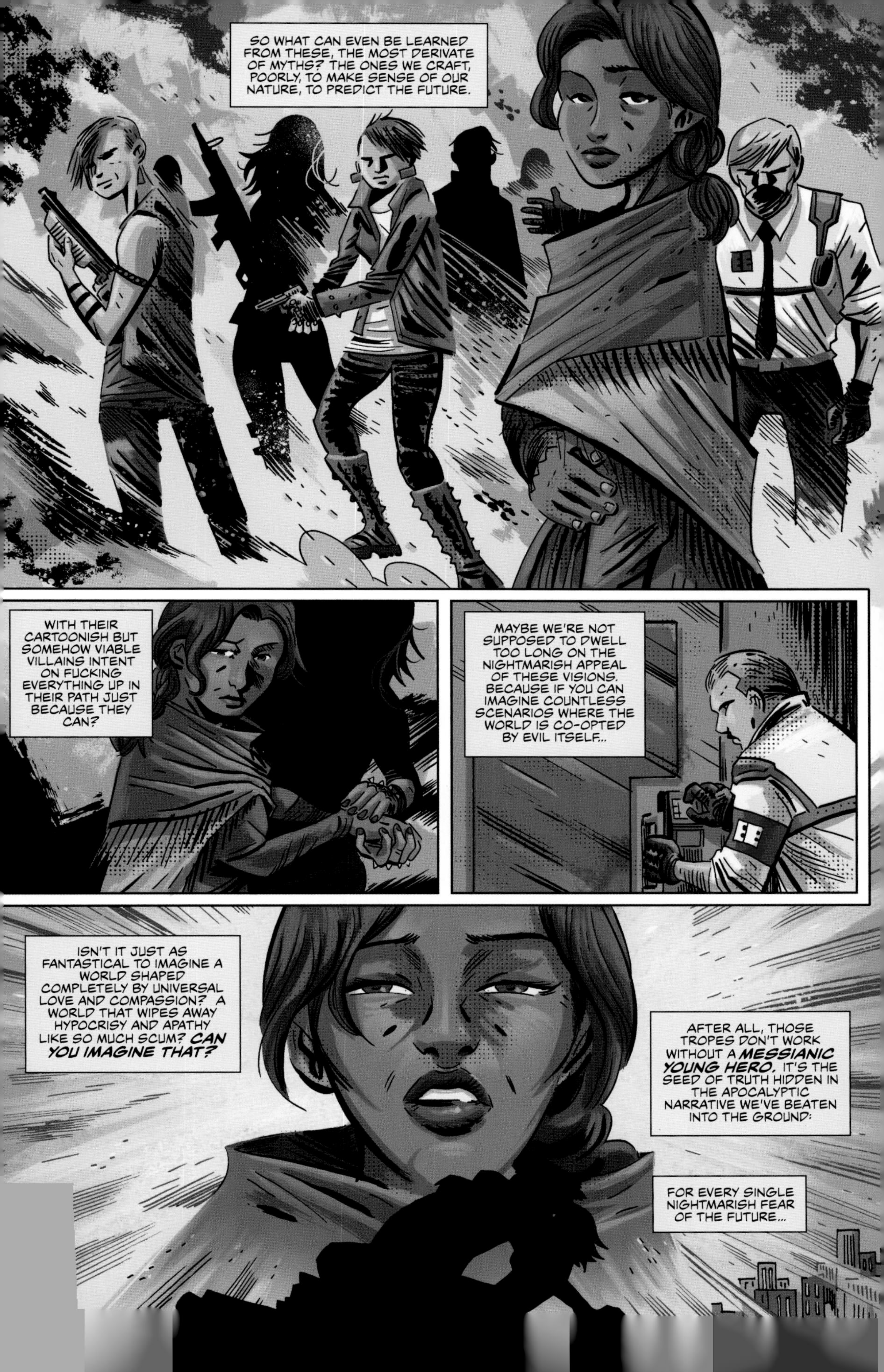
SO WHAT CAN EVEN BE LEARNED FROM THESE, THE MOST DERIVATE OF MYTHS? THE ONES WE CRAFT, POORLY, TO MAKE SENSE OF OUR NATURE, TO PREDICT THE FUTURE.
WITH THEIR CARTOONISH BUT SOMEHOW VIABLE VILLAINS INTENT ON FUCKING EVERYTHING UP IN THEIR PATH JUST BECAUSE THEY CAN?
MAYBE WE'RE NOT SUPPOSED TO DWELL TOO LONG ON THE NIGHTMARISH APPEAL OF THESE VISIONS. BECAUSE IF YOU CAN IMAGINE COUNTLESS SCENARIOS WHERE THE WORLD IS CO-OPTED BY EVIL ITSELF...
ISN'T IT JUST AS FANTASTICAL TO IMAGINE A WORLD SHAPED COMPLETELY BY UNIVERSAL LOVE AND COMPASSION? A WORLD THAT WIPES AWAY HYPOCRISY AND APATHY LIKE SO MUCH SCUM? ***CAN YOU IMAGINE THAT?***
AFTER ALL, THOSE TROPES DON'T WORK WITHOUT A ***MESSIANIC YOUNG HERO.*** IT'S THE SEED OF TRUTH HIDDEN IN THE APOCALYPTIC NARRATIVE WE'VE BEATEN INTO THE GROUND:
FOR EVERY SINGLE NIGHTMARISH FEAR OF THE FUTURE...

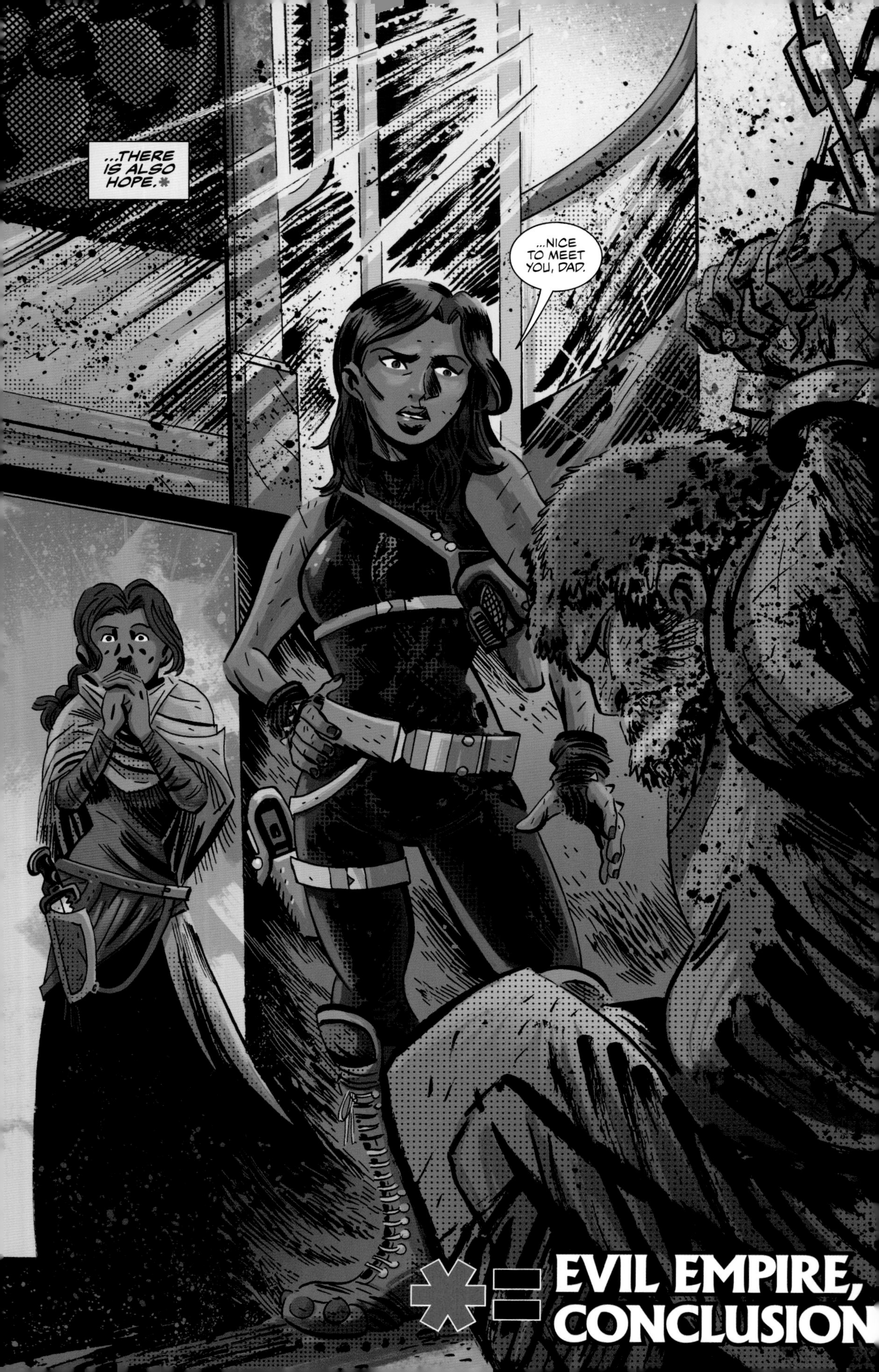
...THERE IS ALSO HOPE.*
...NICE TO MEET YOU, DAD.
*= EVIL EMPIRE, CONCLUSION

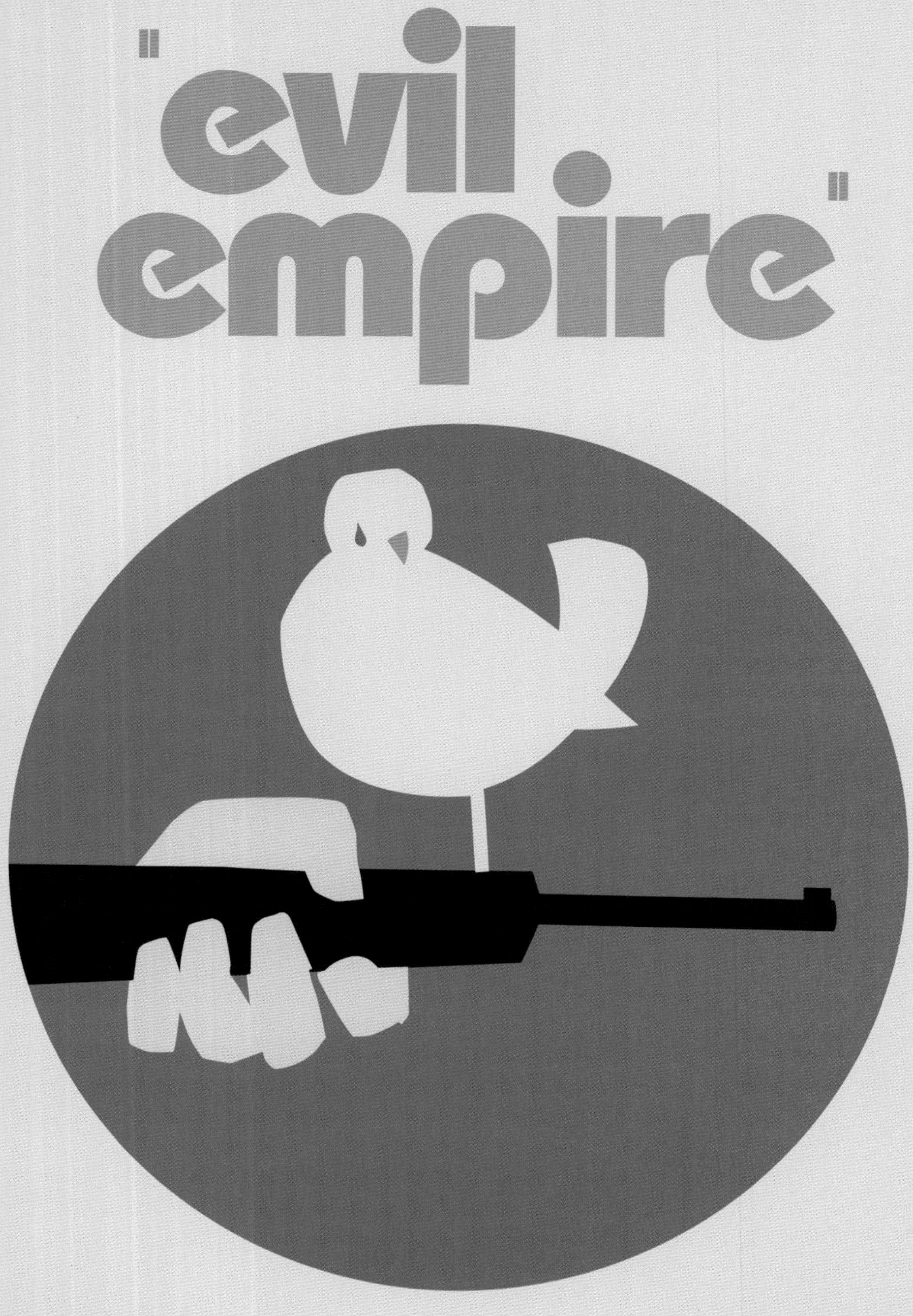
"evil empire"

JAY SHAW ISSUE NINE COVER

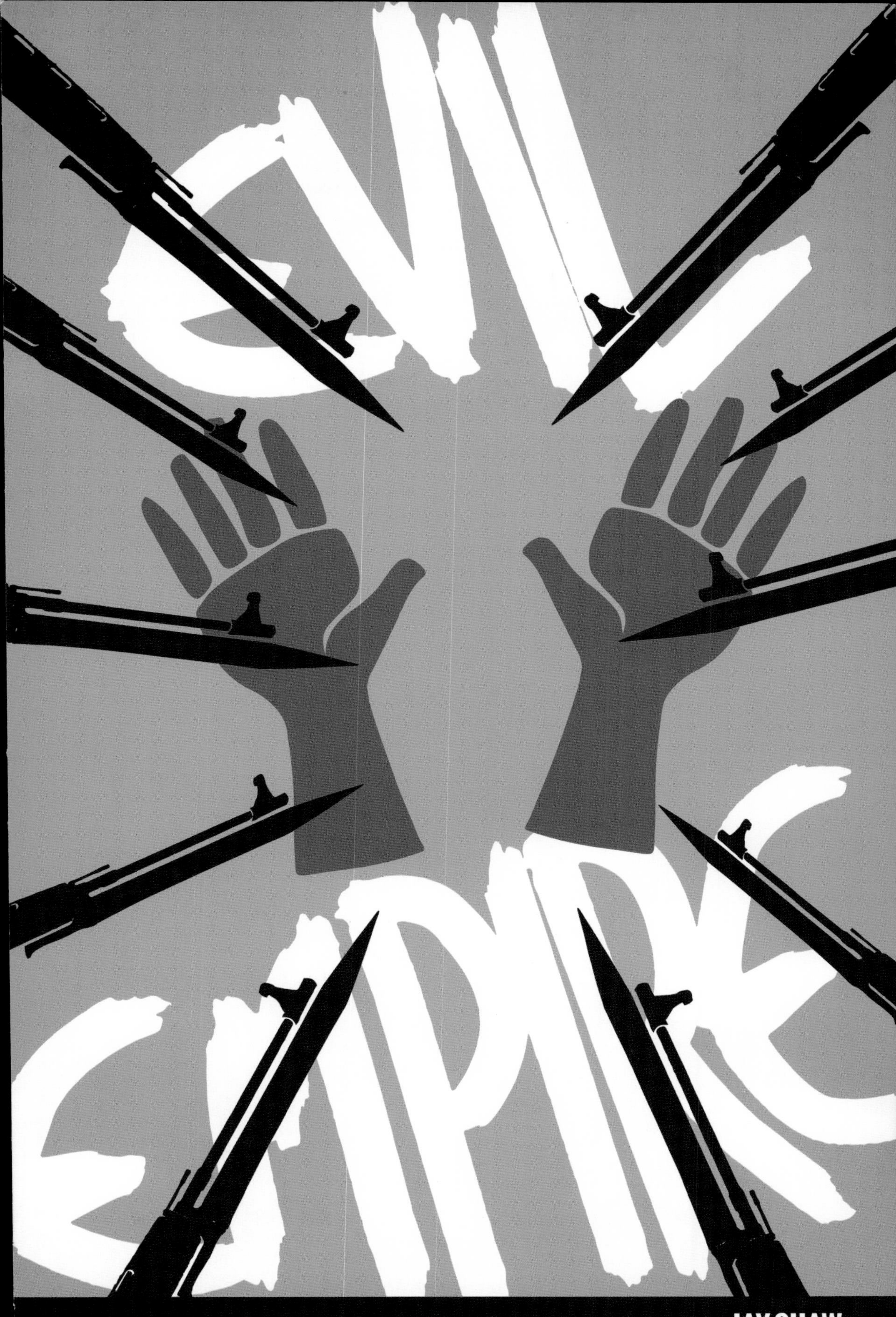

ISSUE TEN COVER **JAY SHAW**

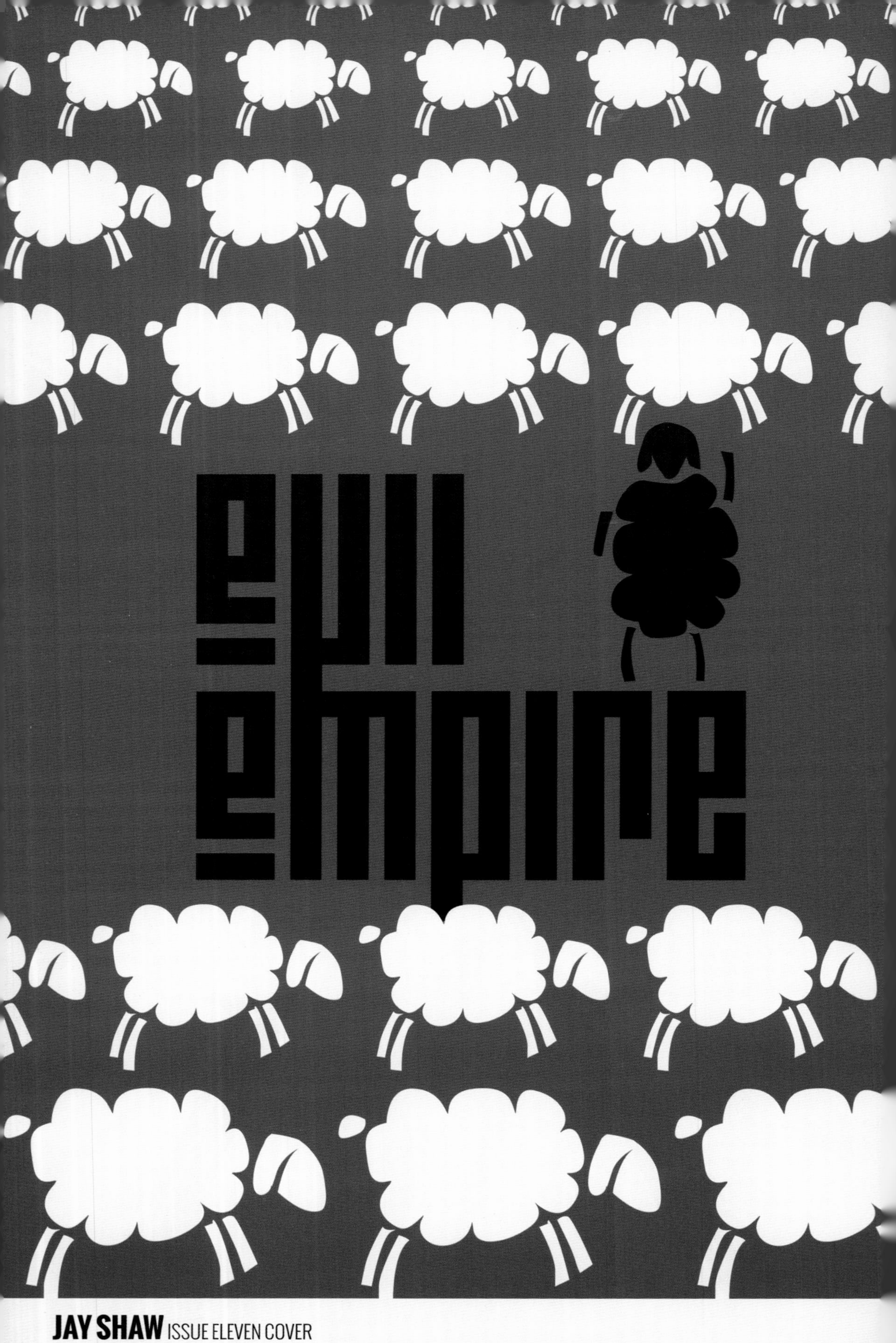
evil empire

JAY SHAW ISSUE ELEVEN COVER

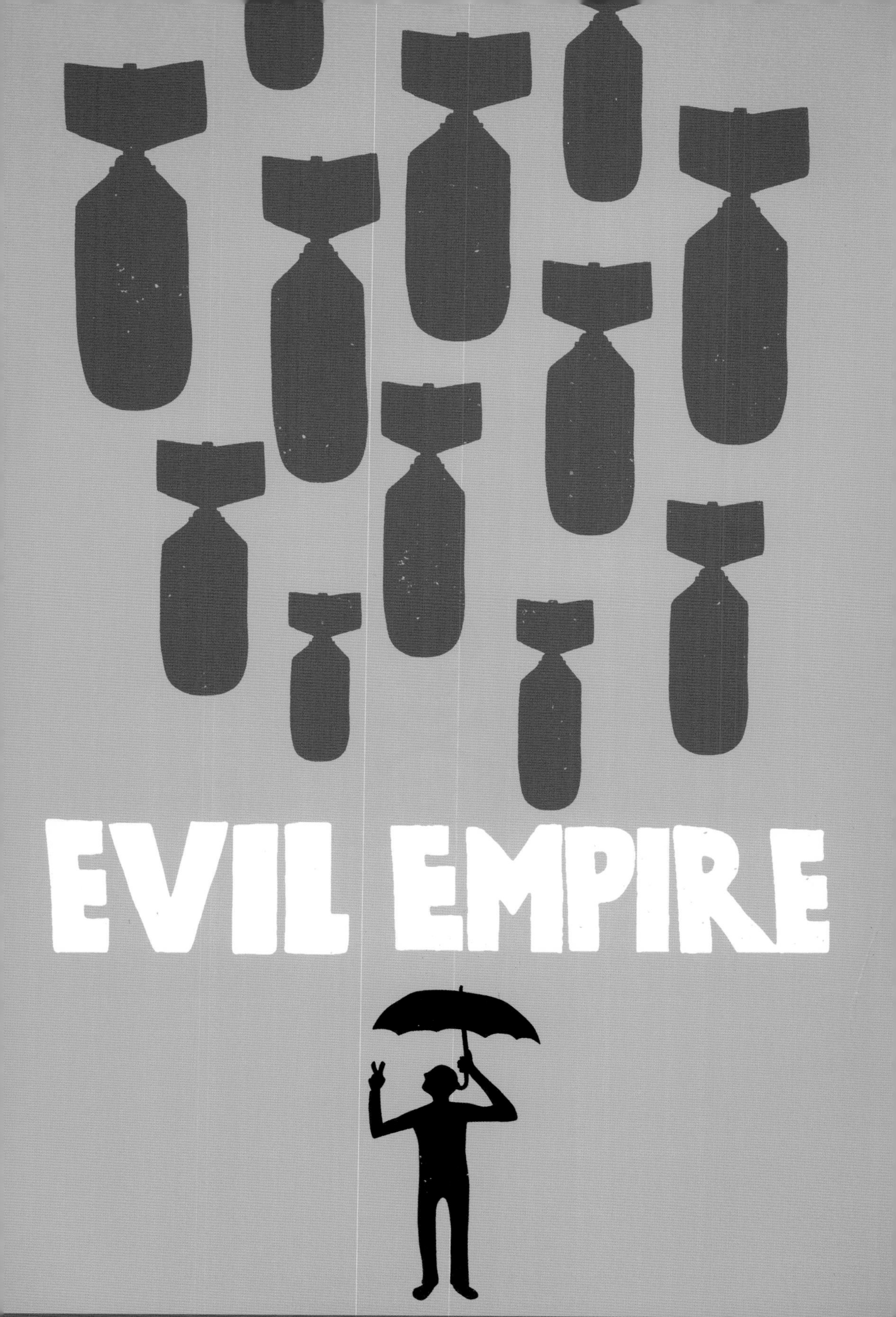
EVIL EMPIRE

ISSUE TWELVE COVER **JAY SHAW**

It's rare when evil itself gets
.....exc. 7.0 **wiped out completely.**